THE NEW UNIONISM IN THE NEW SOCIETY

Public Sector Unions in the Redistributive State

LEO TROY
Distinguished Professor of Economics
Rutgers University

George Mason University Press
Fairfax, Virginia

Copyright © 1994 by
George Mason University Press
4400 University Drive
Fairfax, VA 22030

Distributed by arrangement with
University Publishings Associates,ᴿᴹ Inc.

4720 Boston Way
Lanham, MD 20706

3 Henrietta Street
London WC2E 8LU England

Library of Congress Cataloging-in-Publication Data

Troy, Leo.
The new unionism in the new society : public sector unions in the
redistributive state / Leo Troy.
p.   cm.
Includes bibliographical references and index.
1. Trade-unions—Government employees—United States—History.
I. Title.
HD8005.2.U5T76   1994
331.88'1135'0000973—dc20   94–2667 CIP

ISBN 0–913969–69–9 (cloth : alk. paper)

 The paper used in this publication meets the minimum requirements of
American National Standard for Information Sciences—Permanence
of Paper for Printed Library Materials, ANSI Z39.48–1984.

"Attitudes toward unions, pro and con, are emphatic enough. But of serious thinking about unions – what kind of institutions they are, and why, and to what purpose – there is precious little." (Irving Kristol)

"Little wonder that it is rarely perceived that unionism in the United States now is as revolutionary in consequence as it is conservative in intention." (Charles Lindbloom)

Acknowledgements

I thank the Public Service Research Foundation and the Smith Richardson Foundation for grants which made this study possible. In particular, I wish to express my appreciation to Mr. David Y. Denholm, President of the PSRF and Michael Greve, at the time of the award at Smith Richardson for their patience in awaiting the manuscript. I wish to thank, too, Mr. Peter Katsirubas, Editor of the *Government Union Review* for his help and advice. I acknowledge the help, too, of my colleague, Neil Sheflin, in preparing the charts and the appendix table comparing the densities of the New and the Old Unionism by state.

Responsibility for the content of this study is solely my own.

Leo Troy

Contents

CHAPTER I.

The New Society

A New Society began to evolve during the past generation and its leading characteristic is the redistributive state. The transfer of income from one group of the population to another has become the major economic and social function of government's domestic programs. I call this the New Socialism.

Unions of public employees, the focus of this study, play a major role in the New Society and its redistributive goals. Meanwhile, the union movement, public and private, and the labor markets in which they function have also changed. The changes in unionism, labor markets, and ideas governing their actions are the new environment in which the American union movement now functions. These changes have come about slowly obscuring the break with past assessments of what unions are, what they do, and why. Chapter I presents an overview of these developments.

Structural Change in Unionism and Labor Markets

The character of organized labor changes over time, just as any social institution. Its most recent and its most momentous, since the founding of the American labor movement in the 19th century, took place during the last three decades. Its central features were the rise of unionism in the public labor market and its decline in the private market. The disparate trends constitute a structural break, or transformation, in the composition of organized labor – the very stuff of unionism.

The metamorphosis transcends a quantitative alteration. The change has also been marked by a fundamental shift in what unions do and why, their philosophy. These changes have given birth to a new union movement, the New Unionism. It is distinct from the private sector movement, the Old Unionism, in origin, character, goals and future prospects.

The burgeoning of the New Unionism in membership and labor market penetration began in the 1960s and continues into the present. It marks a watershed in the annals of American labor history even more momentous than the rise of unionism in manufacturing, epitomized by the rise of the Congress of Industrial Organizations (CIO) in the 1930s. The CIO extended organization to millions of workers, but its success was limited to extending the union movement to more blue collar workers. Moreover, in less than a generation, those gains were steadily eroded; the market penetration and membership of blue collar unionism has plunged. In contrast, the ranks and labor market penetration of the New Unionism have climbed.

The emergence of the New Unionism ranks with the founding the labor movement itself in 1886, with the establishment of the American Federation of Labor (AFL). Each represents a new departure in labor history: The AFL in organizing blue collar workers on a permanent basis for the first time, and the New Unionism in organizing white collar and service occupations in government on a major scale. (Government unions have also organized blue collar occupations, but these are a small proportion of their membership.)

Ultimately, the New Unionism's impact on the economy and society will be more far reaching than the Old. But, it may be asked, how can a union movement in a market which accounts for about 16% of total employment be able to wield such influence? Furthermore, it will be asked, how can the New Unionism's 6.7 million members, who represent less than half of government employment (just under 40%), exercise such leverage?

There are several explanations. First, the New Unionism (together with unorganized public employees) now administer government spending which is approaching 45% of the national income, and the percentage keeps increasing. A corollary is that the New Unionism, made up as it is, by professionals and other white collar workers, is in a stronger position to shape and influence social ideas and trends than the blue collar who are the backbone of the Old Unionism. Another reason for asserting that the New Unionism can exercise influence well beyond its numbers is that it has already wrought radical, if yet largely unnoticed, changes in the economy and society. It has done so in collaboration with other social and political forces, principally in the Democratic Party. The philosophy of this collaboration is what I term "social unionism" (Chapter V).

There is also historical precedent for minority organized groups to gain control of authority and policy. In 1945 the British union movement (private and public combined) accounted for only 39% of the labor market (Bain and Price, Table 2.2, p. 40, 1980) when the Labor (Socialist) Party won control of the government and ushered in an era of sweeping nationalization of industry and the socialization of social services. Today, the New Unionism in the U.S. has a market share of nearly 40%, but its goals exclude the ownership of the "means of production," in contrast to the British union movement. Meanwhile, the nationalization of industry has been largely reversed in Britain, but the sweeping socialization of services provided by government has not. The comparison in government provided services is the appropriate comparison with the goals of the New Unionism of our time, especially in view of the commitment of the New Unionism and the Democratic Party to some version of socialized medicine.

The gulf dividing the New and the Old Unionism, what they are, what they do and why, has been overlooked by the conventional analysis. Typically the conventional analysis has treated the spectacular growth of public sector unions over the past three decades as merely an extension of labor organization and collective bargaining into the public labor market (Freeman, 1986; Burton and Thomason, 1988). In theoretical terms the conventional approach has interpreted the explosion in public sector unionism as the most recent example of the "spurt" theory of union growth (Chapter II). In brief, the spurt theory argues that, historically, union growth comes in periodic episodes, rather than in a steady expansion. Examples of the spurt theory were the rise of the Congress of Industrial Unions (CIO) in the 1930s and 1940s, and the spurt of unionism, AFL and independent, in the early part of this century. In relying on the spurt theory to account for the enormous growth of unionism in the public economy, the conventional approach treats private and public unionism as a unitary movement, obfuscating and misinterpreting their fundamental differences.

The composition of the union movement changed dramatically with the arrival of the New Unionism. On the eve of this structural change in labor organization, in 1960, 94% of all union members were in the private sector and 6% in the public labor market. Today, 40% of the total union population are part of the New Unionism, diminishing the corresponding share of the Old Unionism to 60%. These disparities are even more accentuated when compared to the shares of employment accounted for by labor markets in which the two movements function. While public employment accounts for only 16% of the total labor market, the New Unionism accounts for 2 1/2 times that proportion of all union members (private and public). At the same time, the percentage of the labor market organized (in terms of paid membership) by the New Unionism is also (coincidentally) just under 40%. This is nearly four times its penetration rate in 1960 (10.8%), when the New Unionism "jumped off." The New Unionism's penetration rate of government employment (of just under 40%) already exceeds the highest rate ever scored by the Old Unionism (36% in 1953) and can be expected to climb higher as the new century approaches (Troy and Sheflin, 1985; Troy estimates). The New Unionism also represents in bargaining (in contrast to membership) a record high percentage of government employees, nearly 45% (Bureau of Labor Statistics, 1992). Meantime, the Old Unionism's market penetration is under 12% of the labor market, a figure even below 1929!

These measures set the two union movements apart in yet another dimension: One is a growth "industry," the other a declining one. The New Unionism is also more durable than the Old, as trends over the past three decades establish. Looking to the future, while the New Unionism's growth will slow in line with recent trends, the Old faces further decline, also in line with recent trends. Clearly, the contemporary public sector union movement is something other than a "spurt" in labor organization which just happened to occur in the public labor market. It is a New Union Movement and a basic element of the new environment.

The New Unionism breaks with the history of unionism most decisively in its diminution of public authority – sovereignty (Chapter III). This is one of the most remarkable consequences of the New Unionism for society; it is a key underlying the New Unionism's role in redistributing income. The diminution of sovereignty cannot be dismissed as a red herring, as is the wont of the conventional wisdom. According to the politically correct position, bargaining with government is essentially equivalent to reducing managerial prerogatives in private bargaining. The predecessors of the New Unionism in the public sector could not challenge and reduce sovereignty as does the New Unionism.

Public policy has been the causal force in the structural change which produced the New Unionism (Chapter II). However, this was not the first occasion in labor history that government policy produced structural changes in unionism. The enactment of the National Labor Relations Act in 1935 changed the character of the Old Unionism (Sheflin,

Troy and Koeller, 1981). Historically made up primarily of skilled workers in several nonmanufacturing industries, the NLRA facilitated the extension of unionism to large numbers of less skilled workers in manufacturing, epitomized in the rise of the CIO. A follow up study showed that the transition to the new environment created by the NLRA had been completed no later than 1939 (Sheflin, 1984). Put another way, the change in the factors governing union growth underlay the organization of manufacturing.

Although public policy occasioned the structural break within the Old Unionism and the structural break from private to public sector unionism, its long run durability differs between the private and public labor markets. In the private sector, markets subsequently overwhelmed the National Labor Relations Act. Within 20 years of its enactment, competition and the rise of the service economy, gradually eroded the efficacy of the NLRA. Market forces "repealed" the interventionist power of the National Labor Relations Act and initiated the continuing steady decline of the Old Unionism. Between the mid-1930s and the mid-1950s market forces separated the Old Unionism from its historical industrial base and the rising service industries (Keddy, 1988). The Old Unionism, shut out of the private service labor market and its white collar workers began the persistent decline in market penetration from their 1953 peak to their present low level. Even if the Old Unionism had not lost a single member since the peak year of 1953, the erosion in the percentage of workers unionized would nevertheless have shrunk because of the emergence of the private service labor market. The new service labor market also proved to be a barrier to the Old Unionism internationally, not just in the U.S.

The shift in public policy in the 1930s and the changeover to the service labor market in the 1950s took place within the private, the market, sector of the economy and thus only affected the Old Unionism. The first environmental change, the policy change of the 1930s, temporarily overrode market factors, only to succumb later. The second environmental change, markets, undermined government's interventionist power to foster the Old Unionism. Market forces have relentlessly played themselves out not only in this country, but after a lag, in the labor markets of all other advanced industrial nations as well (Troy, 1990a). Similar structural breaks in the pattern of union development applied to all other advanced industrial nations, including Canada, the nation which the politically correct declared had escaped the "American disease," the decline of the Old Unionism (Troy, 1992; for a contrary view, Visser, 1991).

In marked contrast to the government policy in the private labor market, government policy is largely immune to market forces in the public labor market. Consequently, government policy in the public labor market continues to foster the expansion of the New Unionism. Public policies also spurred the growth of government employment. This added to the "pool" of membership for the New Unionism. Over the last three decades, since the 1960s, the number of government employees rose by more than 10 million, providing an enormous pool from which the New Unionism could and did draw members. Beginning in the 1960s government employment also increased sharply relative to private employment. Within a decade government's share of total employment rose so rapidly that by 1970 it was about 18% of the total, compared to just over 15% in 1960. As for the future, there is little on the horizon, including privatization, to threaten the stability of public labor market and the New Unionism. Indeed, at this time there are more government workers than production workers in manufacturing.

Structural Change In Socialism: The New Socialism

Just as unionism and labor markets have undergone change so, too, have ideas about the role of state in the economies of advanced capitalist nations. These are a crucial part of the new environment in which the New Unionism operates; the ideological change has also boosted the expansion and affected the character of the New Unionism.

The scope and type of state participation in the economy have changed the traditional concepts of socialism and capitalism. In general, the conventional understanding of socialism is of government ownership of the means of production – the factories, machines, buildings and raw materials used in making goods. This core idea is a 19th century idea and applies to both democratic or totalitarian versions of socialism. Both versions are therefore outdated and lag the structural change socialism. The essence of the New Socialism is government ownership of an increasing share of the national income, not the means of production. The core of the New Socialism is the socialization of income. Professor Milton Friedman defined the new form of socialism as follows:

> What is socialism? In its purest form, socialism is government ownership and control of the means of production. Ownership of anything implies the right to the income produced by that thing.

All means of production in the United States – people, land, machines, building, etc. – produce our national income. By that test, government owns 45 percent of the means of production that produce the national income. The U.S. is now 45 percent socialist (Friedman, 1989).

In 1929, total government spending was 12.6% of the national income; in 1990 it reached 43.2%, nearly 3.5 times as great as in 1929. In 1960, government spending accounted for under 1/3 of the nation's income (32.6%). In financial terms, it is evident that the public sector grew far more rapidly than did the private and the growth continues. National income is used for the comparisons because it comprises the total income originating in the production of goods and services attributable to labor and property used in production and before the deduction of taxes, as Professor Friedman had pointed out.

Paradoxically, the New Socialism thrives within economies based on private ownership of the means of production, both of goods and services. In contrast, the Old Socialism (democratic or totalitarian) and capitalism were engaged in a winner take-all struggle. Up to a point, the New Socialism and capitalism, as now practiced, have a complementary relationship. The limitations on the New Socialism are the extent of income socialization which will be tolerated and which is consistent with an acceptable rate of economic efficiency and growth.

The new version of socialism is a more subtle and effective method for reforming society than the socialist policies of the past, whether democratic or dictatorial in political form. The New Socialism links the productive power of capitalism to the redistributionist power of the State. It is more powerful than historical socialism because it junks the unworkable, ideological baggage of the social ownership of the means of production in favor of the redistribution of income. It is a direct method of achieving socialism, whereas the traditional concept was indirect, requiring first public ownership of the means of production in order to gain control of the income produced. Experience demonstrated that the indirect method backfired, and economic growth lagged or declined as a result. The New Socialism leaves undisturbed the private ownership of productive resources because experience has demonstrated that also leaves decision-making to those who promote economic growth. To do otherwise would be to starve the cow (the means of production) which provides the milk (income).

The New Socialism is pragmatic in that it draws its philosophy and policies from experience. In contrast the Old Socialism derived its principal inspiration from Marxian dogma and analysis. Its industrial policy was state ownership of the means of production, a 19th century strategy which was carried into the 20th. Its focus was manufacturing because manufacturing industries were responsible for the great upsurge of income and wealth produced by the industrial revolution in the 19th century, and which employed the new industrial (blue collar) working class, in Marxian terms, the exploited proletarian masses. In the past, leaders of the Old Unionism in this country advocated public ownership of transportation and communication, but not out of ideological reasons, but because they regarded these industries as "natural monopolies." They did not advocate public ownership of manufacturing, the industrial keystone of the "means of production."

Public ownership of the means of production, by going to the source of income would, in the analysis and dogma of the Old Socialism, transform an unfair to a fair society and abolish the "exploitation" of the industrial working class. In Marxian terms, output would be determined by the maxim "from each according to his deeds," and income would be distributed "to each according to his needs." The idea of relying on each person to produce according to his deeds as the motivation for production, flawed in concept, also never worked. On the other hand, "to each according to his needs," survives in a vitiated form, most recognizable as "the caring society," or Fairness. Although the "caring society," can be trace its roots to religious, ethical and philosophic roots as well, it is also genealogically related to the Marxian maxim "to each according to his needs."

To achieve the goals of Fairness, the New Socialism seeks public ownership of income. This approach is a far more powerful than the Old Socialism's because it harnesses the productive power of private ownership to Fairness. Quite simply, the arithmetic demonstrates that there will be more income available for social engineering from private than from publicly owned means of production. The New Socialism therefore rationally rejects public ownership of the means of production.

History demonstrates the validity of the new approach. Capitalism, instead of increasing the misery of the working class and generating the army of the unemployed, generated an unprecedented rise in the real living standards of workers and armies of the employed. Workers under capitalism prospered, despite myths to the contrary. Ironically, the fate which Marxian socialists forecast for workers under capitalism, befell workers under socialism. Societies in Eastern Europe which built on its principles have collapsed. In Western countries, many of the artifacts of the Old Socialism, the nationalized industries, have been privatized because of their financial and economic inefficiencies, and the trend continues.

By linking the productive and income producing capacity of capitalist enterprise to the redistribution of income, the New Socialism has become a viable and durable form of social engineering. The New Socialism recognizes government production as failure in generating income, while it recognizes government redistribution of income as a highly efficient system for creating a Fair society.

Clearly, the New and the Old Socialism are ideologically a light year apart, to mix a metaphor. The Old addressed income distribution indirectly, that is, by the socialization of production, while the New Socialism addresses income distribution directly by socializing income. The Old Socialism was a product of the 19th century thinking when the production marvels of the Industrial Revolution demonstrated the wealth potential of the new industrial machine. Production was therefore the obvious choice of the Old Socialism in its grand plan for changing the distribution and creating the new society. However, economic change has made the socialization of production an ideological relic of the past. On the other hand, the New Socialism, by addressing income distribution directly, is up to date and, with some limitations, has a promising future.

The New Socialism also depends upon a different working "class" than the Old. While the Old Socialism expected to draw its support from blue collar workers, or in its own terminology, "the toiling masses," the New draws its support from white collar workers. Industrially, this is a shift from manufacturing to (government) employment. What is produced, who produces it and how it is earned have changed the economy and labor market which the Old Socialism analyzed in the 19th century. Meanwhile, the meaning of private property and capitalism have also underwent rapid and radical change, distancing capitalism further from the socialist analysis of the past. These developments discredited the 19th century preconceptions of the Old Socialism and explain why they are unsuited to the dynamics of a modern economy. A new version of socialism was needed and it has appeared in the socialization of income.

The structural change in Socialism is visible in the increased importance of the public labor market as well as in the increasing share of government spending. Public employment – federal, state and local – increased markedly between 1960 and 1980, from 15.4% to 18.0% of all non-farm employees. By mid-year 1991 it had receded to just under 17%. However, 1991 represents about a 70% increase in market share over 1929, a benchmark year when government employment and involvement in the economy were still very limited.

The New Socialism is also distinct from the welfare state, although it is an outgrowth of welfare state ideas. The New Socialism deals with redistribution and government spending on a great variety of services. In that sense, government spending is the provider or becomes the surrogate for the production of those services. On the other hand, the perspective of the welfare state was the consumption of services. Finally, the quantitative difference in the scale of public spending between the New Socialism and the Welfare State also separate the two.

In contrast to the perspective presented here, the conventional wisdom treats the redistributive function of government as merely an extension of the public sector economy. In this it errs in the same manner as its account of the New Unionism as merely an extension of unionism into the public labor market. To describe the public economy as merely the public segment of the economy obscures the sector's redistributive (socialist) characteristics. The conventional terminology treats these economic and financial activities with euphemisms (mixed economies, or simply the public sector) which obfuscate their socialist character. Euphemisms mask other socialist ideas such as the language of tax laws which declare that income from property is "unearned," while income from labor is identified as earned.

The Union Connection

Unions have historically been associated with the variant forms of socialism. It is consistent with that experience to find that the New Unionism is closely tied to the New Socialism. Its members and the employees it represents are the labor force providing and facilitating the redistribution of income. Paradoxically, the Old Unionism (in the U.S.) has been one of the key institutions of the capitalist system. Historically, the philosophy of the Old Unionism stressed acceptance of capitalism and rejected the Old Socialism. American workers never subscribed to the class struggle, "all being conscientious objectors" (Kristol, 1991, p. A10). The goal of the Old Unionism was and remains the redistribution of income within the private economy, from employers to workers.

The New Socialism is also not acceptable to the Old Unionism. The socialization of income separates the Old from the New Unionism in the most fundamental way, their philosophies. Because the current version of the philosophy of the Old Unionism shares with the New a demand for more government intervention in the economy and society, superficially there appear to be no differences. However, they do differ and significantly. The Old Unionism favors regulation of the private economy, what I call neo-mercantilism. It favors government regulation of labor markets, an industrial policy to support its protectionist foreign trade policies, and government intervention in the economy to maintain high levels of employment (Keynesianism). On the other hand, it does not share the New Unionism's policies to redistribute income from the private to the public economy.

The distinctive roles of the New and the Old Unionism in their separate sectors of the economy, the socialized and the capitalist sectors, put the two movements in competition (Chapters IV and V). Just because each are unions, or because many from both wings are affiliated with the American Federation of Labor and Congress of Industrial Organizations (AFL-CIO) only obscures their competition; it does not alter it. The New Unionism and the Old compete for resources in all open, democratic countries. Their relationship is therefore more competitive than cooperative. The Old Unionism and private decision-making in the economy are currently on the defensive, while the New Unionism and public decision-making (spending) are on the offensive. Meanwhile, the balance of power within the union movement is shifting toward the New and away from the Old Unionism. The New Unionism has already become the dominant wing of the organized labor movement in Canada and in other countries, notably Britain and France, and can be expected to gain ascendancy in the U.S. early in the next century.

Even when it becomes the dominant wing of organized labor, the New Unionism itself would be too weak to create the New Society. However, in the tradition of pressure and special interest groups in a pluralistic society like America, it is able to wield enormous influence in supporting and expanding income redistribution. Politically, the New Socialism is a political amalgam comprising the New Unionism, the dominant liberal wing of the Democratic Party, and various other left-liberal special interest groups. It is a combination of "grass-roots coalitions of labor with other community groups ... to ... generate a broad based social reform movement" (Battista, 1991, p. 497). Among these partners are the extreme environmentalists. They are of particular interest because their policies and those of the New Unionism will result in little or no economic growth. Curiously, this contrasts sharply with the Old Socialism which expected its New Society to generate economic growth in order to further the interests of the working class.

In the past intellectuals have recognized the special connection between unions and new societies, but such is not the case with the New Unionism and the New Society being developed out of the socialization of income. Perhaps it is the pragmatic approach of the New Unionism and its allies, but whatever the reason there is neither a manifesto outlining the New Society or the role of the New Unionism in achieving it. However, intellectuals' analysis of past attempts to link unionism to new societies has application to the linkage between the New Unionism and the New Society.

One of the most notable examples was the late Harold Laski. In a series of lectures published in 1949 as *Trade Unions in the New Society*, honoring the memory of his deceased friend and noted American union leader, Sidney Hillman, Professor Laski outlined the future role of trade unions in a democratic socialist society. His sketch of the anticipated future seemed on the verge of fulfillment in the aftermath of World War II with the great election victory of the Labour (the Socialist) Party in the United Kingdom. Although his expectations were not fulfilled with respect to socialized production of goods, with some modifications his analytical framework can be usefully applied to the New Unionism in the contemporary New (Redistributive) Society.

The transition to Socialism in Britain was to be achieved through the ballot box, not revolution as Marx had anticipated, and instead of the dedicated vanguard of the working class, the Communists, leading the way, the trade unions were to be the key to Laski's New Society. However, Britain again disappointed socialist planners. Thus, Marx, based on his materialist interpretation of history, had expected Britain, as the most advanced capitalist nation of the 19th century, to lead in the historically determined march from capitalism to the New (Communist) Society. However, Britain did not lead. The same failed expectation befell Laski's New Society a century later. Instead of becoming the "wave of the future," the basic elements of Laski's New Society, the trade unions and the socialized industries, steadily lost their central role in the economy and society. Nationalized industries were financial failures; many became privatized during the 1980s and others, rail and coal, may well follow in the 1990s.

Meanwhile, since 1979 British unions have steadily declined in membership and market share. Although this fate was common across all advanced industrial countries irrespective of the modes of ownership, socialized production accelerated the process when it confronted the New Age of Adam Smith and competitive world markets. The parts of the Old Socialist program which showed staying power were those which are now key components of the New Socialism, social services. The dissolution of the unrealized part of Laski's New Society, public ownership of the means of production, was engendered by the economic inefficiencies of the nationalized industries, the clash of interests between consumer-taxpayers and state enterprises, and, as Phelps Brown pointed out, new attitudes of British workers which he termed the democratic "counter-revolution" of our time (Brown, 1990).

At about the same time that Professor Laski was diagramming a New Society for Britain based on the Old Socialism, in the U.S. Professor Sumner Slichter of Harvard asserted (1948) that the Old Unionism had reached a position of sufficient power to warrant his expectation of a "laboristic" society which would replace capitalism (Chapter IV). Details of the "laboristic" society are scanty, but apparently he meant that the redistribution of income between employers and unionized workers would be determined more by powerful unions than by markets. However, his forecast proved to be mistaken; the Old Unionism peaked soon after he made his forecast and has since plummeted (Chapter II). Nevertheless, Slichter's Laboristic New Society, like Laski's New Socialist Society, may well be applicable if we switch from the Old Unionism to the New Unionism as the principal actor, and substitute the goals of the New Redistributive Society for the Old Socialism or the New Laboristic Society.

The New Society

No blueprint or even a sketch paralleling Professor Laski's for the Old Socialism or Professor Slichter's New Laboristic Society exists for the New Unionism and the New Redistributive Society of our time. The New Redistributive Society rests on different building blocks than either Laski's New Society or Slichter's Laboristic Society. First, the trade union component of the New Society is the New Unionism, a unionism far different than the Old Unionism on which both Laski and Slichter premised their expectations. The New Unionism is made of government employees, while the trade union component of Laski's Old Socialism and Slichter's Laboristic Society were private sector workers. Moreover, the occupational make-up of each also differs. White collar workers are the mainstay of the New Unionism, while blue collar were the backbone of the Old. The occupational difference alters the social perspectives of the two unionisms. The outlook of the New Unionism is dominated by the use of bureaucratic techniques to achieve goals, not a dramatic and wholesale change in social relations under either Laski's socialism or Slichter's laboristic economy.

Unlike unionism under the Old Socialism, the New Unionism is already established in the socialized (government) sector of the economy. The New Unions are not erstwhile private unions transferred into the public domain by the nationalization of industry; its their natural habitat. The New Unionism functions in a different industrial context than unions in Laski's nationalized industries. No industries have to be nationalized; there already exists a large and growing government sector as expressed in government spending relative to national income and employment. The industrial base of the New Unionism are the service, not the goods industries. Some of these services are new, some old, retained from the period of the welfare state; some are substitutes or supplements to services hitherto provided by the private sector, but now offered by government, and many are supplied by the private sector but paid for by the public. Services, not goods production, are the industrial "wave of the future." They offer a promising and growing domain for the expansion of the New Unionism and the New Socialism.

A second difference between the building blocks of the Old and the New societies is that the redistribution of national income from the private to the public sector of the economy is "invisible." The nationalized industries of Laski's Old Socialism are easily identifiable symbols while the socialization of income is much less visible.

Another aspect of the "invisible" quality of the New Society is the absence of any clearly identifiable ideological philosophers, such as have dominated the Old Socialism. From Marx on, the Old Socialism had many noteworthy ideological and identifiable proponents. In contrast, there are no towering advocates, "academic scribblers," to use Keynes' term, writing about the New Socialism and the New Society. Indeed, these concepts have yet to receive any general recognition that they exist! Nevertheless, they do and "Fairness" is the guiding philosophy. Under pristine Marxism, income transfers were to be made "from each according to his deed, to each according to his needs." Now income transfers are from each according to his income, to each according to his entitlement.

Fairness also replaces the goal of equality of the Old Socialism and the paternalism of the welfare state. Substituting fairness for welfare enhances the acceptability of the programs enacted. Indeed, the word welfare has developed a bad connotation, a case of social halitosis, while fairness implies a comprehensive and elastic social scheme evoking images of equity, as distinct from equality. A current example of the power of the word is the title Congress has given to proposed legislation on striker replacements in the private sector, the Workplace Fairness Act of 1991. Likewise, with respect to the 1992 presidential election, a *Wall Street Journal* headline read, "Congressional Democrats Choose Tax Fairness, Health Care as Issues on Which to Make a Stand" (Birnbaum, 1991, p. A. 12). Similarly, Novak has observed that [s]ocialism may be dead in the (former) U.S.S.R.; socialism may be dying in Sweden; but its last stand in America is the belief that inequality of income is 'unfair'" (Novak, 1991).

Because of the doctrine of Fairness and its pragmatic programs, the New Society appeals to a constituency wholly alien to the Old Socialism or a laboristic society, the middle class. In fact, the New Socialism is the socialism of the middle class! It can be called the Socialism of the middle class because so many if not most of its programs – entitlements – are for the middle class. Contrast this with the appeal of Marxian socialism to the proletariat who had nothing to lose but the capitalist chains which bound them, and a world to win.

The middle class and the New Unionism are not at odds; in fact they depend upon one another marking yet another distinctive element of the New Society. The middle class are major consumers of public services, generating the demand for increased production of services by public employees and ultimately, in many instances, union members. Nevertheless, there is no widespread middle class support of the New Unionism. The reason lies in the fact that the middle class are also taxpayers. Similar reasoning explains the antagonism of members of the Old Unionism to the goals of the New.

While the New Society is futuristic in outlook, paradoxically it also evokes social arrangements of an earlier time, the Middle Ages:

> The society of that time rested on relations and duties, not on isolated individuals and rights. ... the typical man did not compete. The several economic

activities in a medieval community were regarded as services to the ... community in which he [the typical man] held his estate (Pound, 1959, p. 4).

Like its medieval counterpart, the contemporary doctrine of fairness is based on the relationship of the typical man to society. However, unlike that earlier relationship, contemporary society requires few reciprocal duties or service from recipients of its services. Thus, contemporary rights to entitlement programs comes from one's "estate," or position, in the New Redistributive Society.

The New Unionism's philosophy in the New Society is "social unionism." It has been defined by one important union as "unionism which is rooted in the workplace, but understands the *importance of participating in, and influencing, the general direction of society*" (Canadian Auto Workers, undated; emphasis in the original). While the source of this definition of social unionism and its goal of a New Society comes from a Canadian union, it applies to unions in the U.S. as well. At this point, Canadian unions lead in the explication of social unionism.

Despite its abjuration of a formal and doctrinaire approach to the New Society, the New Unionism does have a philosophy. As Laski put it in describing the philosophy of the Old Unionism, the political issues involved in attaining union objectives "make it imperative for trade unions to have a policy, which may be empirical in its daily approach, but must, nevertheless, be informed by a body of long-term principles, by what, in fact, is a philosophy ..." (Laski, p. 33). Laski went on to point out that the "body of long term principles" which becomes a "union philosophy ... is generally more likely to develop after the trade union has twisted and turned to adapt itself to a developing situation than while the situation, in all its rich variety, is trying to find some stable basis of equilibrium in society" (Laski, p. 28). Such a dynamic period is now upon the New Unionism and the American society. This dynamic, the New Environment, is forging the philosophy of the New Unionism, social unionism, whose goal is the socialization of income.

Paradoxically, the New Unionism of our era may fulfill Harold Laski's goal of income redistribution. Laski did not foresee either the New Unionism of our time or that American unions could practice the philosophy of social unionism. In fact, he had derided American (private) unions' adherence to "business unionism," the philosophy which dominated the outlook of the Old Unionism in this country until the New Deal. He denounced "business unionism" as not only incapable of fulfilling the workers' wider goals, but even in standing in the way of that fulfillment. The paradox is that the very reasons he gave for the shortcomings in the philosophy of business unionism have become the basic elements of social unionism. Thus, he castigated business unionism because

> ...it discourages the worker from relating his job to the complex of social relations in which he is involved and because its insistence upon denying to him the reality of a wider hope conditions him to the very state of mind which ... privileged groups desire him to accept that their privilege may go unchallenged (Laski, p. 39).

In his view, business unionism, the pre-New Deal philosophy of the Old Unionism, "kept workers in their place" and distanced them from programs which would transform society. Laski condemned business unionism for divorcing collective bargaining from the unions' "civic" responsibilities (social unionism) and, even worse, for lulling union members into accepting the interests of private property over the wider social interests of workers. Collective bargaining, he argued, cannot resolve all the issues workers face either as workers or citizens; only a larger outlook and goal with a program are capable of doing that.

Contrary to that assessment of collective bargaining, in the public labor market, collective bargaining has not only altered sovereignty (Chapter III), but is day-to-day impact accomplishes the larger outlook of social unionism – "participating in, and influencing, the general direction of society." Succinctly, collective bargaining by the New Unionism is the process by which income redistribution from the private to the public sector comes about.

This makes the New Unionism and its link to the New Society so pedestrian in appearance. There is nothing about it which compares to the "sturm und drang" often associated with the Old Socialism. The New Unionism will not bring workers to the barricades to win the New Society, but it will have deep-seated and long lasting consequence for the American economy and society. As Charles Lindbloom put it in describing the Old Unionism in this country many years ago, but really more applicable to the New Unionism of our time: "Little wonder that it is rarely perceived that unionism in the United States now is as revolutionary in consequence as it is conservative in intention" (Lindbloom, p. 20).

It is evident from this overview of the New Environment of our time, that a far reaching transformation of organized labor, the labor market, the economy, and social doctrines, has been unfolding in this country. The transformation has changed what unions are, what they do and why. Such issues are the substance of this study.

CHAPTER II.

The New and the Old Union Movements

Origins

Labor analysts typically describe and analyze the American Labor Movement as a single entity. Until the 1960s, this procedure was historically satisfactory, if not entirely accurate, because organized labor was essentially a private sector institution (the Old Unionism) and could, therefore, be dealt with as single body. This treatment was applied not only to the U.S. union movement, but also to those abroad, so all international comparisons were based on the assumption of unitary union movements across countries. When the new public sector unionism appeared in strength, changing the make-up of the union movement, the assumptions and comparisons became invalid. But analysts in general continued to examine unions across countries as though nothing had changed. As a result they misread actual trends in unionism across countries and reached false conclusions. Specifically, the international decline in the Old Unionism was masked by the rise of the New leading prominent analysts to declare that the U.S. was unique in the decline of unionism among advanced industrial nations (Troy, 1990a,b,and c). These generalizations marred analytical procedures in evaluating unions' over-all (macro) effects on the private labor market since the union variable was "contaminated" with public sector data. Obviously, organized public and labor markets must be treated separately, as micro-studies measuring union effects on wages have done. Since analysts distinguish between the two markets in order to measure the relative wage effects of public as compared to private sector unions, surely the requirement extends to other analytical purposes: What the New Unions are, what they do, and why.

I treat the private and public union movements separately because they are, in fact, separate movements, affiliation with a common federation notwithstanding (Troy 1990c). Their histories, even the labor organizations comprising them, their attributes and goals, and the factors governing trends in each sector outweigh their common characteristics. Indeed, sectoral union movements share transnational rather than intra-national trends in membership and market penetration as well as other characteristics.

Differences between the New and the Old Unionism begin with their origins. In all market economies, unions originated in the private labor market and during most of their history were concentrated in that market. Private sector unions date back to the 18th century when they were established as substitutes for government (mercantilist) regulation of labor conditions. Before that, government regulation of labor (and all other) markets had been the standard economic policy for centuries among European nations. These regulatory practices were brought to their colonies in North America and continued in the into the early history of the country. When mercantilist controls began to disintegrate during the 18th century, under the impact of economic development, inflation generated by wars, and a gradual shifting toward laissez-faire economic policy, labor markets increasingly free of government controls emerged and with them trade unions. Workers formed unions for the purpose of thwarting market forces by regulating the terms and conditions of employment hitherto carried out by custom, law and government. Paradoxically, therefore, trade unions in the private sector owe their origin to markets even though they are an anti-market (monopoly) force.

A similar history accounts for the formation of the first unions ever, in Britain, earlier in the 18th century. Private sector trade unions were first established in Britain before the middle of the 18th century (the Webbs, 1950). In this country unions first appeared during the last decade of that century (Commons, 1946). In both countries, unions arose among skilled blue collar workers in an effort to blunt the effects of increasingly competitive markets on wages and working conditions. The Webbs' use of the term, trade union, indicated that the first occupations unionized were skilled, not the unskilled. Otherwise, they would have used the term "labor unions," as later came to be the case when unions of unskilled workers were set-up. While the skilled groups felt the impact of spreading markets and the division of labor, they were largely unaffected by the industrial revolution. In fact, the two developments, the industrial revolution and the formation of unions, proceeded largely independently of one another (Mantoux, p. 78). Initial efforts to organize the growing number of unskilled in the industries initially impacted by the industrial revolution, textile manufacturing, had little success. Only later, when private unions made inroads into the semi-skilled and unskilled workers did the term labor union arise. In due course the two terms lost their distinction and became interchangeable. Legislation, notably the National Labor Relations Act, introduced the term labor organization; the word union is absent from the law. Currently, all three expressions are interchangeable and are treated as equivalent in this study.

Definitions of Unions

While the three terms, trade union, labor union and labor organization, are generically the same, this study defines unions differently in the private and public sectors of the labor market. Such a distinction is not made in the extensive literature on unions; indeed, even the word union is seldom defined.

The importance of the defining unions was clearly perceived by the Webbs, who were not only among the earliest chroniclers of unions, but also among the most thorough. Appraising what unions are in private and public (socialist) labor markets caused them to revise their initial definition of a union. The Webbs originally defined a trade union as a "continuous association of wage-earners [organized] for the purpose of maintaining or improving the conditions of their employment (the Webbs, 1950, p. 1 and note 1). Subsequently, they revised their definition because fellow socialists' objected that their definition did not distinguish between the private (capitalist) and public (socialist) sectors of the labor market and economy. They objected specifically to the inclusion of the phrase, "of their employment," in the definition, because to them the expression implied acceptance of the perpetual existence of the capitalist system of private property and wage payment. They persuaded the Webbs that their original definition excluded unions in a socialist economy. Put another way, the Webbs recognized that what unions are, what unions do, and why in a private labor market would diverge from what they are, do, and why in the public (socialist) labor market. The same reasoning applies to the mixed private-public labor markets and economys of today. Unions in the public sector conceptually stand apart from the private sector and should therefore be defined differently.

In response to their fellow socialists' criticism, the Webbs altered their definition of a trade union and replaced the phrase, "of their employment," in their definition with the phrase, "of their working lives." As the Webbs explained, the change implied two things: First, that trade unions are different in capitalist and public (socialist) labor markets. Therefore, in the present context, the definition of a union in the (socialized) public sector should on theoretical grounds, differ from the definition of a union in the private sector. Likewise, on empirical grounds, diverse theoreticians like Harold Laski and Ludwig von Mises (1951) have shown, unions are expected to perform differently in a public (socialist) labor market than in a capitalist one.

The definitional difference between private and public sector unions is a distinction with a difference. The attention to definition should not be regarded as pedagogical dancing on the head of a semantical pin; it distinguishes, as the conventional wisdom does not, why the New Unionism differs from the Old. While competitive private markets shaped the meaning of the Old Unionism in the private economy, public sector, the New Unionism, owes little to market forces. Instead, public policy, in furtherance of the goal of "fairness" in the labor market and industrial relations, initiated and shaped the New Unionism. Public policy justified the need for unions and collective bargaining in the public sector, at least in part, on the contention "that it is simply *unfair* to permit, indeed encourage, private sector bargaining while denying similar rights to public employees" (Westbrook, 1986, p. 358, emphasis added). In contrast to private sector unions, public sector unions are essentially the product of political decisions and public policy. Therefore, what they are, their definition, should also differ from the definition of private sector unions, just as the Webbs intended.

However, in the historical literature and statistical records on unions, public sector organizations, such as those in the U.S. Post Office Department, were simply included in the general statistics of unions. This practice was generally accepted because until the rise of the New Unionism, public sector organizations were on the "fringe" of the (private) labor movement and many were affiliated with the American Federation of Labor.

In the private sector, I define a union as a continuous association of wage and salaried workers organized to redistribute income from private employers to their employees through collective bargaining.

In the public sector I define a union as a continuous association of salaried and wage employees organized to redistribute income from public employers to their employees through political and economic means;

and to redistribute income from the private to the public economy. The definition reflects the dual actions of bargaining and the important political aspect of that bargaining.

The definition differs from the Webbs, because theirs applied to skilled blue collar occupations (hence the term, trade union) and public ownership of the goods industries. Under the influence of 19th century concepts of socialism, they thought of public ownership only in terms of such industries as coal mining, manufacturing industries, transportation, communication and utilities (see Fuchs, 1968 on the definition of goods industries). The Webbs did not anticipate the displacement of these industries by service industries and the predominance of white collar occupations. The definition used here can apply to either goods or services. In the U.S., public ownership in goods is limited, but does include, under the concept used here, communication and utilities. Thus, it includes the U.S. Postal Service and the Tennessee Valley Authority. Currently, the USPS is governed by private labor law, the National Labor Relations Act, and the TVA by federal public sector law, although since its inception in the 1930s, administrators of the Authority have applied the policies of the National Labor Relations Act.

The political dimension of the New Unionism's bargaining distinguishes it from the Old Unionism. The political aspect in the definition of the New Unions binds them as a group separating them from the market aspect of the definition of the Old Unionism. It also binds the New Unionism more closely as a group. In contrast, the market dimension of the Old Unionism spawns diversity in goals and practices among the constituent unions. For example, those unions adversely affected by imports seek restraints on free international trade. On the other hand, unions in exporting industries take an opposite view. By contrast, the public labor market fosters less division of interests among the constituent organizations: There is less industrial diversity among the three levels of government, with functions often being the same at all levels, thereby fostering greater unanimity of purpose among the unions. For example, while education is still a primary function at the local level, the unions involved all seek federal and state funding to augment local expenditures.

In his discussion of the characteristics of the public sector unions Freeman also calls attention to their political dimension as a distinction between them and the private sector unions: "A fundamental difference between public and private sector collective bargaining is that public sector unions can affect the demand for [their] labor through the political process, as well as affect wages and working conditions through collective bargaining" (Freeman, 1986, p. 42). However, Freeman does not extend this insight to declare public sector unionism as the New Unionism, as set forth in this study. While his characterization is consistent with the definition presented here, it does not go far enough. It does not take into account the most significant intent of that political activity – to redistribute more of the national income from the private to the public sector of the economy.

Private unions, too, have used political power to raise both the demand for their services and the wages paid through political power, as evidenced by the Davis-Bacon and Walsh-Healey Acts. However, the effect has but a small impact on the redistribution of income from the private to the public economys. Moreover, these private sector unions and their members regard themselves as private, not public sector institutions. Nevertheless, their actions suggest that there is yet another branch of the labor market, unionism and industrial relations, the "quasi-public" sector which merits study. A sketch of this evolving sector is presented in Chapter III.

The New Unionism of this study also differs from the unions in nationalized industries (of Europe). Unions in nationalized unions are branches of private unions. The New Unionism of this study originated in the public sector and rejects socialization of the basic goods industries, the keystone of the Old Socialism and therefore the tenets of unions in the nationalized industries.

The New Unionism

Literally the term, the New Unionism, is not original to this study. Richard Freeman, too, refers to public sector unionism as the "New Unionism" (Freeman, 1986, p. 44), but my use of the term differs radically from his. My usage identifies the New Unionism as a new genus in labor organization in this country and abroad (Chapter I). In contrast, Freeman uses the expression to refer to two developments: First, the spectacular growth of union membership and market penetration in the public sector labor market since the 1960s; and, second, to identify this momentous episode in union history as an illustration of the "spurt" theory of union growth. According to Freeman, the surge in public sector unionism exemplified the theory of union that "[u]nions typically grow in sudden spurts after years of stagnation ... [and that] this is true of public sector unions in the United States" (Freeman, 1986, p. 44). His discussion addresses the expansion of public sector unionism as an aspect of the general expansion of labor organization, rather than the creation of a new union movement, as the title of his paper makes clear: "Unionism Comes to the Public Sector." Other analysts, Burton and Thomason (1988), and Stieber (1973) regarded the growth in public sector unions in the same way as Freeman. None treated the growth of public sector unionism as a new union movement, as I do. Burton and Thomason examined and critiqued Freeman's analysis of public sector unionism and they, too, treated his term, the New Unionism, as nothing more than an aspect of the general growth in unionism. The premise and application of the "spurt" theory are limited to union growth in the private sector, episodes which differ in causality of the growth of the New Unionism.

The conventional explanation of the growth of public sector unionism attributes its spurt either to government intervention (Freeman, 1986) or a sudden propensity of public employees for union representation and collective bargaining (Burton and Thomason, 1988). I also regard government, public policy as the responsible factor in the creation of the New Unionism. However, my explanation differs radically from the conventional one. Governmental policy impacted the organizational antecedents which became the New Unionism, rather than individual workers encouraging them to join unions. In contrast, in the 1930s governmental policies fostered the organization of hitherto unorganized workers, and the workers themselves showed a strong demand for unionism. That episode in union history was, indeed, an example of the spurt theory of unionism. The rise of public sector unionism, the New Unionism, beginning in the 1960s is not an example of the spurt analysis and is therefore to be distinguished from the rise of the Congress of Industrial Organizations (CIO) in the 1930s, and earlier episodes of major expansions in the Old Unionism.

The explosion in public sector unionism is the result of a process unique in the history of unionism, what I call "organizing the organized." Paradoxically, therefore, neither the major organizations nor the millions of members of the New Unionism are newly organized workers. The New Unionism is the result of public policies of the 1960s which compelled the transformation of existing associations and organizations of public employees into full-fledged unions. The major unions in the New Unionism are, in fact, organizations transformed into unions as a result of those and these successor organizations comprise the bulk of the New Unionism. Thus, instead of a spurt of employees suddenly joining unions, the associations which became unions had only a Hobson's choice: become unions or disappear.

Although the process of organizing the organized was unique, the process itself was not unique to the U.S. A parallel development took place in Canada beginning in the mid-1960s, just after the process started in the U.S., and was initiated by policies adopted by Canadian governments, federal and provincial, in emulation of U.S. policies. These policies had the same result: the transformation of public and professional associations with large memberships into labor unions. In contrast to these developments, the process of union growth in the 1930s and 1940s, and in earlier episodes was the process of organizing the unorganized.

My use of the term "the New Unionism" also differs from Heckscher. His book, *The New Unionism*, deals with employee involvement in the management of the company (1988). It deals with the private not the public sector and concerns the unions' role in the management of the enterprise.

From Back To Center Stage: Unionism's New Center of Gravity

The rise of the New Unionism over the last thirty years ranks in importance with the permanent establishment of private sector union movement, the founding of the American Federation of Labor (AFL) in the last century. It has now moved from back to center stage in union affairs and will in the not distant future become the center of gravity of the union movement as a whole. The balance of power within the union movement as a whole will shift from the private to the public sector.

Historically, these developments have come about quickly. The New Unionism's speed of development far outpaced the AFL and the CIO. Moreover, while the CIO extended the Old Unionism to more blue collar workers, the Old Unionism remained exactly that, a blue collar movement. In contrast, the rise of the New Unionism transformed the union movement as a whole by enrolling millions of government employees, most of them white collar workers. Thus, it changed the very stuff of unionism, diluting its blue collar and private character.

The transformation the nature of the union movement as a whole has been accelerated by the divergent trends in the New and the Old Unionism in membership and market share. These trends have altered the relative strengths of the two union groups. As the New has grown, the Old Unionism has declined, further altering the relative strengths of each. When the conventional wisdom, in this case a noted labor arbitrator (!), sought to explain the decline of the Old Unionism they singled out private sector employers as the responsible cause in these colorful and pungent terms:

> The assault on unions being waged by many of the nation's private employers has no counterpart in most of the public sector. In the private sector, anti-union employers are stirred to action by the smell of blood of a wounded and weakened labor movement, but in the government employment sector most unions are healthy and strong (Aaron, 1988, p. 315).

Actually, however "bloody-minded" private employers may be, they are only marginal in the explanation of the decline of the Old Unionism, as I have shown (Troy, 1990a,b,c). As for the vigor of the public sector, instead of opposition from public management, the New Unionism finds the welcome mat laid out, not to mention helpful cooperation in the bargaining process. Indeed, it is questionable whether the bargaining relationship has any resemblance to the adversarial tone in the private sector of industrial relations (Chapter III).

Like the life-cycle of the industries in which they are established, the Old Unionism is now in a state of permanent decline. It is not because of "bloody-minded" private employers, but primarily because the economy is making an anachronism of so much of the Old Unionism, as it did in the past. Thus, individual unions associated with industries whose life cycle has come and gone share the fate of those industries as is illustrated by an abbreviated historical roll call of unions associated with the rise and fall of private sector industries: Elastic Goring Workers, Carriage Workers, Chandelier Workers, Straw and Ladies Hat Workers, Stogie Makers, Steel Plate Transferrers, Tip Printers, Glass Flatteners, Sheep Shearers, Mule Spinners, Cigar Makers, Broom and Whisk Makers, Tube Workers, Tack Makers, Sawsmiths, Gold Beaters, Pocket Knife Grinders. Major contemporary unions, like the Auto Workers and Steel Workers, are going through a long term process of decline, albeit not oblivion. Today these once powerful unions are less than one-half their peak size and still shrinking as their associated industries shrink.

On the other hand, the public sector is a growth industry, with employment on an ascending curve, so the New Unionism has expanded throughout the sector as a whole, among all governmental sectors and at all levels of government. Labor Department data for 1991 indicate a continuing expansion of the New Unionism as a whole with membership at record levels and penetration near record levels, 37% in 1991 (U.S.

Department of Labor, 1992, Table 58, p. 229) and 40% in 1976 (Troy, and Sheflin, 1985, Appendix Table A, p. A-2). Census data on state and local governments confirm the growth of membership at both the state and local levels between October 1982 and October 1987, but a slippage in local government unionization compared to a small gain at the state level (U.S. Bureau of Census, June 1991, Table A. p. V). It is unclear whether the slippage is actual or the result of statistical methods. However, it is certainly consistent with the sharp decline in federal funds shipped to the states during the Reagan years. This forced states and local governments to fend increasingly for themselves and would seem to account for the slow down in the New Unionism at the local level. However, in about 40 of the 50 states, state employment rose more than population between 1980 and 1989, according to Census data. The average for all states showed state employment up 19% compared to a population increase of 9% over the decade.

At the state and local levels, nearly 80 percent of all public employees work in seven governmental functions – education, fire protection, hospitals, police protection, public welfare and sanitation. Most organized of full time employees are fire protection (65%), teachers (58%), police (54%), and sanitation (50%). At the federal level defense (civilian employment), postal environment and housing, and health services are the major functional sectors of employment. A short roster of the unions which are part of the New Unionism illustrates their extensive organization of public employment: the National Education Association, the American Federation of Teachers, a large number of non-instructional associations of school employees, the National Treasury Employees Union, the American Federation of Government Employees, the National Federation of Licensed Practical Nurses, the American Nurses Association, the National Fraternal Order of Police, numerous independent police associations, and the International Association of Fire Fighters.

The divergent trends of the Old and the New Unionism are international. The patterns which have occurred in the U.S. are to be found among all advanced industrialized nations. In the U.S. the Old Unionism, now has dropped below its 1929 market penetration of 12%. Its record high in 1953 was 36% of the private labor market. Since 1970 the Old Unionism has given up more than 7 million members and further losses can be expected. By the beginning of the new millennium, the Old Unionism's market share will most likely drop to about the ratio it registered at the beginning of the 20th century, about 7% of employment. In Churchill's words, the full circle in the Old Unionism's market share exemplifies "the symmetry of history." In sharp contrast to the Old Unionism, since the 1960s, the New Unionism has climbed to new heights in both market share and the number of members. At this time, New Unionism's market share of 37% more than triples the Old Unionism's 12% and its membership is 6.6 million compared to 9.9 million private sector union members (U.S. Department of Labor, 1992, p. 229). Further, if modest, gains in the New Unionism are likely as we head toward the new century.

These contrary developments have radically changed the "center of gravity" and the balance of power within organized labor: They have altered the relative importance of the New and the Old Unionism, and therefore the basic structure of the American Labor Movement as a whole. Coupled with the growth/stability of public sector unionism, the "center of gravity" and balance of power in union membership is steadily shifting from the private to the public sector of the labor market. And these shifts in unionism will have far reaching consequences for workers, political institutions and the economy.

Again, these developments are not unique to the United States (Troy, 1991; 1990a). While private sector unionism is declining across all advanced industrial nations, the New Unionism is growing or stable. As the life cycles of the Old and New Unionism unfold, the membership of the New Unionism will eventually become the dominant element of organized labor in the United States, as it already has in the labor movements of most advanced industrial countries. Unionism in Canada, Britain, France and probably in Italy has already undergone that structural shift. Apparently the only major Western European country in which the Old Unionism still prevails is Germany, and that mainly because of the export driven manufacturing industries. Switzerland's union movement also remains primarily private sector, both because of exports and a policy which maintains a relatively small public sector. In all advanced industrial nations, the New Unionism has scored not only a higher market penetration than the Old, but currently exceeds the highest market penetration ever achieved by the Old Unionism.

Of particular interest are developments in Canada because of a similar economy, the Free Trade Agreement between the two countries and, of course, our proximity. The politically correct assessment of Canadian and U.S. comparisons championed the Canadian experience with the

Old Unionism as an example for the U.S.. That assessment believed that Canada's Old Unionism had escaped the "American disease," decline. Actually, the contrary proved to be case, as I have already indicated.

However, Canada is an exemplar of what the U.S. can expect in the public labor market. In Canada the New Unionism overtook the Old during the decade 1975–1985. (The absence of annual data make the dating uncertain, but it was probably 1980, one year after the peak in membership of the Old Unionism.) The change in position came about because of growth of the New Unionism and decline of the Old (Troy, 1990a). The remarkable feature of the Canadian record is that despite more interventionist policies in the private labor market, these failed to prevent the decline of the Canada's Old Unionism. Moreover, the Old Unionism's decline in membership and market share extends over nearly as long a period as the American (Troy, 1991b). This is surprising because the U.S. led Canada by a longer period in structural changes in the labor market which have been responsible for most of the declining membership and market share of the Old Unionism. While the peak membership of the Old Unionism in the U.S. came in 1970, the Canadian peak was reached nine years later, in 1979. Private unions' market share hit its all-time high in 1953 in the U.S. and in 1958 in Canada (Troy, 1991 b).

On the other hand, Canada's very interventionist policies in the public labor market have raised the New Unionism's market share to record levels as well as converting the Canadian movement dominated by the Old one dominated by the New Unionism (Troy, 1990a). Its effect on Canadian political life is indicated by its contribution to the election of the New Democratic Party to govern Ontario, Canada's most important province. In the U.S., a comparable role in the exercise of political power has been wielded by the New Unionism. Examples are New York City and State, as is evident in the electoral process and the fiscal crises of each.

U.S. trends are clearly headed where the Canadians have already gone. Chart 1 shows that in the short span of three decades, the "center of gravity" of American union membership has already shifted dramatically. Between 1960 and 1991, the New Unionism grew so rapidly that it now constitutes nearly four of ten union members, up from less than one in ten in 1960. In 1960 public sector membership accounted for less than six percent of the total and in 1991 nearly 40 percent, almost a seven-fold increase. This remarkable development also came about with none of the stresses, strains and industrial warfare which characterized the periods of union expansion, the spurts in growth which occurred in the private sector in the past.

By the beginning of the 21st century, the New Unionism will comprise over forty percent of the total Labor Movement compared to fewer than 2% of its predecessor public sector groups in 1900. Early in the next century the New Unionism will replace Old as the dominant wing of Labor-U.S. in membership. If the 20th century was the century of the Old Unionism, the 21st will be the century of the New Unionism in the U.S. and in the Western world generally.

Public Policy and the New Unionism

What accounts for the dramatic change in public sector organization over the century between the beginning of the 20th and the beginning of the 21st? How could a union sector accounting for less than 2% of total U.S. membership in 1900 become (an estimated) 40% by the year 2000. The answer, in a word, is government. Government policy favoring unionization was the over-riding factor which produced this transformation.

The origin and rise New Unionism differ from the Old and therefore cannot be explained by the same factors as those applied to private sector unions. When industrial relations specialists have constructed a theoretical framework to explain the development of unions, they have historically addressed the private sector only (Dunlop, 1948). The Old Unionism was the dominant wing of organized labor and the focus was therefore justified. Updates to account for the explosion of the New Unionism typically treats it as example of historical spurts in membership. For reasons given above, this theory is inapplicable.

John Dunlop identified four areas or issues which industrial relations specialists have historically used to explain the development of (private) unions. Explanation of their origins; patterns of growth; ultimate goals; and the motives of workers to join (Dunlop, 1948, pp. 164–165). In applying these criteria to the New Unionism, I conclude that they provide an analysis of the New Unionism which, like so much else already noted, sets it apart from the Old.

The origin of the New Unions emanated from public policy. Indeed, it is not an exaggeration to assert that the New Unionism is a product of "Fairness." As one analyst put it, "it is simply unfair to permit, indeed encourage, private sector bargaining while denying similar rights to public employees" (Westbrook, 1986, p. 358).

The growth of the New Unionism consisted predominantly in the transformation of existing public and professional associations into unions, or what I have described above as "organizing the organized," rather than organizing the unorganized.

The ultimate goal of the New Unionism, whether or not explicit, is the socialization of income, the redistribution of more of the national income from the private to the public sector.

I believe that public sector employees are motivated to join the New Unionism because as members of organizations which became unions, they were swept into union membership in the transformation process. The benefit/cost ratio has also been favorable. By benefit I mean total compensation, and by cost I mean the relative ease of joining, the freedom from lay-offs, unemployment and time lost in strikes compared to private workers and the absence of employer opposition. Indeed, public management, the political management in particular, actually encourages membership, even in the absence of agreements requiring membership as a condition of employment.

Because the decisive factor in the origin of the New Unionism is the visible hand of government favoring unions and bargaining, government intervention shows why it is necessary to include a political dimension in the definition and bargaining activities of the New Unionism, and therefore why that definition given above must be distinct from private unionism. While public policy encouraging unions and bargaining has contributed significantly to the development of the Old Unionism, indeed even causing a structural break in its development, its origins were independent of policy and were owed to markets (Chapter I). In fact, during the unions' formative years in the 19th century and into the early 20th, public policy toward labor organization was either hostile or indifferent.

Public policy has also played a different role in the durability of the New and the Old Unionism. Public policy has been much more effective in enhancing the staying power of the New Unionism than the Old Unionism. In the private economy, public policy has had an asymmetrical impact on the Old Unionism. At the inception of policies enacted to foster unionism and bargaining they stimulated growth. Later the power of these policies dissipated under the impact of competitive markets (Troy, 1992). Thus, the legal immunities granted by the Railway Labor Act of 1926, the Norris-Laguardia Act of 1932, the National Labor Relations Act of 1935, the policies of the National War Labor Board of World War

II, and many judicial decisions spurred the Old Unionism in its expansionary phase of the 1930s and 1940s, but could not later arrest the declining life cycle of the Old Unionism in both membership and market share.

In contrast, public policy has fortified the New Unionism's extensive "natural" immunity to competitive markets with symmetrical protection in good economic times and bad. A measure of the "natural" immunity of the public labor market it the virtual insusceptibility of public labor markets to unemployment. Department of Labor statistics show that the unemployment rate of government workers is in the 2% range (*Employment and Earnings*, Jan. 1991, Table 11, p. 175) while unemployment rates in the private sector more than tripled that rate. A 2% unemployment rate in the private market would be accompanied by overpowering inflation. The stability of public sector employment quite naturally affects the stability of the New compared to Old Unionism in membership, market share and the organizational structures themselves. Few, if any local units of the New Unionism have folded while the number of local and other units of the Old Unionism have disappeared over the past thirty years. Not only do these facts augur well for the future durability of public sector unionism, but they reinforce the expectation that the New Unionism will become the majority movement in the next century. Even in the face of what politicians euphemistically called "budget cutbacks," public employment and the New Unionism have yet to shrink. Typically, "budget cutbacks" translate into a slowdown the rate of public expenditures, not an absolute reduction; and layoffs typically culminate in no reductions of total employment.

Freeman, too, recognized public policy as the decisive factor in the origin and growth of public sector (the New Unionism):

> What changes led to the sudden organization of traditionally non-unionizable public sector workers? First and foremost were changes in the laws regulating public sector workers (Freeman, 1986. p.45).

A different explanation for the New Unionism has been offered by other analysts, notably Burton and Thomason. In their review of the origin and growth of the New Unionism (which they term public sector unionism), they reject public policy as the dominant causative factor, choosing instead "organization over legislation" (Burton and Thomason, 1988, p. 27). By that they meant "the long tradition of public sector unionism" (Burton and Thomason, quoting G. Saltzman p. 27) as the driving force leading to the expansion of public sector unions beginning in the 1960s. I find that mystifying since public sector unionism, prior to the

1960s, consisted of scattered groups at the state and local level, while at the federal level, the "tradition of public sector unionism" was concentrated in the Post Office. Although the contemporary New Unionism may not be as distant a relative to pre-1960s public sector unions as modern man is to *homo habilus*, the kinship is far removed. It is also paradoxical that when academic supporters of unionism, the Old and the New, seek ways to revive the Old and enhance the New, they invariably call for the visible hand of government intervention in the labor market (Troy, 1991a). Finally, it highly likely that most public employees were members of associations which in philosophy were pressure groups hostile to unionism.

Even more convincing of the power of policy to promote unionism is the example of Canada. Canada offers a laboratory case and a quod est demonstrandum (q.e.d.) of the power of an industrial relations system to produce a sustained expansion in the New Unionism. There policy induced a structural break in the body unionism so large that within the decade 1975–1985 the "center of gravity" and the balance of power within the Canadian unionism shifted from the private to the public sector (Troy, 1990b).

More evidence of the power of public policy to stimulate the New Unionism comes from an analysis of municipal unionism over the period 1977 and 1982 (Zax and Ichniowski, 1990). That study compared five different government services in over 10,000 departments which were without bargaining laws at the beginning of the period but which adopted them by 1982. It found that the changes in unionization attributable to law accounted for nearly all the differences in average density rates between states with and without laws encouraging unionism and bargaining. Previously, Ichniowski had concluded that in the absence of policies favoring unions, it takes "forever" to unionize (Freeman and Ichniowski, 1988, p. 3). Indeed, he wrote, "... that the nature of the bargaining law is the most important factor in influencing unionization rates" (Ichniowski, in Freeman and Ichniowski, 1988, p. 29). However, what these researchers did not consider was how much of the "new unionization" was attributable to "organizing the organized," the conversion of independent associations into unions. My assessment is that the adoption of state policies requiring local governments to bargain compelled a Hobson's choice by existing associations – become unions or vanish from the scene. This means that the process by which public policy encouraged the formation of unions in the private and public sectors have historically been different. In the private sector, policy led to the organization of the unorganized. In the public sector, policy favoring the organization of the organized dominated the process; organizing the unorganized was a secondary reason.

The attitude of public sector employees toward joining unions may have contributed to the upswell in the New Unionism in the 1960s and early 1970s. As one commentator wrote: "... the time was ripe for organization. There is very little question that the climate of protest during the 1960s, reflected in the civil-rights movement and anti-war demonstrations, and society's general tolerance of the disruptive actions of such groups were significant factors in encouraging the new [public] employee militancy" (*Morgan Guaranty Survey*, Feb. 1974, p. 8). Still, as the same commentator wrote, "Just why [public] employee attitudes ... underwent so far-reaching a change is not altogether clear." In more recent times, surveys of nonunion workers in both the U.S. and Canada show that about two-thirds would not vote for a union in a secret ballot election (Harris, 1984; CFL, 1991). Even though the sample in each country was primarily from the private sector, public employees were included in both surveys. These results indicate the efficacy of public policy in generating unionism, especially in the public labor market.

In the U.S., public policy toward unionism in the public labor market evolved slowly, only culminating in a radical shift in the 1960s. At the beginning of the 20th century, government policy toward unions of public employees ranged from negative to mildly tolerant. There were few labor organizations among government employees and most of these were in the federal service, the U.S. Post Office Department, the naval shipyards, government arsenals and in the Government Printing Office. In addition to the limited presence of labor organization in the federal government, there was also a small union presence among some municipal employees in Chicago, the police in Boston (culminating in their disastrous strike of 1919) and among some state and county hospitals (Carroll, 1923, pp. 96–97; Spero, 1972; Ziskind, 1940). Over-all, however, the number of organized employees in the public labor market was meager and hardly noticeable among the growing union population of private sector workers as the 20th century unfolded.

Records of continuous membership of public sector unions date from the starting year for all unions, 1897 (Wolman, 1924, Table I, p. 112; Wolman, 1936, Table I, p. 193; Troy and Sheflin, Appendix A, 1985). Based on these records and Spero's pioneering work on public sector unionism (1972, Chapter 7), I identify the first continuous national public sector organizations as those in the Post Office Department. At the local level of government, there were organizations of Teachers and Fire Fighters and some scattered local unions of employees in municipal services. Few of these locals, however, had any collective bargaining agreements (Commons, 1913, pp. 106–119 and p. 184). It is unclear whether the locals Commons referred to were independents or affiliates of national private sector organizations, such as the International Brotherhood of Electrical Workers. If they were the latter, then they presaged the development of the mixed union, a change in union form to be discussed below.

The initial government stimulus to public employee organization in the federal service was the enactment of the Lloyd-Lafollette Act of 1912. The Act's jurisdiction was limited to the Post Office Department. To be eligible for protection under Lloyd-Lafollette, unions had to renounce the right to strike. The Act reversed the policies of the (Teddy) Roosevelt and (William Howard) Taft Administrations which prohibited federal employees from engaging in union activities on pain of dismissal. Until 1912, postal workers were the only group in the Federal service which had formed organizations to any extent; local affiliates were established in many Congressional districts and therefore were able to exercise more political influence than any other group of federal employees. Lloyd-Lafollette permitted employees in other federal departments and agencies to petition Congress individually or in groups. As these groups became established in other executive departments and agencies the protection of the Act was extended to them as well.

The policy of Lloyd-Lafollette was to tolerate labor organization in th e Federal service. Although it fell short of the outright encouragement to join unions later given by President Kennedy's Executive Order 10988 in 1962, it certainly was benign in its "neglect" of labor organization because it had a marked impact on the growth of federal labor organization, as indicated by the steady growth of union membership and new unions in the federal government (Troy and Sheflin, 1985, Appendix A). However, Lloyd-Lafollette should not be regarded as laissez-faire in government policy toward federal employees. It provided positive encouragement, albeit far less than what was to come. Limited though it was in comparison to what was to follow in 1962 and afterward, Lloyd-Lafollette not only stimulated the growth of membership in existing unions and in the formation of new unions, but also contributed to the stability of unions in the federal service, once established.

Another step in the extension of unionism in the Federal service was the adoption of the Keiss Act in 1924. This legislation applied to employees in the Government Printing Office, an agency under the direct control of Congress. Most of the employees affected were in the printing trades. The Act led to rapid growth of unionism among the printing trades unions in the GPO and eventually led to the virtual total unionization of the agency.

Between the enactment of Lloyd-Lafollette (and Keiss) and President Kennedy's Executive Order 10988, there were no changes in public policy toward employees of the federal government. They were specifically excluded from coverage under the National Labor Relations Act, as were employees of state and local government. The latter were not even considered within the reach of federal law at the time. A half-century later this jurisdictional picture changed. As a result of the Supreme Court's decision in *Garcia* (469 U.S. 528, 1985), Congress can now regulate employee relations of state and local government. The details of that case and its implications for the New Unionism and the New Industrial Relations System are discussed in Appendix A.

E.O. 10988 shifted policy from tolerance and "benign neglect" under Lloyd-Lafollette to an activist and decisive policy encouraging the formation of unions and the commencement of bargaining, or what was termed negotiations, in the executive departments and agencies of the federal government. President Kennedy's Executive Order 10988 initiated what we now know as the New Unionism. The Order was promulgated on January 17, 1962 and became effective in July of that year. The Order was adopted in fulfillment of the President's pledge to the AFL-CIO in the course of the 1960 election campaign to foster union organization and bargaining in the federal service. Thus, the initiative leading to the formation of today's New Unionism came from principally from the Old Unionism rather than the government employees themselves. The Kennedy Administration decided to use the Executive Order as a substitute for legislation because of uncertainties about Congressional approval of its plan to foster the organization of federal employees of the executive departments and agencies, and the speedier application of an Order compared to legislation.

The Order applied to most civilian employees of the executive departments and agencies of the Federal Government. It was patterned after the National Labor Relations Act, but fell substantially short of that law's legal encouragement of unionization and collective bargaining. This policy difference measures the legal gap between public and private systems of industrial relations, a gap which the New Unionism wishes to close, by a process I call "convergence" (Chapter III).

E.O. 10988 was followed in 1969 by E.O. 11491 and that Order was further amended in 1971 and 1975. Cumulatively, these executive orders further strengthened the position of organized labor in the executive branch of the federal government. Title VII of the Civil Service Reform Act of 1978, effective January 11, 1979, replaced these executive orders with the statutory sanction of organized labor relations in the federal service long sought by organized labor. These steps also brought the federal labor relations system much closer to the private sector model of industrial relations, although strikes and compulsory membership (the union shop) continued to be prohibited, and continue to be banned. Compensation was likewise not subject to bargaining, but the unions' inability to claim credit for prevailing wages and benefits through economic action – strikes – is hardly a limitation on their status as unions. Instead, they can and do claim credit for gains in compensation through their political leverage. The process illustrates the importance of the political dimension of my definition of unions in the public sector.

Prior to the Civil Service Reform Act of 1978, the postal unions were removed from the jurisdiction of Executive Order 11491. Under the Postal Reorganization Act of 1970 the postal unions were transferred to the jurisdiction of the National Labor Relations Act and postal services were transferred from an executive department, the U.S. Post Office Department (which ceased to exist) to the Postal Corporation, operating a new entity, the U.S. Postal Service. The shift in legal jurisdiction is an important step toward convergence in industrial relations, a major goal of the New Unionism (Chapter III).

Under the 1970 Act transferring the postal unions to the jurisdiction of the NLRA, the unions were authorized to negotiate all issues negotiable in the private sector, except compulsory membership and pensions. These were hardly necessary since membership as a percentage of employment was nearly total and pensions benefits far exceed those of comparable workers in private industry. The postal unions continued to be denied the right to strike, but were given final and binding arbitration, a procedure sanctioned by court decisions (Stern, 1988, p. 56; Olson, 1988, p. 252). Just as they had received special recognition in the enactment of Lloyd-Lafollette in 1912, so nearly sixty years later, the postal unions were again given special treatment in federal labor policy. In this instance, it was recognition of their economic as well as their political power. The changeover followed an illegal strike of 200 thousand postal workers at major installations across the country. Although the Taft-Hartley Act (the Labor Management Relations Act of 1947) declared strikes by federal employees illegal and strikers subject to immediate dismissal and ineligible for reemployment for three years, President Nixon did not take the line which President Reagan took eleven years later in the Air Traffic Controllers' strike. In the postal strike, the postal workers successfully defied the federal government. Perhaps this is not surprising given that the Postal Service is the single largest enterprise in number of employees in either the private or public labor markets. Meanwhile, strikes continue to be illegal in the Postal Service as in the rest of the federal sector.

The direct relationship of public policy to union growth is evident from the statistical record. After Congress adopted the Lloyd-Lafollette Act in 1912, membership rose sharply. It jumped from 61,000 in 1912 to 92,000 in 1917 and gained steadily thereafter. By 1962, on the eve of President Kennedy's Executive Order 10988 membership of the postal union' was 447,000. E.O. 10988 was the defining moment of the New Unionism in the U.S., just as the National Labor Relations Act of 1935 was a defining moment in the history of the Old Unionism. Comprehensive unionization in the federal government got underway with President Kennedy's Executive Order. In 1961, there were under 120 thousand members of public employee organizations in the federal service; by 1970 the number had jumped four-fold, to over 480 thousand.

The postal unions, too, benefitted. In the twenty years following President Kennedy's order, membership in the Post Office advanced 447 to 606 thousand, or over 35 percent. The proportion of postal workers organized, 75 percent of employment in 1962, rose to 92 percent in 1982 (Troy and Sheflin, 1985, Table 3.93, p.3–21). Currently, organization is higher, probably around 95%, close to the maximum potential making the Postal Service the most organized enterprise in the country, public or private. In addition to membership and representation gains, the Executive Order initiated the conversion of the postal unions to the New Unionism. This process culminated in the transfer of these unions to the jurisdiction of the National Labor Relations Act. This experience indicates that not only did the associations of public and professional associations take the step toward the New Unionism, but so did those labor organizations which had been established prior to the 1960s.

The relative impact of E.O. 10998 on federal employees outside the Post Office was even greater, but that came about because the postal workers were already well organized before the Order was promulgated. Outside the Postal Service, average annual dues paying membership rose from 181,000 in 1962 to 434,000 in 1982, a gain of almost 140 percent (Troy and Sheflin, 1985, Appendix A, p. A-1). Since then, it has remained stable.

Federal policy was emulated by many states and local governments and these, too, spurred the unionization of state and local government employees on a scale heretofore unknown in the U.S. Although New York City and the State of Wisconsin anticipated the federal policy, the real impetus to state and local governments' visible hand encouraging unionization and collective bargaining among their employees emanated from President Kennedy's Executive Order 10988.

For all public sector unions, membership increased over 175 percent, 1962–1982; the number of members rose 2.8 million. The gains in union membership at the state and local level of government were larger than at the federal level. Larger membership gains among state and local governments, compared to the federal, reflect the larger size of employment, a longer history of group relationships in education, and an even more pro-union labor policy among key states and municipalities. Since 1982 the New Unionism has gained further members and reached a record high in labor market penetration.

American public policies encouraging unionism in both the private and public labor markets reverberated in Canada and with parallel results: The transformation of associations into unions (the New Unionism), and a spectacular growth in membership the public sector labor market. In emulation of President Kennedy's Executive Order, the Province of Quebec (1964) and then the Canadian federal government adopted legislation (1967) and policies fostering public sector unions. These were quickly followed by the other provinces giving Canada a comprehensive policy encouraging the expansion of public sector unionism and bargaining. Just as in the U.S., the visible hand of government was the defining action in the rise of the New Unionism in Canada in the 1960s. Moreover, the "student" outdid the "teacher" and Canadian policies promoting the New Unionism outperformed the American, as the Canadian enacted laws which were even more helpful to unionism. In a very short time, the New Unionism of Canada accounted for a much larger share of the labor market (density) and also displaced the Old Unionism as the center of gravity in Canadian membership.

Clearly, the change in policy at all levels of government in the U.S. (and Canada) was a watershed in the history of public sector unionism. It is decisive factor in dating the establishment of the New Unionism in the 1960s. And the enormous gains in public sector unionism which flowed from government intervention speak for themselves as an argument for treating the New Unionism as something apart from the scattering of public sector organizations which preceded it.

Because of these distinctions, it is analytically reasonable to divide the history of public sector unionism in this country (and Canada) into two segments, with the 1960s being the watershed. Prior to 1962, statistically I only include self-declared public sector unions in the records of union membership for the U.S. (Troy and Sheflin, 1985, Appendix A, p. A-1). I excluded public sector employee associations, most notably the National Education Association (NEA), from that population.

Under the impact of public policy and the competition of other labor organizations claiming jurisdiction over their members during the 1960s, public employee and professional associations transformed themselves into collective bargaining organizations. The outstanding transformation was that of the National Education Association (NEA) from a professional association to a union. Together with the transformation of the American Federation of Teachers (AFT) and other instructional groups, "[t]he dramatic shift in image form the milquetoast-like teacher to the militant unionist which has accompanied the adoption of collective bargaining procedures by teachers at all levels of instruction is one of the well-publicized developments in public-sector labor relations" (Stern, 1988, p. 72). In the process the two major organizations of teachers, the NEA and the AFT have become indistinguishable from one another (Stern, 1988, p. 73). Other associations made the transformation to unionism by merger with established unions, some of them in the private sector. Since 1962, for purposes of this study, no distinction is made between labor organizations termed unions and those termed associations.

As important and as impressive as were the gains in total membership of the New Unionism, more significant was who became members. Of most importance was the large scale unionization of white collar workers, especially teaching professionals. According to one estimate, as of 1984 nearly 70% of the New Unionists were white collar workers, and over one-half (53%) were professionals. Teachers in particular stand out as the reason for this profile. In contrast, 23% of the Old Unionism's ranks were white collar, of whom 6% were professionals. Women accounted for 53% of the New and 27% of the Old Unionism. Blacks account for about the same proportion of the unionized population among both the New and the Old Unionism (Freeman, Ichniowski and Zax, Table 9, p. 392, in Freeman and Ichniowski, 1988).

Except for the railways, the New Unionism also is far ahead of the Old Unionism in the penetration of distinct groups. The most recent census of governments (1987) reports that 61% of instructional staff employed full time were organized. A breakdown shows that 88% of all township teaching staff were organized. Among school districts, by far the largest employers of teachers, the proportion organized was 59% (Bureau of Census, 1987, Table 2, p. 2). The most organized group in the country is the Postal Service, an estimated 95% unionized. In the private economy, the railways rank at the top, probably around 85% – 90% organized. However, while the railways are privately owned, their history of government regulation makes the industry's labor relations very similar to the public sector's.

The New Unionism is also more highly concentrated than the Old. Two unions alone, the NEA and the American Federation of State, County and Municipal Employees (AFSCME), AFL-CIO, currently account for about 40% of total membership in public sector unions, a concentration not now or ever duplicated by the Old Unionism. The concentration of membership in a few organizations affords the New Unionism much more effectiveness in mobilizing its political and economic powers. Should the NEA join the AFL-CIO, the affiliation would further concentrate the power of the major public sector unions within the Federation because so few account for so much of the membership.

The New Unionism's distribution across the 50 states puts it in a far more powerful position than the Old Unionism. The New Unionism is more evenly distributed among the states and even more important, has a far higher penetration rate. As shown in Appendix Table A-1, its penetration rate is higher in every state. Moreover, its rate of penetration ranges from nearly eight times as high as the Old (Vermont) to more than double (Virginia). Indeed, what is remarkable about the ratio of density of the New compared to the Old Unionism is that the disparity is typically greatest in states with the weakest representation in the Old Unionism. Thus of the states with at least five times the density in the public labor market compared to the private we find Vermont, Florida, New Hampshire, Rhode Island, Maine, Utah, Massachusetts, and South Dakota. The strong presence of the New Unionism in such states points up the significance of public policy in encouraging membership, and the immunity of the New Unionism to competitive forces.

Among the unions responsible for the high market penetration rates of the New Unionism are the teachers' unions, mainly the National Education Association, and the postal unions. The high market penetration endows the New Unionism tremendous with political and economic power within their respective domains, the teachers' unions in state and local governments, and the postal unions in Congress. The national size of the NEA (now the largest union in America, having recently replaced the Teamsters as number one) enables that teachers' organization to exercise great power nationally, as well. Should the NEA affiliate with the AFL-CIO, its political strength would grow since it could be expected to assume the leadership of the Federation's large public sector membership, not to mention its potential ascendancy to leadership of the Federation itself. The organization of teachers on so a large scale and their importance to the New Union movement can reasonably be expected to significantly reinforce what the New Unions think and do. However, the affiliation of the NEA with the AFL-CIO is not imminent.

As a result of massive government intervention at federal, state and local levels since the 1960s, the membership and market penetration of the New Unionism grew rapidly. In contrast, over the same period the Old Unionism languished and the New and the Old union movements have since continued to follow different trajectories. As the data and analysis have shown, over the past three decades, under the beneficent climate of virtual market immunity and government policy, the New Unionism has boomed, while the Old Unionism has wilted under competitive forces.

Characteristics of the New Unionism

Types of Organizations

The contemporary Labor Movement in the public sector stands apart from the aggregation of organizations which preceded it. In addition to different origins, the organizations making-up the New Unionism are also new, but not new because they were newly established. Many are new because they evolved either from previously existing associations or labor organizations. Those New Unions which have evolved from previously established labor organizations such as the American Federation of Teachers and the Fire Fighters I shall identify as "proto-unions." Others are new because they are a mix of existing Old Unions which became partly private and partly public sector union, which Steiber has called the joint or mixed union (Steiber, 1973). The joint or mixed union is a new type of labor organization on the American labor scene.

Structurally, therefore, the New Unionism consists of three distinct types of labor organizations. First are the transformed professional and public employee association. Second are the joint or mixed unions. Third are organizations founded well before the birth of the New Unionism many of which were affiliates of the original AFL, the original CIO and after 1955, the AFL-CIO. I refer to them as "proto-unions" because they seldom could negotiate and strike as do the New Unions. In general, their labor market behavior resembled that of the professional and public employee associations prior to the 1960s.

The distinction between the "proto-unions" and the mainstream of organized labor, the Old Unionism, was noted as well by Spero:

> Organized labor itself has not always fully accepted the public worker. To a large extent the feeling on both sides is the result of the restrictions which government as an employer places upon the freedom of its employees to engage in political activity and strike. These restrictions mean that public employees are able to go along with fellow workers in industry only up to a certain point .... Time and again government employee unions have had to abstain from voting on political actions in which all other unions took part (Spero, 1972, pp. 475–476).

Likewise, when it came to collective bargaining, Spero commented that "[a]lthough unions in private industry have always regarded collective bargaining as the life blood of a free labor movement, unions in the public service have only recently [circa 1948] begun to show interest in the process" (Spero, 1972, p. 341).

The internal structure of all three types of organizations parallels that of the private sector union movement and is clearly taken from or simply parallel to the structure of the Old Unionism. Therefore, public sector labor organizations, irrespective of origin, shared the philosophy of the private sector unionism on how to structure themselves. The associations' structure of local, district, state and national units, was laid out long before they became unions and stem from the same or similar sources as the Old Unionism. Their structure was shaped by the size of the country, the political structure (local, state and federal governments), and the multiple labor markets in which they functioned.

The most important type of organization in the New Unionism are the evolutionary descendants of the independent professional and public employee associations. These are exemplified by the National Education Association, the American Association of University Professors, and the Civil Service Employee Association of N.Y. State, now an affiliate of the American Federation of State, County and Municipal Employees, AFL-CIO (AFSCME). In number, there were probably as many separate independent associations as there were unions affiliated with the AFL-CIO in the 1960s. While a few of these organizations had taken some steps toward becoming like unions during the years between the end of World War II and the 1960s, they were still far from full-scale unionism (Spero, 1972, pp. 223–226; Krislov, 1962, p. 511). When they faced the competitive threat of unions in the 1960s, the independent associations faced a Darwinian choice – either to adapt their organizational behavior or to become extinct. Choosing organizational life, the independent associations then faced yet another choice, either transforming themselves into independent collective bargaining agencies, unions in a word, or becoming affiliates of existing unions, mostly AFL-CIO unions. Significantly, before the 1960s, neither the Old Unions nor the "proto-unions" made headway in absorbing the associations; indeed, they apparently rarely tried (Spero, 1972, p. 224).

Despite the fact that they retain the word "association" in their names, contemporary associations in the public labor market are unions, both *de jure* and *de facto*. Most are subject to the jurisdiction of the Labor Management Reporting and Disclosure Act of 1959 and are therefore required to file the organizational and financial reports required of all unions, demonstrating that the public and professional associations are labor organizations within the meaning of the law. However, they are not subject to the National Labor Relations Act, because they are in the public sector. On the other hand, their identification and operation as unions is unrelated to affiliation with the AFL-CIO. Independence from the Federation has no bearing on whether a public sector labor organization is a union. This is true as well of labor organizations in the private sector.

A comparable genealogy of independent associationism-to-unionism was virtually absent from the history of the Old Unionism. One important exception was the Air Line Pilots Association (ALPA), AFL-CIO. However, it ought to be recalled that ALPA developed and functioned in a regulated market, a market therefore very similar to the public market, and this doubtless affected its development and evolution from an association to a union just like those in the public sector.

The second component of the New Unionism, the mixed or joint union, is a new type of labor organization in the history of unions in this country. Paradoxically, it was generated largely by the decline of the Old Unionism over the last three decades, as private sector unions tried to compensate for their declining membership by taking in members in the public labor market. In contrast to their experience in the private sector, this defensive move was relatively an easy task: They emulated by the practice of "organizing the organized."

Technically, it is true that some private sector unions have a long history of enrolling government workers, but they organized on the basis of unionizing the same crafts as in the private sector. As Spero described it, the unions regarded those government workers "as craftsmen or laborers who merely happen to be employed by the government" (Spero, 1972, 474). This indeed was an extension of unionism from the private to the public sector rather than the creation of a new unionism. Quantitatively it was a very small part of those private sector unions' membership. Moreover, these government affiliates of standard craft unions and the "proto-unions" (which form the third leg in the structure of the New Unionism and will be discussed below) which belonged to the AFL found in necessary "[t]ime and again ... to abstain from voting [in AFL proceedings] from voting on political resolutions and to refuse to participate in political actions in which all other unions took part" (Spero, 1972, p. 476). Thus, political participation (as distinct from lobbying), now so characteristic of the New Unionism, distinguished the earlier public sector organizations from the contemporary New Unionism.

Among the leading standard craft unions which enrolled workers in federal shipyards and arsenals on an occupational basis were the Machinists. Other craft unions followed the same practice, such as the printing unions which organized the printing trades in the Government Printing Office. The Machinists established a separate district organization for their members in the federal government (Spero, 1972, p. 95), indicating yet another distinction, this one made by the parent organization itself, between government employees with the same craft as those in the private sector.

These earlier arrangements differ widely from the present practices of private unions for garnering public employees differs in two respects.

First, private sector unions are not seeking to organize the craft, but rather to acquire new members without regard to their occupation because their core, private sector membership has been fading rapidly. Instead of being a policy of expansion, the present efforts of the Old Unionism to acquire government workers is compensatory. Second, they are not organizing the unorganized as in the past, but the already organized employees of independent associations. At times this has embroiled the mixed or joint unions in jurisdictional battles with the New Unionism.

In some cases, the mixed or joint union has acquired so many members in government that they have changed the character of the union. The outstanding example is the Service Employees International Union (SEIU) – AFL-CIO. Thusfar, most joint or mixed unions remain primarily private unionism in character. Leading examples are the Steelworkers, the Auto Workers and the Teamsters. The first two once numbered their private membership over the million mark, and as they have slipped in size in the private economy, they moved into the public sector union market, in efforts to compensate for their losses. However, their gains have been far below to restore them to their previous exalted status. The Teamsters, while still over 1.5 million members strong have reached out to the public sector to find new members, but its acquisitions have been small. Thusfar only one major union has made the transition from a predominantly private to predominantly public organization, the aforesaid Service Employees International Union, AFL-CIO. Currently and for some years already, most of this union's membership is made up of public sector employees both in the U.S. and Canada. As a private sector union it was known as the Building Service Employees Union. As a predominantly public sector union, it changed its name to the SEIU. It is altogether a different organization from that set forth in its original constitution and jurisdictional claims. Likewise, on the state level, the largest public sector union in the State of New Jersey is a private sector union nationally, the Communications Workers of America, AFL-CIO, but in New Jersey is a predominantly public sector in membership.

Like the transformed public associations and the joint unions, the third component in the structure of the New Unionism, the proto-unions are also the product of a transformation. These public sector organizations were established in the same manner as private sector unions and many were chartered by the AFL, the CIO and then the AFL-CIO. However, in their pre-1960s history they actually functioned more like the pre-1960s public employee associations than the Old Unionism. As Spero noted, for public organizations affiliated with the AFL there was a "gap between affiliation and full integration with organized labor on the part of government employee unions" (Spero, 1972, p. 475). Of course, the gap between the proto-unions and private unionism was larger for those public sector organizations which were not affiliated with one of the major Federations.

Among the major reasons for distinguishing the "proto-unions" was their opposition to strikes and overt collective bargaining. For example, the American Federation of Teachers (AFT), the American Federation of State, County and Municipal Employees (AFSCME), and the International Association of Fire Fighters (IAFF), currently major elements in the New Unionism, once officially opposed the strike either as policy or in their constitutions. However, this is not to say that at times locals of these organizations did not strike, but the number was small and the duration brief. For example, Spero estimated that in 1946, a record high strike year in the private sector because of the post-war readjustments to inflation, .0034% of municipal work time was lost compared to 1.5% in the private sector. Ziskind's count of over one thousand strikes in public employment, apparently from the 19th century into the New Deal years, included 30% which lasted a day or less, suggesting that they might better have been classified as protests, not strikes (Ziskind, 1940, p. 189). In addition to the proto-unions' disapproval of the strike, the general tone of public opinion of the time as well as public policy and the leadership of the nation also opposed strikes by public workers. The President most supportive of unionism, Franklin D. Roosevelt, opposed the strike by public employees, and, in fact, their right to organize into unions (Walsh, p. 54). When the National Labor Relations Act was enacted in 1935, federal employees (who could have been included) were excluded from the jurisdiction of the Act. By all the major indicators, the proto-unions of the pre-1960s era were different from the contemporary New Union movement.

The changeover in attitudes toward strikes of the proto-unions coincides with the rise of the New Unionism; it is one of the characteristics of the New Unionism. In 1961 the Bureau of Labor Statistics reported a total of 28 strikes causing just over 15 thousand days of idleness at all levels of government. Both strikes and idleness jumped sharply through the next two decades, peaking at 593 strikes in 1979 and just under 3 million days lost (Walsh, Table 8, p. 55). The absence of subsequent comprehensive data on strikes by public sector employees reduces the analyst to speculation as to trends since 1979. However, it would not surprise me that at the record of strikes fell during the 1980s and early 1990s in the private sector (an established statistical fact), their trend has probably been up in the government sector.

As for collective bargaining, in 1940 the president of AFSCME wrote that "[it] is the general feeling of our general executive board ... that there is less value in the use of contracts and agreements in public service than in private employment, and, further, it is felt that we should rather proceed by promoting legislation covering job security, wages, hours and conditions of employment" (Spero, quoting Arnold Zander, 1972, p. 216). While AFSCME and its leadership later changed their view on bargaining, the number of written agreements between public sector organizations and governmental bodies remained very few in number (Spero, 1972, p. 218) until the rise of the New Unionism. Currently, bargaining is much more the characteristic form of relationship between governmental units and unions than in the past. (See, for example, Census of Governments, 1982, Vol. 3, No. 3, Table 1, p. 1, on the number of state and local governments with a labor relations policy.)

The proto-unions were originally cast in the mold of conventional private sector unions, but they, like the independent professional and public employee associations, whom they most resembled for much of their life-span, also went through a metamorphosis and converted themselves into labor organizations prepared to bargain and strike – into full fledged unions. The American Federation of Teachers, an affiliate of the AFL since its founding in 1916 historically regarded itself as a professional association, just like the NEA, and only renounced the right to strike in the 1950s (Wildman, 1971, p. 132). Despite the word "association" in its name, the International Association of Fire Fighters is a union; it made the transition to unionism before the public and professional associations (Spero, Chapter 11, 1972).

Yet another distinction between the New Unionism and the proto-unions is the relationship between the unions and the public employers. Today is rests extensively on a legal basis and negotiation has increasingly replaced consultation, in contrast to the past.

The legal and social environment affecting the proto-unions and the New Unionism is also markedly different. The shift in labor policy of the early 1960s was far more interventionist than previous policy, clearly separating it from the earlier permissive policy (Lloyd-Lafollette). Likewise, the inauguration of the Great Society programs and expenditures in the 1960s marked a new and more decisive departure in social policy from the New Deal's social welfare programs which preceded. The Great Society programs stimulated large gains in public employment which in turn helped to fuel the rise of the New Unionism, a development noticeably absent under the New Deal.

The political activities of the proto-unions and their evolutionary descendants separates them as well. Not only are the current unions far more active politically, but their political activities under the law differ by a light year. Under the Hatch Act, proto-unions of federal employees were severely circumscribed in their political activities. Today's New Unionism's political involvements are restrained in name only. Meanwhile, the New Unionism is financially far more powerful than its proto-union predecessors and is able to make that financial muscle effective in the political market-place.

The New Unionism is also distinct from the aggregation of unions operating in the public labor market which preceded it because of quantitative as well as qualitative reasons. The New Unionism consists of a far larger number of labor organizations and membership than before the 1960s; its scope of representation at all three levels of government is far greater; it represents a greater number of occupations and governmental functions than the proto-unions ever did; it has organized a much more significant segment of the public labor market; it is more geographically widespread than before the 1960s, when it was more concentrated in and around Washington, D.C. in the Post Office. Indeed, the membership and market penetration of the proto-unions was largely concentrated in the federal service, including the naval shipyards and government arsenals. At the same time, state and local union representation was minimal and the number of governmental functions organized was very limited. In contrast, the New Unionism at the state and local level constitutes the bulk of public sector membership. In general, the New Unionism comprises a significant and rising share of total union membership (refer to Chart 1). It also has extensively organized functions at all levels of government and among a wide array of white collar occupations, including supervisory and professional employees, and also includes service workers. At some point a quantitative difference becomes a qualitative one and on this basis the pre-1960s and the post-1960s public sector union movements are clearly different.

The proto-unions and the New Unionism also differ widely in their challenge to sovereignty. The challenge of the proto-unions was negligible compared to the New Unionism (Chapters III and V). Similarly, if those organizations had a philosophy, a questionable matter itself, it was essentially a copy of the early version of the Old Unionism's, specifically the Old Unionism's pre-New Deal version, the philosophy of "more" (Chapter IV). In fact, it would be correct to say the proto-unions did not have their own philosophy, but rather tagged along that of the Old Unionism. The New Unionism's philosophy and policies clearly set it apart both from the proto-unions of earlier years and that of the Old Unionism (Chapter V).

Association-to-Union: Model for Reviving the Old Unionism?

Because of the success of the independent association-to-union transition in the public labor market, some analysts urged the AFL-CIO leadership to establish associations as a way of reviving the Old Unionism (*New York Times*, 1990). The theory was that associations would be a preliminary step to eventual full unionization, such as occurred in the public labor market. The Lou Harris study for the AFL-CIO in 1984 recommended that the Federation try to attract nonunion workers by sponsoring employee associations which would offer medical, legal and other benefits as well as information on job opportunities and counseling on workplace problems (Harris, pp. 72, 73). Harris found a positive response among a majority of nonunion workers (which included government employees, federal, state and local) even if a $50 fee was charged. However, when the Harris survey mentioned affiliating these associations with the AFL-CIO, the nonunion respondents, a majority of the nonunion workers' interest in joining an association faded from support to opposition. Nearly 60% said they would not join under those circumstances. This was not surprising in the face of another Harris finding that 65% of nonunion workers (including government employees) would not vote for a union in a secret ballot election.

Despite this evidence, the Harris report to the Federation declared that the "plan for sponsoring an employee association which would provide specific benefits, at a fee, over and beyond what any union has ever provided, has real possibilities" (Harris, p. 39). This analysis expected that following the example of the public sector, the union sponsored associations in the private sector would eventually make the transition to full unionism.

However, these recommendations failed to recognize historical and fundamental differences between the "ersatz," union generated associations and those which had existed in the public sector. The latter were indigenous and ongoing groups long before they became unions; they were not hastily formed organizations designed to head-off unions. Most had been established as professional, civil service and simply public employee organizations intended to lobby public officials over employment rules and conditions. The AAUP and civil service associations had other goals as well. Had it not been for the dramatic public policy changes in the 1960s, perhaps these associations may never have become unions. Indeed, their rich experience in dealing with public officials already fulfilled the political track of negotiation I identified above and are part of the definitional difference I have presented between public and private unions. A similar historical background is virtually absent in the private sector. Moreover, the relative importance of associations in the two labor movements is enormously different. The number of associations which transformed themselves into unions in the private sector involved a very few organizations, whereas in the public sector, the process involved a major part of the new movement and most of its current membership. The independent associations not only antedated the rise of the New Unionism, but one, the National Education Association, actually preceded the founding of the centerpiece of the Old Unionism, the American Federation of Labor. The NEA was established in 1857, initially as the National Teachers' Association, 29 years before the AFL was established in 1886. (The Federation itself dates its origin in 1881, as the Federation of Organized Trades and Labor Unions). In 1870 the National Teachers' Association was changed to the National Educational Association; later this was altered to its present name.

There was a few examples of the transformation of labor organization in the private sector similar to the association-to-union transformation in the public sector. However, they did not involve independent, but rather company established associations. In the 1930s and 1940s, after the validation of the National Labor Relations Act, many organizations originally established by employers made the transition to unionism either because of absorption by existing unions or by becoming independent local unions. In one case they developed into a full-fledged national union, the contemporary Communications Workers of America, AFL-CIO. The CWA began its career as an offspring of organizations set up by the American Telephone and Telegraph Company and its subsidiaries. The associations set up by AT&T evolved into a national federation of telephone associations and eventually into the CWA. The most striking difference between the association "movement" in the two sectors were their origins. The private associations were spawned by their employers and could not withstand the legal tests set by the National Labor Relations Act and the National Labor Relations Board. Like the independent public associations of recent times, they, too, faced a Darwinian alternative, change or extinction. However, the challenge came mainly from the law, not as in the case of the independent professional and public employee association, competition from rival labor organizations. It must also be understood that the independent public employee associations did not confront the issue of employer domination as did the private associations which had been set up by employers. The public sector associations were established by the employees themselves. One, the National Education Association, did have to make one important change in its structure in order to compete and that was to drop principals and supervisors from their ranks.

The public associations and the private associations of yesteryear and those proposed by Harris and others differ also on their occupational make-up. Public employee associations consisted of white collar or service employees, while both the historical and proposed associations in the private sector did or would consist of blue collar workers. Moreover, until the early 1960s the associations of public employees, like the National Education Association, stood apart and aloof from trade unionism. Indeed, they were actually hostile to the trade union movement. Professional associations typically described themselves as opposed to the principles and practices of trade unionism. This attitude was reinforced by their occupational make up – white collar workers whose historic antipathy to unionism and bargaining is well know. That occupational difference even separated the proto public sector unions from most of the affiliates of the AFL. Today's New Unionism's collar make-up continues to be a major reason for recognizing it as conceptually a separate entity with different concerns from a blue collar dominated Old Union movement.

There is a potential legal barrier to forming union sponsored associations in the private sector which also makes the public model of association-to-union inapplicable: Are union sponsored associations legal? Under the Amended National Labor Relations Act, section 8(b)(1) declares that it is an unfair labor practice for a labor organization [union] to restrain or coerce employees in the exercise of the rights guaranteed in section 7, the right to organize. Would union sponsored employee associations survive the legal tests of the Act and the Board? Likewise, employer encouragement of employee groups to foster management-labor cooperation, which could become the nucleus of an association, may be declared illegal interference by the National Labor Relations Board. To date I am unfamiliar with any discussion dealing with the issue of union sponsored associations, but it seems to me that on its face union sponsored associations would violate the National Labor Relations Act. No such legal challenge appeared in the public model of association-to-union transformation.

In summary, there is no parallel in the histories of the New and the Old Unionism for the Old Unionism to capitalize on the experience of the New in the association-to-union transformation to full-scale unionism and collective bargaining. In fact, the evidence is to the contrary. An attempt was made in Canada in the 1970s, well before it was even proposed in the U.S., to organize via an association-to-union in the private finance industry and failed. From the foregoing sketch of the historical background of "associationism" in the two labor markets, it is evident that they had little in common beyond the word "association" itself. What proved to be a significant development for the public sector labor market, the transformation of associations to unions, and for the rise of the New Unionism, has virtually no counterpart in the evolution of the Old Unionism and has no future role in its revival, if, indeed, there is to be one in the private sector of the labor market.

Patterns of Organization

Chapter I has noted that the New Unionism has become the dominant wing of the organized labor movement in Canada and in other countries, notably Britain and France, and that it can be expected to gain ascendancy in the U.S. early in the 21st century. Paradoxically, this shift in the "center of gravity" of unionism in the U.S. and Canada was not the result of forming new labor organizations! In fact, the New Unionism is conspicuous in the absence of newly established unions and relatively few of the extant members are the result of organizing the unorganized. Instead, the New Unionism, as already pointed out, is very largely the product of transforming existing organizations into the contemporary movement, organizing the organized, a process unique in the history of American Labor. The process was simplified by the characteristics of the independent associations. Although not unions and opposed to unions throughout their history, they had the right profile for conversion to unionism. As Krislov concluded from his study of state employee associations, they had organized a significant number of employees, their structure and governance was similar to unions, and they engaged in membership recruitment and lobbying just as unions always have (Krislov, 1962 p. 511).

Likewise, the New Unionism is the product of the conversion of proto-unions to full-scale unionism, and the rise of the mixed union. Of the three, the first contributed the largest membership to the New Unionism. That pattern of expansion is unmatched in the evolution of unionism in this country. Canada, likewise, underwent a parallel progression of associations into the New Unionism with the transformation of associations contributing the largest segment of the membership. This pattern of development in both countries furnishes yet another definitive reason for rejecting the surge theory of union growth: The surge was to a major extent a transformation, or organizing the organized. Paradoxically, therefore, the evidence claimed to substantiate the surge theory actually substantiates the process of organizing the organized. In both Canada and the U.S. the instrument in the process of organizing the organized was a revolutionary change in public policy encouraging union organization and bargaining by public employees. In the U.S., the watershed change was signaled by President Kennedy's New Frontier policy expressed in Executive Order 10988 in 1962. That policy was then emulated in Canada beginning in 1964 and generated a parallel and even more extensive unionization of the public sector labor market in that country.

Organizing the organized is in sharp contrast to the history of the Old Unionism, especially during the 1930s and 1940s. Then, as before, the Old Unionism thrived by organizing the unorganized. Formation of the Congress of Industrial Organizations (CIO) and expansion of the American Federation of Labor (AFL) during the 1930s and 1940s also altered the "center of gravity" of unionism. The shift at that time moved the balance from skilled, non-manufacturing blue collar workers (mostly in the AFL) to mass production skilled and less-skilled workers in the CIO. It was a structural break in the evolution of unionism in this country (Chapter I). In contrast to the rise of the New Unionism, that era does exemplify the surge theory of union growth because it consisted of the organization of the unorganized. That experience also demonstrates that the surge theory applies to the private, not the public labor market. In the 1930s and 1940s, many new unions were established and enrolled hitherto unorganized workers, particularly in manufacturing. Such was not the case of the New Unionism in the 1960s and afterward. Moreover, subsequent gains in the New Unionism came from building on existing representation, not episodes of organizing the unorganized.

Another difference in the organizational history of the New and Old Unionism is the relative paucity of jurisdictional fights in the development of the New Unionism. In contrast, such fights characterized the relations between the AFL and the CIO from the 1930s until their no raiding agreement in 1954 followed by their merger in 1955. In the public sector, the American Federation of Government Employees-AFL peacefully surrendered its jurisdictional claim over state and local employees in 1936 enabling the AFL to charter a new union, the contemporary American Federation of State, County and Municipal Employees, to organize those groups (Spero, 1972, p. 212).

The New Unionism's general invulnerability to competitive forces indicates that it will not endure the future "aches and pains" of maturity of the Old Unionism. The symptoms of the Old Unionism's aging process identified by Richard Lester in his *As Unions Mature* are internal stability, centralization and bureaucratic control, coupled with external accommodation and moderation. Because of the Old Unionism's maturity, Lester postulated that in the decade or so after his 1957 study, (private) unions' growth curve would level off or drift downward (Lester, 1957 pp. 106, 110). After the fact, private unions peaked in 1970 and have declined precipitously since, more than, perhaps, he anticipated. Most likely, both the peak and decline in membership would have set in sooner had it not been for the war in Vietnam. Market forces, notably structural changes in employment and output, global competition and deregulation, shrunk both membership and union penetration. Because these factors have far less impact on the labor market of government employees, the identical aging process which has made the private union movement ill-prepared for the new Age of Adam Smith, will have only a limited effect on the fortunes of the New Unionism.

The diverse fortunes and patterns of organization of the New and the Old Unionism are shown in Charts 2 and 3. Chart 2 tracks the membership of the New and Old unionism, 1970 to 1991. It shows that since its all time high in 1970, the Old Unionism has slumped over the next twenty years. In contrast, the New Unionism's membership hit a new all time high in 1991. In membership terms, the 7 million members given-up by the Old Unionism over the past two decades numbers about 1/2 million more than the total size of the New Unionism.

Chart 3 presents the market share (density) of the New and the Old Unionism in the year when each touched its all time high and in 1991. Again, one must look back, this time about a generation, to 1953, in the history of private sector unions to find its peak. At that time, its market penetration reached 36%. Even more startling its current rate of market penetration is just under the 1929 rate. On the other hand, public union density a new all time high in 1989 at 36.7%. It dipped slightly to 36.5% in 1990, indicating that while membership grew, employment increased a little more rapidly. Perhaps the dip heralds the beginnings of a slowdown in union penetration of the government labor market, but this is too little data on which to reach a firm conclusion. In 1991, it rose again. Meanwhile, it should also be noted that the New Unionism's densities in are above the 1953 record of the Old Unionism.

Two Labor Movements

Since there are two distinct types of unionism, there are also two labor movements. Collectively, I refer to both groups taken together as Labor-U.S., or Labor-America. I define a union movement as a group of unions sharing similar characteristics and a common philosophy. Differences in philosophies more than any other reason distinguishes the New from the Old Union movements. While there are common interests and elements in their goals, the differences, especially in philosophy outweigh their common interests.

Pragmatic differences also divide the Old and the New Unionism within the AFL-CIO. Affiliates compete over public sector workers. The competition is low key, certainly in comparison to the historic rivalry of the AFL and the CIO until their no raiding agreement and subsequent merger in 1955. Although private AFL-CIO unions have been organizing employees and absorbing public sector associations in competition with AFL-CIO public sector unions in recent years, there is, as yet, no jurisdictional battle looming comparable to that which led to the formation of the CIO. Doubtless the history of the jurisdictional fights between the AFL and the CIO prevents a recurrence. Equally important, the AFL-CIO has a procedure for resolving jurisdictional disputes between affiliated unions, and nearly all the major unions in the country are affiliated with the Federation. As long as there is no serious jurisdictional competition over the unorganized public employee, the association of public and private union movements in a common federation can be complementary and will prevent any rupture arising from their philosophical and jurisdictional differences.

In appearance, the modern American labor movement, the American Federation of Labor and Congress of Industrial Organizations (the AFL-CIO), looks like a unitary movement. However, it is not. The fact that private and public unions are affiliated with the same Federation does not imply that there are no differences between the two types of unions, or contradict the existence of two labor movements and their differences in philosophy. While administratively (and in other respects) a single body, actually the AFL-CIO today is a house divided between the Old and the New Unionism. However, I do not expect a split into two federations, paralleling the split in the AFL and the rise of the Congress of Industrial Organizations (CIO) in 1937. The cost of such a split in the face of the weakening position of Old Unionism and the "acceptance value" of the Federation's name for the rising New Unionism augur for a united Federation of Labor.

The current Federation has undergone changes at various times in its history. Its predecessor organizations were founded as a private sector movement, the AFL in 1886 and the Congress of Industrial Organizations in 1937. To this day the successor to the merged federations, the American Federation of Labor and Congress of Industrial Organizations (AFL-CIO), continues to be dominated by private sector unions, but that is changing as a result of the growth of its public sector affiliates and decline of its private sector affiliates. Such is already the case of the main Canadian federation, the Canadian Labour Congress. In fact, its previous president comes from the public sector.

Because the New Unionism lacks a separate federation, it might be said the New Unionism does not qualify as a labor movement. While there is no separate federation of public employee unions in the U.S., such as can be found abroad, the absence of such an institution hardly disqualifies my characterization of the New Unionism in the U.S. as a distinct movement. Nor does the affiliation of most of the New Unionism with the AFL-CIO change matters. Certainly this is a distinct feature in the U.S., but it is not unique. For example, the same relationship between the New Unionism and a national federation, the Canadian Labour Congress (CLC), applies in Canada and the Canadian New Unionism now dominates that federation. I believe the same is true of the oldest union movement in the world, the British. Like the U.S., most unions in Britain whether public or private, are affiliated with the same federation, the Trades Union Congress (TUC). The TUC is now dominated by the membership of the New Unionism. In all three countries, the U.S., Canada, and Britain, the single federation embracing public and private sector unionism is a product of historical development. In the U.S. the limited scope of public sector organizations prior to the 1960s led many to affiliate with the AFL, the CIO and then the merged federation, the AFL-CIO. However, the New Unionism will dominate the AFL-CIO in membership, should the National Education Association affiliate. The NEA is today the single largest union in the U.S. and, indeed, in North America, supplanting the Old Unionism's Teamsters. Undoubtedly, a prerequisite for the NEA's affiliation with the AFL-CIO would be the merger of the American Federation of Teachers with the NEA. The affiliation of the NEA with the AFL-CIO would likely bring the clash of private and public sector philosophies and policies out in the open, perhaps leading to the establishment of a separate federation of public employees, just as the quarrel over jurisdiction (and personal power) led to the separation of unions from the AFL and the formation of the CIO during the 1930s. Certainly, the distinctions between the Old and the New Unionism are sufficient and at least as logical as those which led to the split within the AFL and the rise of the CIO. While the logic is there for two separate federations, nevertheless, the probabilities are negligible at this time, I believe, because of the experience of inter-union conflicts during the days of the two separate federations of private sector unions, the AFL and the CIO. The strong desire by unions in both sectors to maintain a united front is an historic imperative for organized labor to belong to a single federation. It is important to remember that the CIO was founded in a period of rising expectations and growth for organized labor in the private labor market, a condition opposite to the current situation of the Old Unionism. The growing weakness of the Old Unionism will inhibit such a separation. In any event, the New Unionism will come do dominate the AFL-CIO even in the absence of the affiliation of the NEA. However, the transformation will take longer.

After stating the case for the unlikelihood of a new and separate federation in short term, it is conceivable that in the next century the New Unionism will form a new federation, under the leadership of the National Education Association. The new federation would focus on the goal of redistribution, the core of the New Unionism's philosophy. The new federation would be friendly with the Old Unionism of the AFL-CIO.

Meanwhile, in recognition of the growing strength of the New Unionism, the AFL-CIO has established a Public Employees' Department (PED) within the Federation. Theoretically, this step puts the PED on a par with all other departments of the Federation such as the Building and Construction Trades Department, and the Industrial Union Department. The Building Trades Department reflects the occupational strength of the original American Federation of Labor. The Industrial Union Department reflects the industrial concepts of the Congress of Industrial Organizations. Together, they make up the private sector, or Old Unionism of the AFL-CIO unions. The Public Employees Department reflects the new importance of the New Unionism to the AFL-CIO. However, it is not yet the power center of the Federation. At this time, the PED is hardly in an equivalent power position compared either to the Building and Construction Trades Department, or Industrial Union Department of the Federation, but under new leadership and more public sector members, especially from the National Education Association, the balance of power within the AFL-CIO would swing toward the New Unionism.

Because of the growing significance of the New Unionism and its different philosophy, it is not now accurate to analyze the contemporary Labor Movement and its philosophy either in the U.S., or abroad, in the terminology and concepts of the private sector because there are two Labor Movements, not one, and each, including their distinct philosophies, must be analyzed separately. But before turning to the issues related to the philosophies of the Old and the New Unionism, I examine next (Chapter III) the new system of industrial relations which has emerged with the New Unionism.

CHAPTER III.

The New Industrial Relations System

The Comparative Advantage of the Public System

The New Unionism and the Old Unionism function in different industrial relations systems and are likely to continue to do so for the foreseeable future. Although "in its infancy in the 1960s ... it [the New Industrial relations system] has now come of age (Aaron, 1988, p. 314), but as it matures, the industrial relations system in the public sector will eclipse that in the private labor market in its impact on the economy. Evidence of this are the trends in membership, unionization and the far higher proportion of the labor market organized in the government sector compared to the private. The New Unionism represents (members and nonmembers) over 43% of government employees, compared to 13% of private sector workers. Membership as a percentage of employment is close to 40% in the public and under 10% in the private labor market (U.S. Department of Labor, 1992, Table 58, p. 229).

The disparities in the strength of the New and the Old Unionism will grow as state and local governments, which account for the bulk of all public employees, extend their encouragement of unionization and bargaining. At present, a great potential exists for the unionization of state and local government employees, especially at the local level. Currently only about seven states have no policy encouraging unionization and bargaining, but the 43 State governments' which do have policies favorable to unionization and bargaining, have contracts or agreements with fewer than 30 percent of their employees (Census, 1991, Table D, p. vi). In contrast to the states, most local governments do not have labor policies (Census, 1991, Table C, p. vi), and just over 14 thousand local government units, or 17 percent of the total of some 80 thousand, do have such policies (Census, 1991, Table C, p. vi). Local government employees under agreement or memos of understanding account for 38 percent of employment, over twice the proportion of governmental units with a policy.

Because of the relatively small number of local policies favoring unionism, and the splintering of policy-making among so many governmental units, the New Unionism sees its system at a disadvantage compared to the private. However, that legal disadvantage is reduced by the fact that under the first and 14th amendments of the Constitution, "it is now clear that there is a federal constitutional right to form and join a union and that federal courts will provide relief for state and local employees when these rights are violated" (Westbrook, 1986, p. 341). However, legal recognition of the right of public employees to form a labor organization does not include legal sanction of exclusive representation and the right to bargain (or consult). Thus, federal legislation (the Lloyd-Lafollette Act of 1912) enabled federal employees to form and join unions, but did not extend the legal right to bargain (Chapter II). The New Unionism also points to the general absence of the right to strike, compulsory membership and dues check-off as disadvantages in the public system of industrial relations.

Despite these claimed disadvantages, compared to the private system, the new public system (including the federal government) accounts for nearly four times as many employees represented in bargaining. And as noted, New Unionism is in the ascendancy, while the Old is steadily declining. It should also be noted that the strike in the private sector has tracked the decline in the Old Unionism, indicating that the strike has been unable to stem the ebb its strength. Without the legal sanction to strike (in most jurisdictions), the New Unionism has flourished, raising the question of just how important it is to organizing in the public labor market. Meanwhile, the New Unionism has increasingly resorted to strikes, whether or not they are legal, but these take place in established representational units and arise out of disputes over new terms and conditions of employment, not organizing.

The extensive immunity of the public sector to competition adds significantly to the comparative advantage of public over private sector bargaining. And even though there are threats to that immunity in the form of privatization and contracting out, and a free trade agreement with Canada and Mexico, which increase the sources of private goods and services as substitutes for public production, these threats to the immunity of the public system of industrial relations and the New Unionism are as yet minuscule.

Until Spero's book was published in 1948, little notice was taken of public sector organizations and their impact on sovereignty was mainly appraised in terms of strikes against the state and its instrumentalities. In his original version, Spero did not envision the challenge to the constitutional prerogatives of public authorities. The republished version of 1972 recognized the changing status of public sector unions, the New Unionism (although he did not refer to it as such). Spero's revised assessment of the impact of the New Unionism is further recognition of the gulf between the old public sector unionism (the "proto-unions") and the New Unionism (Chapter II).

To those who are wary of the growing authority of government, the ceding of power to the New Unionism constitutes a new twist in the term, "power sharing." It is not a change in the sharing of power between constitutional bodies of authority, the federal and state governments, but to the sharing of power between sovereign authority and unelected groups, the New Unionism, arbitrators, and to collective bargaining. Not surprisingly, the sharing of governance is closely tied to the power of the New Unionism to socialize income. Since the New Unionism has expanded its "jurisdiction" to participate in policy making, what should be more natural than ever more vocal and effective advocacy of policies requiring more public funding? An anecdotal and recent example is deluge of (organized) telephone calls made by members of the New Unionism to state officials in Connecticut demanding enactment of a state income tax during the fiscal stand-off in 1991. Public officials favoring enactment of the tax cite the telephone calls as evidence of "wide public support" for their position.

In sharing sovereign authority in many governmental jurisdictions, the New Unions have pushed well ahead of the Old in innovating and changing industrial relations systems; it is a major comparative advantage of the public over the private system of industrial relations. Nothing in the private sector approaches it in this country. It is also worth noting that private management has, in most industries, fought vigorously to maintain its right to make policy decisions, a right which the conventional wisdom would erode by compelling management to negotiate investment decisions (Kochan, Katz and McKersie, 1986). Kochan, Katz and McKersie's advocacy of private unions' participation in managerial decisions on investment and plant location (what they term "strategic decision making") in the private sector would be a step in that direction. Abroad, the closest approach is co-determination in Germany's private sector. While the New Unionism leads the Old in power sharing in the U.S., it still lags the Old Unionism in its lack of the full collective bargaining rights of strikes, compulsory membership, the check-off and bargaining over all other terms and conditions of employment.

The comparison of the Old Unionism's encroachment on managerial rights in the private sector to the New Unionism's diminution and sharing of sovereign authority obfuscates the watershed differences between the two. Surprisingly, Spero, after calling attention to the intrusion of New Unionism into the domain of constitutional authority in his retrospective commentary, contradicted himself and subscribed to this obfuscation: "In a sense [he wrote] this is a public phase of the perpetual conflict in industry over management and union rights." While there is a superficial similarity, the managerial authority and sovereignty are significantly different. Sovereignty is derived from the people in an open society, while managerial rights are derived from stockholders and private ownership; curtailment of the rights of sovereign and private employers are hardly equivalent.

The countervailing forces limiting the encroachments on sovereignty and managerial rights also differ. In the private market, competition brakes the extent of the encroachment on managerial authority. In the public market, competition also plays a role, but a far more limited one in its economic aspects and very slow moving one in its political aspects. General business downturns only slow the rate, but rarely the amount of public revenues, expenditures and employment. Even in the midst of budget deficits, revenues and expenditures typically continue to increase. For example, California's budget projected deficit in 1991, will be accompanied by an estimated rise of expenditures of 11% and revenues of 20% (*Wall Street Journal*, June 24, 1991, p. A 10). At the federal level, "federal spending will consume a peacetime record 24.9% of gross national product by next year, up from 22.3% in 1989" (Mitchell, D.J., 1991, p. A 10). Most recently, the *New York Times* reported that "a decade after property tax revolts in a dozen states and the across-the-board tax cuts of the Reagan era, the percentage of income that Americans pay in taxes is back to a postwar peak" (Nov. 17, 1991, p. 1). So much for the "budget reforms" of 1990.

The comparative advantage of the New over the private industrial relations system in durability, power and influence will increase should the two systems converge, that is, become subject to a common public policy and follow similar practices. The goal of the New Unionism is to eliminate all those differences between the public and private sectors which give the private system any comparative advantages, while retaining and enlarging its comparative advantages. To the New Unionism, the process of convergence means "full collective bargaining rights."

In the ongoing process of convergence, the first step among the "proto-unions" (Chapter II) in becoming part of the New Unionism was the elimination of the self-imposed limitations on strikes and the inception of collective bargaining. Among the quasi-unions the self-imposed strike limitation was adopted for several reasons. The American Federation of Teachers, for example, regarded itself as an organization of professionals who did not strike. In this, the AFT emulated the position of its much larger, older and more established NEA, which completely disassociated itself from the practices and principles of organized labor. The no-strike policy of the AFT was intended to enable the quasi-union to compete with the NEA on a professional level. Other reasons that the quasi-unions followed a no-strike policy were the weakness of the organizations and public intolerance of industrial action by public employees and their organizations. Strikes were forbidden in all political jurisdictions to the no-strike policy merely made discretion the better part of valor. Moreover, public managers, unlike those of today, would quickly apply sanctions if confronted with a strike. One only has to recall Governor Coolidge's handling of the Boston police strike.

In the process of convergence, public sector unions often successfully defied legal prohibitions to strike, demonstrating another feature of convergence – militancy. At the same time, so politically powerful had public sector unions become that rarely did public authorities impose legal sanctions on their illegal "job actions." In the one outstanding exception of recent years when the law was applied, in the Professional Air Traffic Controllers' strike in 1981, the President's action was widely denounced by media and academia sympathetic to the strike, and union leaders, as might be expected, but by few union members. Union rank and filers were unable to identify with the higher earnings and the reasonable offers made the by the Department of Transportation to the striking air traffic controllers. Since the strike was illegal President Reagan replaced the striking controllers. Subsequently, for that action he has since been held responsible by his critics for the decline of private sector unionism in the 1980s, even though the dispute took place in the public sector and public sector unionism has since surged to record levels. The reasoning was that the President had set the tone for anti-union actions by employers in the private sector. In fact, as I have shown elsewhere, employer opposition had little to do with the decline of private sector unionism in this country, that other market forces were more responsible and that the U.S. decline was part of a world-wide trend (Troy, 1990 a and b).

A key aspect of convergence which has already been achieved was the "coming of age" of public sector unions, becoming the New Unionism. From an insignificant "subsidiary" of the American union movement, the New Unionism embarked on an era of unparalleled growth beginning in the 1960s. Indeed, within a short span of years, they swelled to a size larger than the CIO, the Congress of Industrial Organizations, ever attained in its history, 1937 to 1955. Moreover, the New Unionism's spectacular gains were made with none of the "blood, sweat and tears" that went into organizing the CIO. As public sector unions gained the "critical mass" to become a labor movement, the new movement also began fashioning its own philosophy, policies and political agenda.

Convergence is not an abstraction but is now a constitutional possibility since the Supreme Court decision in the *Garcia* case (1985). Should the Democratic Party gain control of the Presidency and retain control of Congress, the prospect of such a law would be greatly enhanced. However, it is also possible that the Supreme Court as currently constituted may eviscerate or over-ride *Garcia*. Because of its potential importance to a future system of industrial relations in the public sector, a summary of the case is provided in Appendix A.

Even before the decision in *Garcia*, legislation was proposed to bring the New Unionism under a single legal umbrella. One approach was to amend the private sector law, the National Labor Relations Act, by changing the definition of employer to include federal, state and local governments. The second approach would have created a new labor law with jurisdiction over state and local government employees and established a National Public Employment Relations Commission, with powers similar to the National Labor Relations Board. The proposed law would have created "unlawful acts," paralleling the NLRA's unfair labor practices, and would restrict the right of public employees to strike. Although, neither bill was seriously considered (Aaron, 1988, p. 324), nevertheless they show the direction and degree of convergence being sought. Needless to say, "[a] coalition of unions, whose members consisted exclusively or in part of federal, state, and local government employees, backed the bill[s]" (Aaron, 1988, p. 324).

Most recently, the Public Employees Department (PED), AFL-CIO, called for national legislation to bring "full collective bargaining" to the organized public labor market. In a resolution adopted at its convention in 1991, the PED stated that:

> Whereas, An irrational patchwork of state laws, local ordinances and executive orders characterize public sector labor relations, with no equitable and uniform standards ... therefore be it resolved ...

> That the PED affirm its support for and commitment to work toward enactment of federal legislation to establish a rational framework extending full collective bargaining rights to all state and local government employees ... (PED, Oct. 3–4, 1991, pp. 19–20).

Even if the public and private systems of industrial relations do eventually fully converge, as is the trend, this does not also imply convergence in the character of the New and the Old Unionism, as some specialists have forecast: "As public-sector unionism matures and as public-sector management and the public become more accustomed to it and the occasional conflicts that arise, it is likely that the perceived differences between public- and private-sector unionism will diminish" (Stern, 1988, p. 88). The differences n philosophies alone (Chapters IV and V) will continue to separate the New from the Old Unionism. In addition and there are numerous other factors which will always separate the two union movement, the employer and the state of competition, to identify two. Actually, the maturation of the public system of industrial relations, even if it converged with the private, will actually reinforce the differences in the two union movements. Convergence in industrial relations systems will enhance the power of the New Unionism, and therefore accentuate its permanent differences with the Old.

The contemporary public sector industrial relations system also differs distinctly from its predecessor (pre-1960s) in the government labor market. This marks another dimension of the structural break associated with the emergence of the New Unionism in the 1960s (Chapter II). The over-riding difference between the new and the old systems of industrial relations in the public sector is the shift from a system in which the rules were spelled out by the sovereign employer, to a system which has diminished that authority. This shift has revolutionized the relationship of the New Unionism and the public employer to an extent inconceivable in the pre-1960s period.

Despite these significant developments, the two most influential studies of unionism and industrial relations in the 1980s gave no more than a passing reference to the New Unionism and its associated industrial relations system. Freeman and Medoff's celebrated *What Do Unions Do?* has but three index references to public sector unionism and these in the context of their analysis of private sector unionism. However, Freeman did address the rise of public sector unionism in a subsequent study (1986), but treated the growth of unionism in the public labor market as an example of the spurt theory of labor organization, not as a New Union Movement, as presented here (see Chapter II).

The other major study of industrial relations during the 1980s, Kochan, Katz and McKersie's, *The Transformation of American Industrial Relations*, totally ignores the New Unionism and the new system of industrial relations, despite its title. This acclaimed treatise has but a single reference to public sector unionism and makes no reference to the change in the U.S. system of industrial relations wrought by the dramatic rise of the New Unionism, as one might expect from the book's title. Instead, their study confines the transformation of industrial relations to the private sector, identifying (and lamenting) the growing dominance of the individual, nonunion system over the unionized system of industrial relations in the private economy. Comparisons between the private and public systems of industrial relations are not considered.

Before examining what the New Unionism seeks from convergence, I review briefly the building blocks of an industrial relations system in general, and the specific characteristics of the current systems in the public and private sectors.

Irrespective of sector, an industrial relations system includes these basic elements: workers, organized and unorganized, employers, unions, the rules, formal and/or informal governing the relations between employers and their employees and public policy (the law) governing the system, the economy and markets, and the interaction of these elements. In organized relationships the rules are embodied collective bargaining agreements, arbitration awards, and the body of law stemming from the agreements and awards.

While these elements are common to both the private and public sectors, the role which each plays can vary in the two industrial relations systems, setting the them apart. The current disparities between the two systems of industrial relations are natural, natural in the sense that the differences are rooted in the characteristics inherent in the two sectors: the employer, competitive forces and markets, and the separation between the management of labor relations and responsibility for fiscal affairs. The divorce of managerial responsibility for labor relations and fiscal affairs in government contrasts sharply with their close association under private enterprise. Competitive forces are tenuous in the public sector, but pervasive in the private. The special characteristics of the public system of industrial relations also make it and the New Unionism affect the economy and society in ways far different and more significantly from those of the Old Unionism and the private system of industrial relations. The most notable are the process of representative government and the socialization of income.

Even when the two systems appear to share common features, the reasons differ. For example, decentralized collective bargaining is common to both systems, but the reasons for decentralization differ. In the public sector, the constitutional and political structure of the country is responsible for the decentralization of industrial relations; in the private sector, the driving force are the decentralized labor markets. While the bargaining structure in both the public and private systems of industrial relations is decentralized, they mirror different reasons, competitive markets versus governmental structure.

The total number of agreements in the private sector is unknown, but it is large and must exceed the number in the public sector, given the number of business enterprises and local and district unions making up the Old Unionism. As of October 1987, the Census Bureau reported nearly 39 thousand agreements in state and local governments (U.S. Bureau of Census, 1991, Table D, p. VI). The content of these agreements differ, notably on compulsory membership and the check-off. Typically, both compulsory membership and the check-off are absent in the public system. Strikes are typically outlawed in the public sector and the ban is prescribed by legislation and not in the bargaining agreement.

However, even in the absence of these terms in most public sector agreements, the public sector system of industrial relations is stronger than its private counterpart. The reasons are the diminished authority of the sovereign employer, the separation of public management from managerial fiscal responsibility, and the public labor market's extensive immunity from markets pressures. Statistical studies of the comparative effects of the New and the Old Unionism would seem to contradict my assertion that the new public system of industrial relations is stronger. These studies have found that the Old Unionism raises wages more than the New (Mitchell, 1988, p. 158). However, I believe that these studies understate the New Unionism's relative impact for two reasons: They do not measure the full extent of the New Unionism's impact on total compensation and, perhaps more important, neglect to discount the compensating wage differentials present in the private sector, but less prevalent or even absent in the public sector. By compensating differentials is meant the disagreeableness of working conditions, or in the case of public versus private employment, greater stability of employment in the public sector results in a higher rate of pay for otherwise comparable jobs in the two sectors. Economists have pointed out that a substantial part of the measured union wage advantage within the private sector actually should be attributed to compensating wage differentials (Duncan and Stafford, 1980, 1982). There is no reason why compensating wage differentials should not also contribute to wage disparities between the public and private labor markets as well.

Meanwhile, the experience of the public sector already has begun to serve as a model for the older private system of industrial relations: "Public-sector bargaining over wages and conditions of employment is no longer the child of private-sector bargaining, even though it was originally its offspring. The now mature offspring has experience and lessons in the area of pay-setting and dispute settlement of potential value to its parent" (Mitchell, 1988, p. 159).

Over time, the differences between the public and private systems of industrial relations have steadily enlarged the comparative advantage of public over private sector bargaining. First among the changes has been the diminished sovereignty of the public employer coupled with the increased transfer of public authority to private parties. In the field of industrial relations, by sovereignty I mean the absolute authority of government to determine employment conditions, including a ban on strikes. Some legal scholars distinguish sovereignty from the doctrine of the delegation of power, that is the transference of public authority to collective bargaining without reducing sovereignty (Westbrook, 1986, 353). Others see the delegation of authority to private parties (unions) to be a dimension of sovereignty. This is my perspective.

Irrespective of its merits, sovereignty was breached when government extended exclusive representation and the right to consult or negotiate with the government employer over the terms and conditions of employment. The point is that once public policy makers decided to foster unionism and bargaining, the result had to diminish sovereignty. To approve or not of this breach is beside the point; the fact is that sovereignty was diminished and that is the starting point of any analysis of the New Industrial Relations System in the public domain.

Because of the singular nature of sovereignty, its power to decide labor relations unilaterally in a nonunion setting and in the earlier history of public sector labor organization, curtailment of sovereignty is the first and most important step in the New Unionism's goal of convergence in industrial relations. Attainment of that goal would reduce the sovereign employer to the same status as an employer in the private labor market in matters of labor relations. And much has already been accomplished by the New Unionism. Once the sovereign employer is whittled down to the equivalent of the private employer in matters of labor relations, convergence in all other matters, especially those subject to public policy, will fall into place more readily.

When government engages in collective bargaining the process itself curtails sovereignty; it is a first step in altering the nature and practice of political governance. To the conventional wisdom this diminution of sovereignty is regarded as no different than the diminution of managerial rights in the private sector. It can therefore treat the curtailment of sovereignty as a difference without a distinction.

However, the curtailment of sovereignty and the diminution of managerial rights in the private sector are not equivalent. In the public labor market, the public employer, the sovereign state, occupies a position not matched by the private employer in employee relations. Sovereignty is derived from the people in an open society, while managerial rights are derived from stockholders and private owners. The sovereign employer sets the legal ground rules for collective bargaining in all labor markets and simultaneously applies them. In the absence of collective bargaining, the state sets all the terms and conditions of employment and relies on civil service procedures in personnel matters. Once collective bargaining ensues, the state employer, especially the policy making component (the political), surrenders some of its previous authority and becomes subject to powerful lobbying, political and bargaining pressures from its labor relations "adversary." Civil service procedures are abbreviated in favor of the bargaining agreement. Even more important, the new relationship makes the once sovereign's (political) employer beholden, often significantly, to its labor "adversary" for election to office. Acceptance of negotiations over the terms and conditions of work immediately clips sovereignty, even if strikes continue to be banned.

Inevitably, the "maturation" of the bargaining process leads to further diminution of sovereign authority evidenced in the expansion of subjects negotiated, introduction of the union or agency shop, dues check-off, and the right to strike, however circumscribed. The agency shop is legal in the public labor market as a result of a Supreme Court decision It held that the agency shop does not violate dissenting employees freedom of speech, as long as the fees are spent on collective bargaining, grievances and contract administration.

While the electorate might wish to accede to a labor policy clipping sovereignty by collective bargaining, it is fatuous to assert either that sovereignty is not curtailed or that it doesn't matter. The ceding of sovereign authority through collective bargaining, albeit limited thusfar, has the potential for significant growth, as its historical record demonstrates. It already has forged a new partnership between the New Unionism and political authorities and has changed the nature of governance without the explicit agreement of the electorate. Clipping sovereignty extends the boundaries of the New Society. The ceding of sovereign authority is the outstanding characteristic of the new industrial relations system and evidence of the power of the New Unionism. Certainly these are significant developments in the theory and practice of representative government and merit recognition as such.

Collective bargaining has clipped sovereignty at all levels of government, but it has diminished it most at the local level. In fact, it has diminished sovereignty proportionately in reverse order of authority, most at the local, and least at state and federal levels. At the same time, the diminution of sovereignty has occurred most, at the local level of government, where employment is also largest. Paradoxically, collective bargaining has reduced sovereignty most at the level of government closest to the electorate, local government. One probable reason for this is the diffusion large number of governmental units at the local level; another is the proximity of local officials to unions representing their employees and therefore their vulnerability to political pressure.

Restrictions on strikes by various jurisdictions are cited by the conventional wisdom as circumventing the challenge to sovereignty, but does it? Actually, restrictions on strikes are, in fact, an explicit recognition that sovereignty has been abridged: The sovereign employer treats the union and the agreement as a treaty between equals, each with reciprocal responsibilities to the other. A public sector bargaining agreement is analogous to a treaty between two sovereign powers.

In addition, prohibitions or other limitations on strikes are typically linked to arbitration, another and even more subtle way of diminishing sovereignty and altering the democratic process. Arbitration transfers decisions affecting the conditions of employment to an unelected "expert" or panel. Elected officials can shrug off the financial consequences because they "had no choice," such as was explained to the writer by the Mayor of his community following a substantial wage increase for municipal employees despite budget "deficits." The City of Scranton, Pennsylvania became insolvent, in part because of an arbitrator's award. In general, arbitrators are said to "split the difference" between public employers and the New Unionism (Freeman and Ichniowski, 1988, p. 6). And this is how the public's fiscal affairs are ordered! And the conventional wisdom declares that these procedures do not encroach on sovereignty!

To the extent the New Society tolerates strikes, its policies alter the meaning of public property, another dimension of the process of curtailing sovereignty. Strikes redefine public property to mean that it is no different than private property and is to be treated according to the same rules. In the absence of that revolutionary change, strikes would remain, *ipso facto*, illegal. By treating public property as no different than private property, the conventional wisdom "reconciles" strikes with public property.

The newly evolving treatment of public property according to the rules of private property, also sets the New Socialism apart from the property doctrines of the Old and the Marxist versions of Socialism. Under the Old Socialism, public property was distinctly different from private property; it had to be, if public ownership of the means of production was to have any meaning, particularly when it came to strikes. Under the Old Socialism, strikes against the private and public property were conceptually different. Under the Old Socialism, strikes against the state provider of goods and services were theoretically illogical and should not occur because of the differences in the meaning of property. According to the theory of the Old Socialism, replacement of private by public property logically eliminated the adversarial relationship between unions and capitalists. Strikes became illogical because *"[t]here is no divergence between the objectives of the trade union and those of the government"* (Laski, p. 10, emphasis added). This theorem of the Old Socialism made public property (nationalized industries) distinct from private property and unions were expected to recognize that difference by not striking against "themselves." When workers in public enterprises did strike against "themselves," as they so often did, government typically surrendered to striking unions as the path of reconciliation.

Under the New Socialism, strikes against public property are not illogical (or illegal) if sovereignty is abridged to permit them. This merely restates the conventional wisdom's claim that bargaining in the public is fundamentally no different from bargaining in the private sector. Instead of public property being different from private property, it is treated as being the same, justifying and requiring strikes against the public employer, in contrast to the doctrines of the Old Socialism. After all, if the sovereign employer is no different than the private employer, then neither is public and private property, so why should the rules on strikes be different? Obviously, the rules of the New Society also are at variance with those of the Marxist Socialism: Under the Marxist version of socialism strikes were worse than illogical; strikers were not only striking against themselves, but were engaging in counter-revolutionary activities.

The most celebrated public sector strike of the 1980s, that of the Air Traffic Controllers, probably was the high water mark in the conceptual convergence in the meaning of public and private property, at least at the federal level, and, therefore, the right of federal employees to strike. Up to this point, "[e]nforcement [banning strikes of public employees] had, in fact, ... [become] so lax and erratic as to approach a de facto recognition of 'illegal' public employee strikes as a regular part of the negotiating process" (Meltzer and Sunstein, 1983, p. 732). Ultimately, the strike failed and its outcome was pointed to as not only a turning point in labor relations in the public labor market, but in the private one as well. Actually, it stemmed the erosion of the sovereignty and the meaning of public property at the federal level, but not in other jurisdictions. Had the outcome of that strike gone the other way, the abridgment of sovereignty and the transformation of the meaning of public property would have grown rapidly at all levels of government.

While the New Unionism usually cites the absence or limitation on the strike as a major deficiency in the current system of public sector industrial relations, the New Unionism's inability to obtain universal compulsory membership agreements and dues check-off across all jurisdictions are, I believe, even more important for its goal of convergence in the short run. These employer contributions to the administration of union finances are a significant dimension to the of power of the Old

Unionism and would likewise contribute to the power of the New Union-ism. Once in hand these arrangements would strengthen significantly the power of the New Unionism to gain the right to strike and convergence in general. Building membership and finances build the political constitu-ency with which the sovereign employer must deal on all matters of labor relations. An important by-product of compulsory membership is its undermining of civil service procedures and management of the public work force. Currently, the ban on compulsory membership applies uni-formly across the federal level, but is not uniform across all states and local jurisdictions.

In curtailing sovereignty, collective bargaining and arbitration have also transferred sovereign authority to the New Unionism. In a retro-spective (1972) analysis of his pioneer study of public sector unionism (originally completed in 1948), Spero described collective bargaining's limitations on sovereignty and the sharing of governance with the New Unionism as follows:

> It is hard to draw the line between working conditions, a subject now conced-edly within the scope of collective bargaining, and decisions regarding issues of public policy, the constitutional prerogative of executive and legislative authorities tracing their powers to the people. ... Increasingly in the public service, matters hitherto regarded as belonging in the realm of official deci-sion are being written into union contracts. (Spero, 1972, p. x).

In his retrospective Spero went on to observe that "[e]mployees in the client-oriented education, health and welfare services have been the most articulate ... [in] dealing with policy issues at the bargaining table ...[and] reject the traditional concept of civil service neutrality and sup-port the new tendencies in public administration toward staff activism and involvement in public affairs" (p. x). Policies in public education are an important domain of local government measured in expenditures, employment and responsibility. It is here, not in some peripheral area of local authority that governance is now shared between public bodies, many of them directly elected by voters in school districts, and the New Unionism. State laws and school codes vest educational authority to school boards, but collective bargaining has steadily encroached on these sovereign responsibilities. Like the process which has eroded managerial authority in the public domain, especially in railways where government regulation has been a surrogate for public ownership, governance has steadily become shared between unions and public rule. The low voter turnout in school board or local elections in general is hardly a reason to deny that the New Unionism does not erode representative democracy (Cohen, 1979, p. 194).

The sharing of governance in education, specifically the curriculum and instruction, is common to both major unions in education, the American Federation of Teachers, AFL-CIO and the National Education Association, Independent. However, it appears that the AFT includes more elements on curriculum in its contracts than the NEA (Geisert, 1984, pp. 36–37). Probably the AFT's more activist stance and greater representation in cities accounts for this. The extension of bargaining from gaining recognition, improved wages, hours and fringe benefits to curriculum and instruction moved rapidly during the 1970s. The move was described by union officials as dictated by matters of "professional significance" (Geisert, 1984, p. 36). The line between professional responsibility for the content of curriculum and instruction and collectively bargained terms and conditions of employment has steadily shifted in favor of bargaining cloaked as professional responsibility. A parallel shift has occurred in school board dealings with unions of supervisory personnel: "Not only do we deal with the teachers who are eroding the board's and management's curriculum and instructional activities, but we now have supervisory unions who also want a piece of that action and have demanded the right to introduce their own ideas on what the curriculum ought to be" (Geisert, 1938, p. 38).

Once sovereignty was breached, the process of steady encroachment began. The end purpose of the New Unionism's continuing effort is to reduce the sovereign employer to the a position as close as possible to the private employer. Legislation broadening the scope of bargaining and extending the right to strike will fulfill that goal. The diminution of sovereign authority and the transfer of governmental authority to collective bargaining also steadily made the organized public employer a much easier "adversary" than its private counterpart. Indeed, the historical comparative disadvantage which sovereignty once imposed on public sector industrial relations, that is during the pre-1960s period, has not only been materially diminished, but actually converted into a positive advantage in the form of a "cooperative" employer, highly advantageous employment conditions, and with little exposure to unemployment. Indeed, the adversarial nature of the private system and the risk of unemployment are not characteristic of the new public system of industrial relations. The literature on what the Old Unionism does and why has focused on private unions' adversarial role in governance. However, there is a distinct difference in the role of the employer on governance and on union goals in the two sectors. In the private sector, employers resist union efforts to encroach on managerial authority, while in the public sector the politician employer (perhaps not necessarily the public manager) may collaborate with the unions to expand the unions' role in governance. The motivation is self-interest, the perpetuation of political control and union support for larger budgets. In the private sector self-interest motivates management to maximize profits and their incomes and therefore to contest union demands for a share in governance. In the private system, governance curtails the authority of employers' to discharge employees for incompetence and nonperformance, whereas in the public sector governance has often reached the point where discharge for incompetence is nearly impossible.

Symptomatic of curtailed sovereignty is the increased separation of managerial responsibility in collective bargaining from fiscal accountability. This is indicated by bargaining's contribution to budget deficits at the state level and insolvencies at the local level of government. Indeed, one analyst (sympathetic to public sector bargaining) could ask, "who is public management," and answer that "in the public sector the formal responsibility often differs from the actual," an ambiguity which, he went on to point out, does not arise in the private labor market (Derber, 1988, pp. 90–91).

Although diminishing the authority of the sovereign employer has proceeded apace, the ultimate goal of convergence has not yet been fully achieved. The task, then, for proponents of full convergence is to reconcile the diminution of sovereignty with collective bargaining. Thus, when the conventional wisdom analyzes the role of sovereignty in public sector industrial relations, it concludes, "[a]lthough there are many genuine issues in determining the best way to structure and conduct public sector bargaining, experience has shown that this type of bargaining is not incompatible with representative government" (Westbrook, 1986, p. 358). In its efforts to reconcile sovereignty and bargaining, this line of reasoning continues "[t]he issue is not whether the government's power is supreme, but how that power is to be exercised. The passage of legislation authorizing collective bargaining is in effect a decision by the sovereign to establish terms of employment for public employees through collective bargaining" (Westbrook, 1986, p. 357). Unravelling this circular reasoning, one must conclude the writer means that the sovereign government simply must share its authority with the New Unionism.

Characterizing this as the "consensus" view, the conventional wisdom justifies this power-sharing in these terms: "The most powerful argument that has led to this consensus is that it is simply unfair to permit, indeed encourage, private sector bargaining while denying similar rights to public employees" (Westbrook, 1986, p. 358). After all, this line of reasoning continues, "[i]f government can be sued upon its consent, it is logical to conclude that the government can bargain with its employees and be bound by the results of the bargaining upon its consent" (Westbrook, p. 357). Indeed, so extensively has government given its consent to bargain collectively that sovereignty has even been dismissed as a significant factor in public sector bargaining (Westbrook, 1986 p. 356).

The conventional approach thereby turns to what it regards as a legal concept separate from sovereignty (a distinction which I reject, as noted above), the legal delegation of authority. The justification for the assault on those legal barriers which still separate the public industrial relations system from the private (coming under the rubric of the delegation of authority) is summed up this way: "Participation in law-making by private groups under explicit statutory 'delegation' does not stand then in absolute contradiction to the traditional process and conditions of law-making; it is not incompatible with the conception of law" (Westbrook, quoting L. Jaffe, 1986, p. 366). Quoting yet another authority, Westbrook reports: "There seems little justification in practice for a continued adherence to a fictitious per se rule against delegation to private authorities" (Westbrook, quoting George W. Liebmann, 1986, p. 366).

Another justification for delegation is that is expertise, or rather the lack of it by public authorities, which justifies delegation of "law-making." Simply put, legislative bodies lack the expertise and time to establish the terms and conditions of employment and are therefore justified in delegating these decisions to collective bargaining. While the conventional approach would equate this with a civil service commission, the two systems are hardly comparable. Civil service commissions deal with personnel administration; collective bargaining goes well beyond that to determine the terms and conditions of employment.

Under the principle of delegation of powers, the attack on the barriers separating the public and private systems of industrial relations would be made piece-meal, rather than wholesale: "An all-or-nothing determination clearly is not appropriate today. An issue-by-issue approach is needed both in drafting effective state legislation on public sector labor relations and in testing the validity of specific provisions with reference to the nondelegation doctrine" (Westbrook, 1986, p. 339). The bargaining provisions must not touch "fundamental" matters for which government officials are politically accountable, but must, on the other hand, provide fairness to the public employee. Not surprisingly the conventional approach concludes that "[m]ost decisions on the terms and conditions of employment do not involved truly fundamental issues" (Westbrook, 1986, p. 375). Illustrative of "superficial" issues are "the allocation of resources within particular programs and agencies" (Westbrook, 1986, p. 375). How this allocation could be construed as not fundamental, while allocation among agencies and programs is regarded as fundamental, is at best obscure. Since fundamental issues of the public fisc at all levels do embrace governance (sovereignty), the borderline between "fairness" and "fundamentalism" is in the eye of the beholder. Thus, "[u]nlawful delegation problems arise only when responsible officials abdicate their responsibilities to participate actively in the process" (Westbrook, 1986, p. 380). The same vacuous standard applies to arbitration in the public sector: "Even when decision making power is given to private persons, as in binding arbitration, the fact that the arbitrator is a private person is one of the least important factors to consider in deciding the delegation issue" (Westbrook,, 1986, p. 380). In practice, experience indicates that the boundary has shifted in favor of "fairness" expanding the scope of public sector bargaining and arbitration with the trend toward convergence steadily picking up steam.

Collective bargaining and sovereignty have been reconciled because limitations on the strike have resolved the conflict "for the most part" (Freeman, 1986. p.169). This can only mean that to the extent strikes in the public sector are legalized, the law recognizes and accepts the diminution of sovereign authority and an important closing of the gap between the public and private systems of industrial relations. Despite his minimization of the sovereignty issue, Freeman nevertheless does agree that "[i]n sum, the particular features of the public sector do, indeed, yield a different industrial relations system from the private sector" (Freeman, 1985, p. 173).

Another approach bringing the public system closer to the private (convergence) treats the diminution of sovereignty as either the equivalent of the reduction of managerial prerogatives in the private sector, or as an exaggeration of the power of the New Unionism (Cohen, 1979). However, that analysis distorts and mutes the significance of the challenge to sovereignty. It is true, of course, that in striving to share in the governance of the work place, the New Unionism superficially seems only to be reducing managerial prerogatives, just as the Old Unionism in the private market. However, its actions have wider consequences: The New Unionism and its associated system of industrial relations curtail sovereignty and change the nature of representative democracy at the local level of government (Wellington and Winters, 1969; Summers, 1976).

Because these changes are incremental rather than large scale, they are not widely perceived. Infringements on sovereignty and democratic representative government are typically presented as merely aspects of collective bargaining akin to the diminution of managerial authority in the private sector, or little different from the actions of other pressure groups in their impact on representative democracy. Professor Sanford Cohen (1979) minimizes the challenge of the New Unionism to representative democracy because not all their strikes have been successful. Such a standard of judgment is flawed, not to say odd. Irrespective of their outcome, strikes, when legal, are public acceptance of a diminution of sovereignty; when illegal they are a acts of defiance of sovereign authority, whether it be the employing public agency, the legislative body enacting policy, or the courts.

While the legalization of strikes represents a "voluntary" (actually, a what else could we do approach) cession of a measure of sovereignty, the most important diminution of sovereignty is involuntary – the insolvency of municipal and other local governmental units. Typically the conventional wisdom has ignored this issue. At the same time, those who *do* recognize that public sector bargaining does diminish sovereignty have emphasized its alteration of the political process (Wellington and Winters 1969; Summers, 1976 and Cohen, 1979). While I agree that collective bargaining in the public sector does directly modify the political process, it also contributes to the convergence of the two systems of industrial relations: Government, in a sense, "goes broke" like many private businesses have under the impact of collective bargaining. Indeed, the bankruptcy procedures in both domains clearly indicate that form of convergence. This approach, the fiscal approach, to the diminution of sovereignty and its thrust toward convergence comes from one of those "fundamental" issues, the absence of political accountability. I would assume that fiscal failures transgress even the conventional distinctions about what is fundamental and what is not. Moreover, it is failure at the local level of government, where, as former Speaker of the House of Representatives, Thomas "Tip" O'Neill, pointed out, all politics begin.

Diminution of sovereignty may not be an explicit goal of the New Unionism, but its philosophy and actions (Chapter V) do reshape the political process well beyond those of an ordinary pressure group. Meanwhile, the New Unionism does intend to reshape its current system of industrial relations and, if successful, will further diminish sovereignty.

The principal comparative disadvantages of the New Unionism in the current public system of industrial relations are limitations on the right to strike, compulsory membership, the check-off, issues subject to bargaining, public policy and above all the persistence of those characteristics which distinguish the sovereign employer from the private employer. Although compulsory membership (the union shop) is as yet beyond the pale, the New Unionism has already won the right to negotiate agency shop provisions in collective bargaining agreements. (An agency shop requires that employees represented by the union, but who are not members, pay fees or dues equivalent to or some percentage of regular dues). Since the Supreme Court's decision in the *Abood* case in 1977, agency shops in the public sector are legal except in states with laws banning them, the right-to-work law states. In 1991, eight right-to-work states were considering legislation permitting the agency shop. If enacted, the legislation would be applicable to both the public and private sectors of the labor market. The states were Arizona, Idaho, Kansas, Nevada, North Dakota, Utah, Virginia and Wyoming.

By law, the funds obtained from agency shop fees and members's dues may only be used for purposes of collective bargaining and not for political purposes. In another case originating in the private sector (*Beck*), judicial proceedings revealed that as little as 21% was found to be spent on collective bargaining. To enable those represented by the union and who object to the expenditure of their fees and dues from being spent on causes to which they object, unions are required to establish a procedure enabling them to reclaim a portion of their fees and dues. However, the fiscal limitations on the unions of such procedures is minimal. Meantime, public sector unions seek legislation which would permit the check-off dues in states where it is not now permitted.

After sovereignty, the extensive immunity from competition in the public economy ranks next as the factor separating the private and public systems of industrial relations and enhancing the power of public sector bargaining and the New Industrial Relations System. While the tenure of managers in the private sector depends on the competitive success of the company (the votes of buyers of the company's products), the tenure of public managers is more assured, despite recurring budget deficits. There is a marked discrepancy between the effectiveness of market voting and political voting in determining the tenure of private and public management. Fiscal failure seems to have limited impact on public managements' tenure in office, although it may now be a factor in the rising demand for term limitations. On the other hand, with some newsworthy exceptions in auto manufacturing, there is a link to managerial tenure and the company's financial success in the private sector.

Currently, public policy also differs between the two systems of industrial relations. Public policy in the private sector is at this time more intrusive than in the public labor market. It is also virtually unitary, that is, the basic federal law, the National Labor Relations Act, covers most private sector workers. The Railway Labor Act has jurisdiction over rail and airline employees, a relatively small number of workers. On the other hand, policies in the public domain are less intrusive and are divided among federal, state and thousands of local authorities. Because policy is more intrusive in the private than in the public sector, the New Unionism sees itself at a comparative disadvantage relative to the Old. However, to a significant extent, the perceived disadvantage is less a matter of policy than of market differences. Thus, policy is unable to impede the markets relentless erosion of the Old Unionism in all advanced industrial countries, despite public policies fostering unionism. In contrast, public policy, though weaker and more diffuse in the public labor market, is reinforced by the immunities of the public labor market from competition. The New Unionism regards the elimination of the policy differences between the two labor markets as the ultimate goal of convergence. And as experience in Canada has demonstrated, a comprehensive and pro-union interventionist policy would add enormously to the strength of the New Unionism and the New Industrial Relations System in the U.S.

Another difference between the industrial relations systems of the public and private labor markets and which redounds to the comparative advantage of the public over the private is the difference in managerial goals. Public managers' goals differ sharply from those of private employers. And because each seeks to maximize different goals, each therefore views costs from different perspectives. Goals, such as enlarging the scope of their responsibilities, may lead public employers to take actions directly opposite to those of private managers. Whereas private managers are ruled by requirements of maximizing profits and minimizing costs, public managers may treat costs in a diametrically opposite manner. Public managers can view the maximization of costs as a means of increasing their responsibilities, the employment and the importance of their bureaucracies. In this way, public managements' goals parallel the goal of the New Unionism to increase the redistribution of income from the private to the public sector. In the public sector, the "bottom line" often includes spending more, not less, and not saving unexpended funds before the end of a fiscal year. Returning funds to the public treasury, instead of being an act of prudence, is more likely to viewed as an act of naivete.

Managerial responsibilities for labor relations are separated from financial responsibilities in public sector labor relations because political and professional (public) management are not checked by market restraints. Unlike private management, public management does not have to show a profit. When deficits are encountered they are blamed on the state of the economy or the political opposition, never on poor management. At times, the unions are blamed, but the resulting mock battles are "fought" so as not to undermine the political support of the New Unionism for the incumbent management. In its managerial "adversary," the New Unionism enjoys a comparative advantage which is inherent in political markets.

The separation of managerial from financial responsibility in the public economy is not the equivalent of the separation of management from ownership in the private sector. While often largely free of the oversight of owners, private corporate managers still must produce profits over the long run to retain their authority. Whatever their deficiencies, the leveraged buy-outs of the 1980s provided yet another check to the authority of private corporate management. Leverage buy-outs often demonstrated that incumbent managements had made inadequate use of the corporations earning capacity. Fear of the buy-out gave rise to the "poison pill" to ward off acquisition. The closest equivalent to the leveraged buy-out in the public domain is insolvency and bankruptcy, with the courts stepping in to re-organize the finances of the entity. Financial controls boards are introduced to ward-off the "poison pill" of judicial reorganization, as happened in New York City (see below). However, unlike the private domain, when bankruptcy would doubtless lead to new management, no such expectation is seriously raised in the public domain.

Political markets – elections, taxpayer revolts and term limitations – may eventually introduce some countervailing power akin to competition in the public domain, but these are less effective than market constraints in the private sector. Needless to say, the fiasco of President Bush's "read my lips" has further undermined the electorate's confidence in the steadfastness of political leadership.

The process of bargaining distinguishes the current public and private systems of industrial relations and the process enhances the comparative advantage of public sector bargaining. The New Unionism employs a "two-track" system of bargaining, one direct and open, the other political and semi-clandestine. While conducting negotiations with public managers in a manner closely paralleling private unions in "open" negotiations, the New Unionism also negotiates, usually simultaneously, with political leaders behind the scene. The "political" bargaining can precede and coincide with the open bargaining. It is more real and substantive than the open.

The importance of political bargaining in public sector negotiation extends beyond wages and hours. It cements the political relationship between the "adversaries." In fact, this association is needed to accomplish certain goals in bargaining. This is especially true of the benefits package because it may even be statutorily beyond the reach of the open negotiations. Changes in the benefits package of public workers typically require approval of legislative or regulatory bodies. For that reason a preliminary approval may be obtained and then afterward the legally implementation follows. Because the size of the benefit package has grown enormously over the years and can hardly be described by the word "fringe" any longer, this aspect of bargaining has also grown in both political and budgetary importance. In contrast, all terms and conditions of employment are the subject of direct and adversarial negotiations in the private sector.

The two systems differ in the extent to which the economic and political dimensions of bargaining determine how bargaining works. While the Old Unionism, too, uses political means to enhance their economic power as evidenced by the Davis-Bacon and Walsh Healey Acts, licensure and trade legislation, the Old Unionism emphasized the economic approach to maintaining and improving the working conditions and living standards of members.

On the other hand, the New Unionism negotiates with a different type of employer, the political employer, and therefore necessarily relies much more on political bargaining. Sometimes this produces severe after effects, such as contributed to the Professional Air Traffic Controllers' (PATCO) strike in 1981. In this case, the bargaining process not only becomes confused as politicians link themselves closely to unions, even though they are not responsible for the outcome. The result can not only be bad advice, but dangerous advice. Such, I believe, would describe the role of Representative William Clay of Missouri in the PATCO strike of 1981. In events leading up to the strike, Representative Clay made the following recommendations to the union at its convention in 1980:

> Your plan must be one which completely revises your political thinking. It should start with the premise that your no permanent friends, no permanent enemies, just permanent interests. It must be selfish and pragmatic. You must learn the rules of the game and learn them well:
>
> Rule No. 1 says that you don't put the interest of an other group ahead of your own. What's good for federal employees must be interpreted as being good for the Nation.
>
> Rule No. 2 says that take what you can, give up only what you must.
>
> Rule No. 3. says that you can take from whomever you can, whenever you can, however your can. ... If you are not prepared to play by the rules then you have not reached the age of political maturity and perhaps you deserve everything that's happening to you (Quoted in Meltzer and Sunstein, p. 765).

If this is the advice of a law-maker, why shouldn't the New Unionism seek convergence in industrial relations? Any notion of public service and the special responsibilities it places on government workers goes out the window as a relic of the pre-historic past. Professors Meltzer and Sunstein described Congressman Clay's advice "guidelines for ruthless self-seeking" (1983, p. 765) and responsible for raising the strike fever which ultimately led to the PATCO strike.

Another, albeit harmless, example of the confusion which politicians can play in public sector bargaining occurred during the negotiations in June 1991 involving the Mayor, City Council and the public unions of New York City. The *New York Times* reported (June 26, 1991, p. A.1) that the Mayor urged union members to "besiege" the Council with protests to prevent budget and employment cuts greater than the Mayor has proposed. Likewise, in New Jersey in 1991, the State Assembly's Democratic leadership "found" monies previously "undiscovered" by the Democratic Administration to ward off layoffs and a threatened strike. The unions shop around among the branches of government to find the best deal and then political pressure brings about something close to their financial or other goals.

While both the Old and the New union groups rely on significant political inputs in their bargaining, the practices of the New Unions are necessarily characterized by a larger political component. This is so not only because of the nature of the employer, but also because of the close political inter-dependence of the "opposing" parties. Indeed, in many ways the inter-dependence of the parties in collective bargaining makes the electorate their common opponent. The legal prohibitions on unions' political activities (embodied at the federal level in the Hatch Act) are noteworthy for their impotence. In contrast, in the private sector, the consumer (the private equivalent of the electorate) must be courted for the enterprise to survive.

A basic difference between public and private sector industrial relations is the New Unionism's usurpation of the process of making policy. Nominally, this is compared the Old Unionism's clipping of private management's prerogatives, but the analogy is inaccurate. Whereas managerial prerogatives preserve a great measure of managerial authority in making and executing policy, public bargaining erodes the authority of democratically elected bodies to make and execute policy. Of all the areas in which the New Unionism seeks convergence in industrial relations, reducing sovereignty to the level of "managerial prerogatives" is the most significant. The goal of convergence is to down size sovereignty to the managerial prerogatives of the private employer.

Differences between the New and the Old Unionism (Chapter II), also separate the industrial relations systems in the private and public sectors of the economy. The Old Unionism is made up primarily of blue collar workers; the New Unionism, primarily white collar workers. The unions making up the two movements also differ in history and development (Chapter II). In both sectors unions enroll and represent a minority of the work force, but the gap is greater in the private sector. The gap in the private sector, the large number of nonunion workers in the labor market who are neither members nor represented by unions, acts as "an army of the employed" to check the bargaining and political goals of the unions. In contrast, the gap, the army of the nonunion employed in the public labor market is far smaller, especially in the federal sector. Therefore, the "army of the employed" in the nonunion public labor market cannot check the bargaining pressures of the New Unionism to the same extent, if at all, as in the private labor market. Because of the disparities in the two union movements and their fundamental divergences in philosophy and policies (Chapters IV and V), convergence in philosophy will not be on the agenda of convergence. Instead of a unitary union movement, the New and the Old Unionism will remain separate and distinct. On the other hand, the two systems of industrial relations will draw closer.

The Public Economy:
Labor Market and Labor Relations Policy

The growing size and diversity of the public sector labor market adds impetus to the New Unionism's pressure for convergence in industrial relations. Given the increasing size of the sector, a large and expanding union movement and multiple governmental jurisdictions, a compelling argument can be made for a unified labor policy to properly administer labor relations. Currently, the sector is divided among a very large number of governmental jurisdictions with diverse labor policies. In addition to the federal government and 50 state governments, there are nearly 83 thousand local governmental jurisdictions. And these thousands of government units have over 14 thousand policies in labor relations (Census of Governments 1987, Table 1, p. 1). In just five years, between 1982–1987, the number of jurisdictions with labor policies increased by approximately 1,000.

The rationale for a national labor policy also draws support from the distribution of employment and union membership, as well as the number and type of labor policies. Among the three levels of government, local government is by far the largest employer, followed by the States and then the Federal government. In 1990 local government accounted for 60%, states 24% and the federal government the balance of government employment. Within the public sector, state and local union membership constitutes close to 85% of total membership in the New Unionism. Meanwhile, many important local and state governments have labor policies which are closer to the NLRA (private sector policy) than the federal.

Not only are state and local governments the largest employers of public employees, but they also are growing faster than the Federal government in the proportion of public employment to the population. The ratio of the state and local government per 10,000 population rose between 1982 and 1987, while the ratio of federal employment to civilian population declined (Census, Aug. 1988, p. IX). The State with the largest number of state and local full-time equivalent government employees per 10,000 population as of October 1987 was Alaska (738.6) and the smallest was Pennsylvania (398.4). The District of Columbia at 886.5 outranked Alaska. The average for the country was 502.

Convergence can be achieved either by subjecting the public and private systems of industrial relations to one law, or a special *national* law covering all public employment, federal state and local. Its content would closely parallel private sector law. As noted, a national law covering all public employees became constitutionally possible after the Supreme Court's decision in the *Garcia* case in 1985 (See Appendix A). Either procedure, a single law for all employees, public and private, or a single law for public employees would be an enhanced Wagner Act, such as the proposed Labor Reform Act of 1977. The new legislation could also retain special treatment – final offer arbitration – for security forces, police and fire fighters. If achieved, convergence in industrial relations would sharply increase membership in the New Unionism. As the Public Employees Department of the AFL-CIO candidly announced:

> A major reason public sector unionism has not grown more is due to a lack of a national comprehensive collective bargaining law. ... State and local public employees must rely on state laws to guarantee collective bargaining rights [and] only 26 states and the District of Columbia have state-wide collective bargaining laws. In those states with such laws 57 percent of public workers are in unions. In the 24 states without comprehensive laws, only 11 percent of the public work force is unionized (PED, March 1991).

A nationalized public sector labor law would also reinforce the political as well as the economic power of the New Unionism to accelerate the trend toward the redistribution of income, the New Socialism, and open wider the vistas of the New Society and its doctrine of Fairness.

Perhaps it may be argued that even an enhanced Wagner Act could not withstand the effects of markets in this, the New Age of Adam Smith, so what protection could a converged labor policy offer the New Unionism? Conceptually, the New Unionism is virtually exempt from competition. Factually, one need look no further than north of the 49th parallel, to Canada, to see a laboratory case in which the power of a fused (public and private) system of industrial relations can virtually guarantee a large, continually expanding and powerful New Unionism in the public labor market even as it proves unable to stem the decline of the Old Unionism. In Canada public and private employees are subject to several varieties of law. Some are under the jurisdiction of purely public or private legislation, but in many cases public employees are subject to the same law as private sector employees (convergence). While the Old Unionism subject to the same law as the New Unionism has steadily shrunk, the New Unionism has continued to grow (Troy, 1992). Thus, the power of public policy to underpin and foster the New Unionism is demonstrably even far more powerful than is acknowledged by the conventional approach.

In the absence of a nationalized policy, the transformation in ideas, labor markets and unionism – the new environment – generates convergence, as, for example, in personnel policies. While personnel policies between the public and private systems of industrial relations differ, the differences are narrowing. While personnel policies in the public sector, from recruitment to promotion and termination, continue to be prescribed by civil service rules and procedures, they are increasingly subverted by collective bargaining agreements. Disputes are subject to overlapping civil service and collectively bargained grievance procedures, but the trend is toward convergence. The New Industrial Relations aims to replace a system based on merit to one based on "industrial citizenship," or "exit-voice," that is, accountability to the collective bargaining agreement.

Grievance procedures are a related area in which the public system of industrial relations is already converging with the private. Decisions in grievances, especially arbitration, impact the meaning of an agreement in the public sector, as in the private sector. Convergence in arbitration practices are most advanced at the state and local levels compared to the federal government. In fact, "over half of the grievance procedures in the state and local contract sample allow binding arbitration" (Ullman and Begin, 1977, p. 328). Ullman and Begin also anticipate expansion in coverage and scope of grievance procedures in the public labor market.

The role of grievance arbitration in the convergence process may be grasped from the following assessment: ... "[G]rievance arbitration has a highly significant role to play in the public sector, and ... courts should accommodate to it in much the same way that they have in the private sector" (Olson, p. 1988, p. 232). Substantively, the new public sector industrial relations system may have leaped ahead of its counterpart in the private sector, according to one study. Thus, in the period up to the mid-1970s, arbitration reviews in the public sector by activist state courts went beyond the scope of arbitrability in the private sector and have since "retreat[ed] to the basic private sector principles" (Olson, 1988, p. 263). One explanation of this reversal is "a reaction to an earlier premise of identity between public- and private-sector labor relations that has been difficult to maintain" (Olson, 1988, p. 263).

At the same time, grievance procedures undermine the civil service system and sovereignty. The awards modify if not set aside a neutral system of personnel management for a system of governance similar to that in the private organized labor market, and as shown by the experience of Scranton, Pennsylvania, further reduces sovereignty. At the federal level, grievance procedures established to supplement civil service processes have eclipsed the old system. Civil service appeals were limited to disciplinary action, however new policies required executive agencies to establish appeal procedures for "adverse actions." Adverse actions covered suspension, discharge, furlough without pay, or reduction in rank or compensation. Other matters now subject to grievance procedures are discrimination, position, classification and the resolution of disputes over the administration of an agreement (Ullman and Begin, 1977, p. 324).

While it might be argued that the private employer system was once unilateral, the same could not be said about the civil service system; civil service had a different origin than private personnel management and has served public administration well since its inception. The application of collectively bargained rule-making undermines that system and is changing the character of public employment. In substituting bargaining agreements for civil service procedures, it substitutes a vastly different system of employee relations for civil service. In this important way, the New Unions are bringing the practices of collective bargaining closer to the private model.

The Quasi-Public Labor Market

Convergence will receive a major boost from the emergence of a new type of labor market, the "quasi-public," or "quasi-socialist" labor market. By quasi-public or quasi-socialist market I mean the market in which public monies fund wholly or in part the production of goods and services through private or non-profit enterprises. In this market, the new environment – the New Socialism and the New Society – blur the differences between public and private production, and property, and add a new and growing dimension to the redistribution of the national income between the private and public economies. In ideological terms, the quasi-public labor market extends the boundaries of "what government can do for you" to new frontiers.

The quasi-public market is wedged between the private and public sectors. Conventionally, the institutions in this market and the employees and the unions are treated statistically as either private or nonprofit in government statistical data, even though their funding depends on substantial receipts coming directly or indirectly from the public bursary. Public construction is an historic illustration of the quasi-public market. Government contracts are awarded to private companies who employ private workers subject to the provisions of federal law, the Davis-Bacon Act, and similar legislation at state and even at some local levels of government. In an early example of "Fairness," the Davis-Bacon Act, enacted in 1931, was inspired by Congressional desire to insure a minimum wage for workers engaged in government construction, alteration or repair of public buildings and public works, including painting or decorating amounting to more than $2,000. The minimum was and remains identified as the "prevailing wage" in the relevant labor market; it is determined by government, the Labor Department. However, the Labor Department uniformly finds not the prevailing market wages, but the prevailing union scales. Davis-Bacon has enjoyed widespread support in Congress, but in recent years it has nevertheless come under criticism even from the General Accounting Office. The GAO has charged that the Act is anti-competitive, inflationary and unfair to female and minority contractors (Whittaker, 1991, p. CRS 3). A number of state and local governments have followed the federal example. Some local governments in the San Francisco area have recently mandated the "prevailing (union) wage" procedure for construction in the private sector (Crovitz, p. 14)! If the legal challenge to this extension of the Davis-Bacon practice does not overturn these local prescriptions, a significant new extension of the quasi-public sector will have been made.

The federal Walsh-Healey Act of 1936 subjected other suppliers of goods in the quasi-public sector to meet prescribed standards of minimum wages, overtime pay, child labor and other requirements. State and local government versions of Walsh-Healey greatly increase the scope of the quasi-public sector.

The quasi-public sector is even larger than these illustrations suggest. The entire so-called "military-industrial" complex can be regarded as part of the quasi-public sector. However, most important for the future is government financial support at all levels of government of the rapidly growing medical and hospital services. These are certain to grow as we approach the 21st century because both major political parties, but especially the Democrats will expand government's role in subsidizing and providing medical and hospital services.

Currently non-profit hospitals exemplify the growing quasi-public labor market in medical services. They are extensively funded out of the public bursary while their employees are subject to the National Labor Relations Act (private sector law). The unions claiming jurisdiction come from both the New and Old Unionism. The American Federation of State, County and Municipal Employees (AFSCME), AFL-CIO has targeted the public, the quasi-public (non-profit) and private hospital medical care services. Its president has estimated that there are nine million workers involved, "the biggest reservoir of untouched, unorganized workers in America" (Cook, 1991, p. 84). Another of the New Unions organizing and representing hospital and medical service employees in the public, quasi-public, and the private sectors simultaneously is Local 1199, Drug Hospital and Health Care Employees. The 1990 Labor Department Register of Labor Organizations shows that Local 1199 to be affiliated with the Retail, Wholesale and Department Store Workers, AFL-CIO, a private sector union, but is also being wooed by a public sector union AFSCME and a joint public-private union, the Service Employees International Union, both affiliated with the AFL-CIO. These jurisdictional cross-overs highlight the mixed or joint union form or organization discussed in Chapter II. In the process of organizing these organizations are likely to generate jurisdictional disputes, despite procedures set up by the AFL-CIO for preventing them. Such disputes are likely to grow given the efforts of the Old Unionism to gain members in the public labor market to offset their declining private sector losses.

The quasi-public domain is not limited to those institutions receiving direct public expenditures. Indirect public support, through tax deductions, governmental grants, student loans and tax-deductible contributions to otherwise private universities and charitable institutions shift a portion of the financing to the general public. It is evident that the domain of the quasi-public sector is not sharply defined and, at the same time, is growing.

While the quasi-public sector derives its funding in whole or part from the public bursary, its labor policies and practices are from the private sector. As just noted, non-profit health care institutions (except medical colleges) are under the jurisdiction of the NLRA. So, of course, are employees of companies with contracts with the government. The combination of government contracts and public funding doubtless accounts for the high unionization rate in the companies which perform government work.

The legal status of strikes illustrate the special character of the quasi-public sector and why the sector's industrial relations can serve as a model for convergence in industrial relations systems. Strikes in the quasi-public sector are treated like those in the private economy even though the service interrupted, like that of a public enterprise, serves a public interest. Just as in the public sector, strikes separate the provider's obligation to provide a public service from the performance of that service, irrespective of its importance. However, unlike the public sector, the quasi-public sector functions under the rules of the private sector which sanction strikes.

Meanwhile, the separation of the obligation from the provision of service is already legally tolerated to some extent in the public sector, and at times condoned even when it is not, the freedom to strike in the quasi-public sector adds a powerful argument for convergence. Of particular interest to the New Unionism at this time is the replacement striker issue in the private and quasi-public sectors. If Congress enacts legislation prohibiting replacement strikers under the National Labor Relations Act (which governs both the private and the quasi-public sectors), the New Unionism would place the same demand on its convergence agenda, even though its application is academic rather than real. The New Unionism will demand equal treatment under the law – convergence – on this as on all other rules of the private system of industrial relations effective in the quasi-public sector, the union shop, the check-off and bargaining over all terms and conditions of employment, for reasons of form, if not substance.

Developments in the quasi-public sector will also affect the Old Unionism, its philosophical orientation and in its membership. Most of the unions in the sector are branches of the Old Unionism, but because the quasi-public sector is extensively funded out of they public bursary, they escape the worst rigors of competitive markets. As a result, the Old Unionism, or at least parts of it, will be converted to the philosophy of social unionism of the New Unionism (Chapter V) and this, in turn, will enlarge the demand for the socialization of income. Added to the expenditures of public monies through public channels will be the demand for public expenditures through private channels. The New Unionism and the Old operating in the quasi-public sector may compete for the public funds, but their over-all impact will increase the aggregate of government spending. At the same time the sector offers the Old Unionism a hope of partial revival. Because the sector is substantially immune to competitive markets the Old Unions operating in it should be able to compensate for some of its losses in membership.

For the New Unionism, the quasi-public sector may also mean more growth. The quasi-public sector is surrogate for the Old Socialism's penchant for the nationalization of enterprise. It thus enlarges their potential scope of operations. For some individual unions, locals, district and national, this could lead to joint affiliation with two established private and public sector organizations. It means that a given union may belong to more than one national union. Joint affiliation is the logical outgrowth of the joint or mixed union. Local 1199 of the Health and Hospital Workers, a union in both the public and private sectors in New York City, may be an example of this development. While it is now affiliated with a private sector union, the Retail, Wholesale and Department Store Union, AFL-CIO, it may attempt joint affiliation with either the Service Employees International Union, AFL-CIO, or the American Federation of State, County and Municipal Employees, AFL-CIO.

It is evident that the quasi-public sector generates some ambiguity about industrial relations system, what unions are and what they do and why. A future research project will be needed to more fully assess its development. However, it seems very likely that unions in this sector have a promising future.

This hypothesis is more than theoretical. Once again Canada offers an example. The Canadian quasi-public sector consists of public enterprises, crown corporations and agencies which are subject to private sector labor law. The sector differ from the U.S. in that the American enterprises are privately owned or are non-profit, but it parallels the U.S. in that private policy is applicable to labor relations. In Canada, the impact of private sector labor policies to public enterprises has had a dramatic impact. Employees of crown corporations and agencies are more highly unionized than the private enterprises subject to the same law, and, *perhaps*, only slightly less unionized than employees in public administration, the most unionized group in Canada. Similarly, in the U.S., the quasi-public sector in medical and hospital care is much more unionized than its private counterpart, especially in large metropolitan areas. I do not know whether union penetration in the quasi-public sector lags the *de jure* public sector in the U.S. Most likely, in large metropolitan areas, it does not.

Government Finance

Increased government spending plays the same role as growing public employment in providing impetus to convergence in industrial relations. Moreover, both fulfill Wagner's Law, a 19th century theory predicting the long-term growth of government finance. About a century ago Adolph Wagner, a German economist, predicted that in advanced economic societies government expenditures would inevitably trend upwards:

> Comprehensive comparisons of different countries and different times show that among progressive peoples, with which alone we are concerned, an increase regularly takes place in the activity of both the central and the local governments. This increase is both extensive and intensive: the central and local governments constantly undertake new functions, while they perform both old and new functions more efficiently and completely. In this way the economic needs of the people, to an increasing extent and a more satisfactory extent and in a more satisfactory fashion, are satisfied by the central and local governments (Quoted in, Taylor, p. 48).

Although one can agree that Wagner's prediction was accurate and that the growth would consist of extending existing functions and undertaking new ones, one can challenge both his explanation for new government activities and the quality of performance. The privatization movement underway in advanced industrial nations underscores the experience that government performance is anything but efficient. However, if anything, Wagner underestimated the prospects for growth in government expenditures.

Wagner expected the increased demand for government services to come only from the people. Indeed, that has been the case. The anomaly of the New Socialism is that it is a middle class socialism (Chapter I). However, Wagner overlooked other sources of demand, initiatives coming from government and politicians, and he did not anticipate the influence of unions to expand that demand.

In the U.S., expenditures by the public economy rose very sharply over the past three decades, in fact, even more than employment. The reason is that many expenditures do not require proportionately additional workers to process the outlays, as exemplified by the interest on the national debt and transfer payments. However, other areas of government expenditures generate employment more rapidly than the output of services, notably education and health services.

The center piece of the redistribution of income from the private to the public economy, the socialization of income, are transfer payments. Transfer payments are therefore also the most rapidly growing portion of government expenditures. Transfer payments are payments for which little or no work is rendered; they are income taken from taxpayers and given to others in the New Society. Social Security is a major transfer, albeit it does require some contributions (taxes, euphemistically titled "contributions") from participants. Following the enactment of Social Security, transfer payments received their greatest impetus from the Great Society programs of President Johnson. While some transfers are not intended to redistribute income, such as interest payments on the debt, they have that effect, but in the opposite direction from most transfers.

Other examples of transfer payments are governmental systems of retirement programs other than Social Security, student loans, medicare and medicaid, unemployment compensation, aid for dependent children, public assistance programs, agricultural price support programs, and benefits paid to veterans. The New Unionism is closely tied to the system of transfer payments of government and seeks ever wider applications of its coverage in the population.

In addition to comprising a transfer from one to another group in the economy, transfer payments also imply another change, the transfer from private to public decision-making and resource allocation. Transfers, therefore, are the keystone of the policy of the New Socialism and the New Unionism. Increased public decision-making is the hallmark of the New Society's canon of Fairness. Indeed, the goal of Fairness in the New Society is to shift decision-making from the individual to the state.

In addition to acting as a mechanism for the redistribution of income (and wealth), government also is a major purchaser of real resources, goods and services from the private sector. These are the governmental transactions most closely identified with the Old Unionism and which give rise to what I call the "quasi-public" sector. These transactions mostly affect unions in construction and defense. With the decline of defense spending, government purchases of real resources will therefore also decline.

Although New Unionism may be thought to be indifferent to the purposes of government expenditures, it necessarily favors government expenditures in the form of transfer payments over the purchase of goods, notably military goods. Purchases of goods mostly involve transactions with the private or the "quasi-public" sector and bring a smaller increase in government employment and in the membership of the New Unionism. Since government purchases of goods principally benefit the Old Unionism, it is one of the areas which separates the two groups in policies and politics (Chapters IV and V).

Many transfers require large bureaucracies, such as the Department of Health and Human Services, a major reason for the New Unionism to favor social programs. This is not to say that the New Unionism opposes all public expenditures for goods; they do not. But the leadership of the New Unionism has generally opposed defense expenditures. Empirically, defense, and other expenditures for goods, are viewed as a competitive demand for the tax dollar and borrowing. Some of the leadership of the New Unionism, like the former president of the Machinists (the Old Unionism), also oppose military expenditures for ideological reasons.

In the public finance of the New Society the word "cutbacks" is the jargon of newspeak. At best, it means slowing the rate of growth of total receipts, expenditures and employment, not absolute reductions as media reporting suggests to the public. At worst, it is simply a catchword intended to deceive the public. Politicians and, of course, the New Unionism treat absolute reductions in public expenditures as unacceptable. This has introduced a new form of budgetary economics, one of uninterrupted expansion in receipts and expenditures, in contrast to private sector economics. Scarcity of resources, central to making choices in the private sector, often is more nominal than real in the public sector, although the phrase "making tough choices" is one of the public sector's favorite catchwords. The belief in an ever expanding public economy is encapsulated in the phrase, "government money," implying that this is a special and unlimited claim on resources. The phrase and the ideology behind it are outgrowths of the extensive immunity of public employment to market forces. During business downturns the demand of government for continuing funding continues unabated. In many instances, governments have resorted to clever bookkeeping to "close budget gaps" – funding current expenditures by long term debt and "off-budget borrowing." Only insolvencies appear to check the "new budgetary economics," hardly a desirable checkmate. Privatization and political opposition, notably taxpayer revolts, are also limited in restraining the growth of government budgets. In general, the sector lacks a countervailing force comparable to the market place in the private economy.

What are the intentions, the philosophical objectives of the Old and New Unionism? I examine the new and the old philosophy of the Old Unionism in Chapter IV. In Chapter V, I turn to the philosophy of the New Unionism.

CHAPTER IV.

The Old and New Philosophies of the Old Unionism.

The Meaning and Types of Union Philosophy

Unions, like any major social institution, have a philosophy delineating their objectives. By a philosophy, I mean that organized labor has an integrated and consistent approach toward its structure, inter-union relations, relations with employers and their general position on economic and social organization. Their philosophy therefore is both inward (internal) and outward (external) looking. The internal philosophy deals with how unions should be organized, relate to one another, and their relations with employers, private or public, that is, in the governance of the workplace. By governance I mean the unions' demand to share in the administration of labor-management relations in the workplace. Unions' external philosophy addresses their "world view" on the economy and society and is long run in perspective. Unions' internal philosophy is both short and long run. For this reason some of its content changes more frequently. What unions are and what they do are shaped by their philosophy.

There is no "official" union philosophy. Perhaps the closest expression of an official philosophy is found in statements of the AFL-CIO and its predecessor federations, the AFL and the CIO. Despite its known commitment to capitalism, paradoxically, the AFL proclaimed a Marxian ideology in the Preamble to its Constitution which was not replaced until its merger with the CIO in 1955. That statement read:

> Whereas, a class struggle is going on in all the nations of the civilized world between the oppressors and the oppressed of all countries, a struggle between capitalist and the laborer, which grows in intensity from year to year, and will work disastrous results to the toiling millions if they are not combined for mutual protection and benefit (Troy, 1982, p. 4).

While Marxian in its analysis of the relationship between workers and employers, the Federation's solution was not. In contrast to the

Marxian rhetoric, that workers have nothing to lose but the chains which bind them, the AFL's solution was not revolution but unionism. It called upon workers to combine for mutual protection and benefit, that is, to form and join unions. On the other hand, the Marxists' position on unions was ambivalent; it ranged between regarding unions as class collaborators or to treat them as groups with the potential to overthrow capitalism. In any event, the American Federation of Labor was anti-Marxian, its preamble notwithstanding, and despite periodic efforts of Marxian's and other socialists' efforts to capture the Federation. Professor Philip Taft, the leading authority and historian of the AFL, dismissed the Federation's preamble as a serious statement, describing it as merely an intellectual artifact of its time (Taft, 1957, p. 37).

The CIO described its objectives as the effective organization of workers, the extension of benefits of collective bargaining, rejection of "alien loyalties," meaning Marxism, "and a continuous struggle for human freedom," (Troy, 1982, p. 4). Fascism and Nazism were also alien ideologies and neither attracted important support in the union movement. The CIO committed itself to the same philosophy as the AFL to organize and bargain for better working conditions. The CIO's outright rejection of Marxism was occasioned, I believe, to distance itself from what was widely regarded as a subversive ideology, and to make clear to the sizeable Marxist following in a number of CIO unions that the goals of the dominant group in the new Federation opposed Marxism. After World War II, the CIO was forced to confront the powerful Marxist following within the Federation and to expel eleven affiliates because of their slavish following of the Stalinist party line.

The merged Federation, the AFL-CIO, announced as its objectives and principles a trade unionist philosophy: securing improved wages, hours and working conditions; assisting affiliates in organizing the unorganized; preventing inter-union jurisdictional disputes; gaining universal affiliation of national and international unions, encouraging the formation of state and local bodies and special departments within the Federation; securing legislation favorable to collective bargaining; protecting and strengthening democratic institutions; and aiding in the promotion of world peace and freedom (Troy, 1982, p. 4).

While the new Federation explicitly reiterated the goals espoused by its predecessors, it also went well beyond these to incorporate the unions' experience under the New Deal. That experience has led to demands for more government intervention in the economy and the labor market. To some extent, this goal was echoed in the Federation's self-study presented in early 1985, thirty years later (AFL-CIO, Feb 1985).

That unions do have a philosophy and that it gives meaning to what they are and what they do is evident from their history. To recall Professor Laski's explanation of the origins of the unions' philosophy: "Their objectives," he wrote, "make it imperative for trade unions to have a policy, which may be empirical in its daily approach, but must, nevertheless, be informed by a body of long-term principles, by what, in fact, is a philosophy ..." and that the "body of long term principles" which become a "union philosophy ... [are] generally more likely to develop after the trade union has twisted and turned to adapt itself to a developing situation than while the situation, in all its rich variety, of trying to find some stable basis of equilibrium in society."

The empirical process "of twisting and turning to adapt to a developing situation" describes how the Old and the New Unionism have constructed their distinct philosophies. Although American unions have derived their philosophic outlook from experience, this is not to say that they have always drawn either the correct inferences or that their response has been timely. However, it has been demonstrated that the unions' empirically based philosophy proved to be historically durable and capable of continuous evolution.

The principal formulators of the Old Unionism's philosophy until the time of the New Deal were the leadership of the AFL, notably Samuel Gompers. Their insights were forged out of experience and a rejection of large-scale social reform. Formulation of the philosophy only incidentally ever involved the membership. Above all, however, the philosophy of the Old, and the New Unionism, did not emanate from the intellectual ruminations of social planners. To the social engineers, the philosophy of labor "begins with an idea, usually an *idee fixe*, about the way in which the world should be ordered, accompanied by a fairly clear notion of how this refashioning is to be done" (Tyler, 1959, p. 5). In contrast to the durability and adaptability of the empirically derived philosophy of the Old Unionism, blueprints drawn up by intellectuals for the "benefit" of the union movement were historically rigid, theoretically elegant and devoid of reality, certainly in the American context. When they did influence unionism, the philosophic orientations of intellectuals led the unions into a dead end. A notable example was the failed producer cooperative movement as a substitute for capitalist production.

It was first proposed in the 1840s and later revived by the Knights of Labor forty years later.

To social engineers, unions are instruments to achieve some grand social reorganization, socialism, or the cooperative society: "The labor movement is viewed as an instrument – more often *the* instrument – for the foreordained purpose" (Tyler, 1959, p. 5). The social engineers' goals were political and long run; they sought to reorganize social relations in the widest sense. In contrast the pragmatic philosophy of the Old Unionism eschewed such fundamental social changes and, instead emphasized the here and now. The union was to be an instrument to raise wages and improve working conditions of union members – to wrest as much as possible from the system. The Old Unionism decided, philosophically, to come to terms with the market system and capitalism. Its philosophy was intended to endow the job with as much monopoly power as the union could possibly create, emulating business practices intended to limit competition. This is one of the reasons that the Old Unionism's philosophy earned its description as "business unionism." Business unionism was devoted to the economic interests of the union member on the job, not his position in a new social order. The Old Unionism's philosophy of business unionism also came to be known as a philosophy of "more."

The Old Unionism's home-made philosophy was limited in scope and probably for that reason it worked. Because of their goal of a New Society, social planners placed the working class as a whole at the center of attention and rejected improvements limited to union members under capitalism, as conceived by the philosophy of the Old Unionism. The Old Unionism' philosophic orientation focused on the interests only of the skilled workers, the "aristocrats of labor." Predominantly these were skilled craftsmen in the construction trades and in railway transportation. (The railway brotherhoods remained independent of the AFL for much of their history and one, the Locomotive Engineers, is still independent of the AFL-CIO, but shared the philosophy of the Old Unionism). Factually, the Old Unionism's constituency *was* initially limited to the "aristocrats of labor;" it did leave out the mass of workers, discriminated against minorities and opposed immigration, especially of Asians.

It was not until the rise of the Congress of Industrial Organizations in the 1930s, that less skilled workers become a part the Old Unionism. With the founding of the CIO, mass production workers, who included all skills, especially in manufacturing industries, also came to share the Old Unionism's philosophy. Even though the CIO extended the unions' scope to mass production workers, the majority of American workers in the private economy remained outside the fold of organized labor, as they do to this time.

The internal philosophies of the Old and the New Unionism parallel one another in their orientation toward inter-union relations and the governance of the work place. They differ fundamentally in origin (Chapter II), goals and approaches to bargaining (Chapter III), and their *external* philosophies (Chapters IV and V). Even if the New Unionism achieves "full collective bargaining" – convergence – in industrial relations, its philosophy toward bargaining will still continue to differ from the Old Unionism, principally because the sovereign employer introduces unusual dimensions to the labor-management relationships (Chapters III and V).

The New and the Old Unionism's external philosophies, expressing their views on economic and social organization, their "world view," differ significantly. The empirical process of trial and error, which applies to the development of the external philosophies of both the Old and the New Unionism, has led each to a different world view. Divergence should be expected given the significant differences between the two labor movements and systems of industrial relations in which they function.

But not only are there are differences, in fact, there are conflicts of interests between the external philosophies of the New and the Old Unionism, even though the clash is not publicly acknowledged. Quite to the contrary, the unity of labor's goals is stressed. Nevertheless the clash of interests exists and their differences define another distinction in the character of the New and Old Unionism. Moreover, that character is delineated despite the absence of explicit declarations, an official philosophy.

The goals of the two union movements diverge on how income should be distributed and the role government should play in the economy. The Old Unionism's principal economic goal is to redistribute income from employers to union members. The Old Unionism had always pressed for government spending on the nation's infrastructure (epitomized in the Davis-Bacon Act of 1931), but since the New Deal, the Old Unionism added advocacy of the use of government intervention to maintain high levels of employment in the private economy and the attainment of some social goals. Currently, its most important new twist is to demand an industrial policy, that is government intervention to foster the development of certain industries regarded as essential to the economy and with prospects of growth. Additionally, it urges government to spend on the reconversion of defense industries to civilian production.

The goal of the New Unionism is to redistribute income from the private to the public sector of the economy, with government redistributing – socializing – income. Its purpose is to increase spending on social programs. While this does overlap part of the objectives of the Old Unionism, the Old and the New philosophies clash over the extent and funding of social programs. Since the success of the New Unionism's goal of redistributing income depends upon increased taxation, the clash of interests between the New and the Old Unionism is heightened by the success of the Old Unionism in raising members' wages. To the extent which the Old Unionism raises members' income, it also increases their tax liability and that forces the members of the two wings of unionism to face the same conflict which confronts all taxpayers and recipients of public social expenditures. On the other hand, while members of the New Unionism also pay higher taxes as their incomes rise, they also recognize that taxes are the source of that increased income and view the marginal cost of additional taxes as easily worth the additional income.

The external philosophies of both the Old and the New Unionism alter the direction and structure of social and economic organization. Both believe in relying on the visible hand of government to attain their different goals, although until the New Deal, the Old Unionism's philosophy relied primarily on the invisible hand of markets – extracting higher wages from employers. Since the New Deal, it has added the visible hand of government to the visible hand of markets to its philosophical outlook. I refer to government intervention to maintain high employment and the support for an industrial policy. From the start, the philosophy of the New Unionism has necessarily been committed to the visible hand of government to attain its objectives.

Over time, unions' short run philosophy on governance cumulatively impacts the economy and society, just as their long run strategies (Williams, 1969; Kovacs, 1965). In the private sector the Old Unionism diminishes market competitiveness and economic growth (Hirsch, 1991). Despite the conflict between its practices and its beliefs, the Old Unionism asserts it favors economic growth. This sets up another issue of conflict in philosophy between it and the New Unionism. The Old Unionism adherence to Keynesianism and government actions which it hopes will spur economic growth and therefore jobs puts it in opposition to a larger share of the national income going to the public economy, as the New Unionism wants.

The New Unionism' policies of redistribution frustrates economic efficiency and has an adverse impact on economic growth and, I believe, one even more severe than that of the Old Unionism. The shift of resources from the private to the public sector transfers resources from the more efficient to the less efficient sector of the economy and in that way slows economic growth moreso than the redistributive effects of the Old Unionism. This outcome is indicated by what Milton Friedman has dubbed "Gammon's Law" in health care expenditures (Friedman, 1991, p. A 20). Gammon, a British physician, announced a theory of bureaucratic displacement derived from his study of the British socialized hospital system which states that in a bureaucratic system an increase in expenditures (input) will be followed by a fall in output. And like black holes in space, they continue to vacuum resources, irrespective of waste. Indeed, a corollary of Gammon's Law is that when government fail to attain its goals, the bureaucracy blames insufficient funding, never the inefficient system and therefore demands increased resources to rectify the shortfall in achievements.

The differences in the philosophies of the New and the Old Unionism have, to date, elicited no comment or have gone unnoticed in the conventional analysis of what unions do and why. This is not surprising and is in fact consistent with our previous findings that the conventional approach has not even regarded the new public sector union movement as a New Union movement (Chapter II), or its associated industrial relations system as an institution separate from the private (Chapter III). Consequently, the conventional analysis has treated the Old and the New Unionism as sharing a common philosophy, that is, to the extent it considers the subject at all.

It might be argued that the absence of an analysis of the philosophic distinctions between the New and the Old Unionism were simply a matter of timing. Thus, Frank Tannenbaum's, *A Philosophy of Labor*, published in 1951, came a decade before the rise of the modern public sector New Unionism. Although timing could be claimed as the reason that Tannenbaum made no distinction in his study, this is not a satisfactory explanation. At the time of his publication there were organizations in the public sector and Spero had already written a landmark study about them (1948), but Tannenbaum made no reference to even the possibility of a philosophy of public sector labor organizations. Indeed, even Spero also made no mention of the matter either in the original publication of 1948 or in his revised edition (1972).

By showing that each of the two labor movements has its own internal and external philosophy, we gain a better and fuller understanding of what unions are, do and why. As Professor Irving Kristol once commented, "[a]ttitudes toward unions, pro and con, are emphatic enough. But of serious thinking about unions – what kind of institutions they are, and why, and to what purpose – there is precious little" (Kristol, 1978, p. 26).

To show the differences in purpose of the Old and the New Unionism, I shall begin with an account of the internal philosophy of the Old Unionism. I shall focus initially on how the Old Unionism's philosophy determined its structure, a key element which was transferred in its entirety to the New Unionism and its predecessor organizations. Next, I shall examine the application of the Old Unionism's internal philosophy to governance in the work place and its influence on the philosophy of governance of the New Unionism. Finally, I shall review its external philosophy, its conception of how the economy and society should be organized. In the next chapter I examine and contrast the external philosophy of the New and the Old Unionism.

Internal Philosophy: Structure

For the Old Unionism the defining experience which generated its internal philosophy was its historical difficulty in establishing itself as a permanent labor movement. It struggled for nearly a century after the founding of this country to develop the philosophy which led to a permanent movement, the American Federation of Labor (AFL). The AFL was founded in 1886, although the Federation itself dates its founding to the establishment of a predecessor association, the Federation of Organized Trade and Labor Unions, in 1881 (Carroll, 1923, n.1, p. 28). However, some scholars regard the two organizations as distinct and therefore date the beginning of the AFL in 1886.

The purpose of the Old Unionism's internal philosophy was to establish a movement which would survive in the market system. Concomitantly, that philosophy would also define inter-union and employer relations. After a century strewn with the wreckage of labor organizations based on a variety of organizing principles and goals, the main body of the unions concluded toward the close of the 19th century that establishing a permanent union movement depended on organizing on the basis of workers's occupation, limiting the unions' objectives to maintaining and improving the members' standards of living and employment, and avoiding grandiose schemes of social reorganization, socialism or producers cooperatives. Specifically, they concentrated on the organization of the unorganized on the basis of skilled occupations, or trades. Hence, as noted in Chapter I, the origin of the term, trade union.

Each union affiliated with the American Federation of Labor would be recognized by the Federation as having the sole or exclusive right to organize a given occupation, or some other "job" or geographic territory (Dunlop, 1960, p. 103). The Federation's recognition of an affiliate's "job territory" came to be known as "exclusive jurisdiction." Exclusivity meant that no other union would be recognized as having a claim (jurisdiction) over the same "job territory." At the same time that the Federation bestowed its recognition of exclusivity over jurisdiction, it also recognized the autonomy of each affiliated union. Autonomy meant that each affiliate pursued its own interests without restraint from the Federation, excepting matters involving organizing or claiming unorganized workers already designated as the exclusive territory of another affiliate.

While exclusive jurisdiction typically applied to an occupation, a few exceptions for industrial jurisdictions, such as mining were accepted. Geographic location was recognized in state federations. Jurisdiction based on occupation reflected the predominantly skilled make-up of the workers in the organizations affiliated with the AFL at that time. By excluding the nonskilled worker, exclusive jurisdiction led to the pejorative phrase, "aristocrats of labor." Nevertheless, exclusive jurisdiction and affiliates' autonomy became the central principles, the internal philosophy, on which the American Federation of Labor was able to establish the first permanent labor movement in the U.S.

The AFL's policy of exclusive jurisdiction also defined to which union an individual worker "belonged." The individual worker, in effect, had no voice in the union to which he should belong. Employers also had no input on the determination of which union his employees should join, aside from any consideration of violating the NLRA (since 1935).

Exclusive jurisdiction also necessarily shaped inter-union relations. Inter-union relations were framed by the AFL's "validation," or recognition of the exclusive claim of an affiliated union to a given occupation. Recognition of that exclusivity was expressed in the union's charter or certificate of affiliation with the AFL. The Federation's upheld each affiliate's exclusive claim by conciliation and if necessary by the expulsion of the violators. Errant affiliates poaching on the claim of other would also be branded as "dual" to the Federation. Unions outside the Federation (independents) which claimed to organize the same category of workers as an affiliate would also be in conflict with the Federation and could therefore also be branded as dual to the AFL. Dualism was the most serious violation of the philosophy governing inter-union relations. The Federation and its affiliates would theoretically make "war" on the expelled or independent violator of that philosophy. In theory, affiliates would raid the outcast organization. In practice, the Federation's power to enforce the claim of exclusive jurisdiction was more nominal than real. Nevertheless, the philosophy of exclusive jurisdiction worked until the rise of the Congress of Industrial Organizations in 1937.

In order to highlight the influence of philosophy over union structure, consider how history treated an alternative philosophy of union organization, the philosophy of one union for all workers. The Knights of Labor (of the late 19th century) included numerous groups within its fold, including trade unions. The Knights regarded themselves as "One Big Union," free of the narrow jurisdictional claims of the trade unions and the autonomy of affiliates which were the foundations of the AFL. The Knights' external goal also differed from the AFL's. It sought the establishment of a cooperative society while the Federation accepted the capitalist system, while seeking more of its fruits. In its heyday, from 1886–1888, the Knights seemed to be the epitome of success in how to organize. At the time few would have guessed that its rival, the AFL, a pygmy in size by comparison, would survive and prosper, while the Knights which may have reached 1 million in adherents by about 1888 would quickly decline and disappear. Yet, that is what happened. Within a few year, by 1893, the Knights' organization had virtually disappeared. Officially, the Knights closed their books in 1917. The short and spirited life of the Knights illustrated how an ambitious philosophy out of touch with the world failed.

In the 1930s, the formation of the CIO posed next and the most serious threat to the AFL's concept of exclusive jurisdiction since inception of the Federation. Eventually another "twisting and turning by the Old Unionism to adapt to the new situation" resolved their dispute sufficiently to bring the AFL and the CIO together in December 1955. The new pragmatic resolution was a revised internal philosophy with a new concept imposed by government regulation of labor relations which amended and displaced exclusive jurisdiction to a considerable extent.

The CIO's internal philosophy on structure was dual to the AFL because the industrial claims of its affiliates necessarily cut across a multitude of craft (occupational) claims of affiliates of the AFL. Although in conflict with the AFL over structure, the CIO's internal philosophy was conceptually parallel to the AFL's: Each affiliate was recognized as having the exclusive jurisdiction over an industry rather than a craft and each operated as an autonomous organization. For the better part of two decades the two Federations fought each other over the principle whose bottom lines were membership, money and power. The conflicting claims, the internal philosophies, of the two Federations were never resolved on the basis of either the craft or industrial claims of exclusive jurisdiction. Instead, the two Federations merged in 1955 by ignoring their historic internal philosophies and substituting a policy laid down by the National Labor Relations Act of 1935, exclusive representation of a bargaining unit.

A bargaining unit is defined by the National Labor Relations Act and by the Board on a variety of bases, including craft or industrial. The representative chosen by a majority of the employees in that unit is recognized by law as the sole, the exclusive, bargaining representative. Based on experience, as before in union history, the newly merged Federation, the AFL-CIO, once again forged a new internal philosophy in defining inter-union relations and relations with employers, a philosophy which accepted exclusive representation as well as exclusive jurisdiction as the basis for inter-union and employer-union relations. At the time of the merger each Federation agreed to recognize the bargaining units which had been established under principles of the NLRA from 1935 to 1955, irrespective of prior claims of exclusive jurisdiction. Since the merger, the legal concept of exclusive representation rather than Old Unionism' philosophy of exclusive jurisdiction, whether craft or industrial, has become the primary basis of union organization and inter-union relations. Conflicts over bargaining unit claims or the "ancient" basis of exclusive jurisdiction would be decided by machinery set up under the constitution of the AFL-CIO.

However, exclusive representation has not precluded continuing disputes over jurisdiction in the construction industry, accentuated currently by the decline of the Old Unionism. For example, District 50 of the United Steelworkers of America, AFL-CIO, has recently been in a serious jurisdictional disputes with the building trades unions of the AFL-CIO over highway construction in southern New Jersey (Ellis,

1991, p. C-1). District 50 organizes construction crafts into an industrial union irrespective of craft – the original issue between the AFL and the CIO. District 50 was originally created by John L. Lewis of the United Mineworkers (UMW) as a threat and rival to the AFL building trades unions about half century ago. It was expelled from the UMW because it supported nuclear power, anathema to those like miners favoring energy from coal. District 50 subsequently joined the Steelworkers, itself an example of union pragmatism in the application of internal philosophy on structure.

Despite the periodic eruptions of jurisdiction feuding, the "twisting and turning to adapt itself to a developing situation," did lead the Old Unionism to change its internal philosophy on structure. Thus, the Old Unionism showed itself capable of adjusting its philosophy, albeit after two decades of turmoil. Like the older versions, the new internal philosophy is also pragmatic. It built on the premise of adopting what works, rather than strict adherence to principle. However, unlike exclusive jurisdiction which evolved from the Old Unionism's experience in the market place, exclusive representation was derived from government intervention in labor relations. And the source is significant: It reveals that government has steadily increased its influence on the content of the unions' philosophy, Old and New, in this instance, on the fundamental issue of how unions should be organized.

Another way in which government has brought its influence to bear on the structure of unions is the emergence of what I have identified as the mixed or joint public-private union (Chapters II and III). The rise of the New Unionism, spurred by public policy, gave birth to this new structural form. The new joint union shows the resiliency of unions in adjusting their structure to new circumstances. In the face of continuing losses of membership in their historical jurisdictions many of the Old Unions have moved to enroll independent associations of public employees. Whether these mixed or joint unions will turn out to be a satisfactory resolution to problems or the beginning of more serious ones remains to be seen. They have occasioned disputes both over organizing (jurisdiction) and philosophy. The issues for these unions are the different interests and goals of public and private members who belong to the same union, in effect, a house divided. In time, these organizations may prove to be unstable unions or in due course the public wing of the joint union will come to change the private aspect of the joint union to a public one.

The structural units of the Old and the New Unionism are the same: local unions, intermediate bodies, regional, national and international unions. All of these forms originated in the private sector of the labor market and were adopted by unions in the public sector. However, the forces which generated the same structural forms in the Old and the New Unionism differed. Market forces led the Old Unionism to respond to market pressures at the local, regional and national level beginning in the 19th century. The impact of markets has also been manifest at the international level as reflected by those unions which have organized workers outside the U.S., principally in Canada. Such unions are known as international unions. Most internationals are part of the Old Unionism. However, their number is rapidly shrinking as Canadian nationalism has led to the dis-affiliation of many Canadian affiliates, despite market imperatives. Among the New Unions, few have public sector workers outside the U.S. Of those which do are the National Education Association (its Overseas Education Association) and the Service Employees International Union, AFL-CIO, which has a very sizeable membership among public employees in Canada. The new Free Trade Agreement between Mexico, Canada and the U.S. may spur the formation of a new and larger form of union structures, North American Unionism.

The size of the U.S. and the Old Unionism's historical experience made local unions the foundation of union organization. Widening markets then dictated the necessity for regional and national structures. Because of its complex organizational structure the American union movement is more decentralized than its European counterparts. This reflected once more the pragmatic approach of the Old Unionism on how to organize and to stay organized.

However, there has been an important change in intra-union relationships. Market forces, increased competition, has led to the diminution of the autonomy of locals with respect to their parent national or international headquarter unions. Local unions have steadily lost power to the national or international headquarters. This would be in keeping with the increased "nationalizing" of social, economic and political affairs in general, the examples of the enhanced authority of bureaucracy in other institutions, and the practical approach of the Old Unionism to bargaining. The "nationalization" of political activity since the New Deal has also brought the Federations, the AFL the CIO and the AFL-CIO enhanced stature and importance as a spokesman for organized labor.

However, autonomy on collective bargaining keeps the Federation out of this domain of union activity, whether the Old or the New.

At the same time, the importance of local labor markets in the construction and other industries has enabled local unions to retain their power in collective bargaining and in inter-union relations. Typically, locals still maintain a significant degree of autonomy from their parent bodies. They select their own officers and negotiate their own agreements, even when industry terms are settled at a higher level of organization. The combined wealth (net assets) of the locals of the New and Old Unionism is about equal to the national and international unions to which they belong, while their income from dues is far greater. Local unions are the most numerous in the structure of both the New and the Old Unionism. I estimate that there are about 40 thousand locals in the structure of the Old Unionism and another 25 thousand in the New Unionism. There are also far more regional, national and international unions in the Old than in the New Unionism. Roughly I estimate there are just over twice as many in the Old than in the New, about 125 to 60.

While markets shaped the structure of the Old Unionism, political structure and its funding shaped the structure of the New Unionism. While the New Unionism and its predecessor organizations did copy the formal structure of the Old Unionism, that structure is geared to the political employer, the federal, state and local governments which make up the political market of this country. In both cases, the principle determining structure is best described by that postulate of modern architecture, "form follows function."

Internal Philosophy: Governance

The Old Unionism's philosophy toward governance of the work place is a corollary of exclusive jurisdiction and by derivation, exclusive representation. From its experience with exclusive jurisdiction the Old Unionism had learned that the principle maximized its organizational and bargaining strength in dealing with employers. Exclusive representation has updated that experience.

Governance is epitomized in the collective bargaining agreement and arbitration awards. The agreement govern the terms and conditions of employment and provide a surrogate "constitution" under which the parties deal with one another. One of the most important "articles" in that constitution is the grievance procedure and its regulation of disputes arising from the agreement. Arbitration awards rendered under the agreement supplement the "constitutional" provisions of the agreement. They interpret the meaning of the agreement in a manner similar to judicial decisions. The purpose of the grievance procedure is to substitute negotiation and arbitration for work stoppages and assure production and income to all parties while disputes arising out of the agreement are resolved. The New and the Old Unionism share the same philosophy toward governance in the work place, although the New has yet to achieve the same measure of governance because of the persistence in some areas of civil service.

The constitutional, or governance aspect of the Old Unionism's philosophy has attracted much interest, discussion and analysis by industrial relations specialists. In fact, Tannenbaum's analysis dealt only with this sphere of the philosophy of the Old Unionism. Therefore, his book's title, *A Philosophy of Labor*, analyzed only a fraction of the "body of long term principles" which become a "union philosophy." Moreover, Tannenbaum did not consider the continuing evolution of the philosophy of the Old Unionism generated by the New Deal even though the change was evident by the time of his monograph.

Tannenbaum defined the Old Unionism's philosophy as the "detailed relationships between worker and employer" which satisfy "the human craving for moral status in a recognizable society" (Tannenbaum, 1951, p. 13), "... of which the trade-union's concern with detail is the most important point [in its philosophy] because it is an attempt to bridge the gap between labor on the one hand and freedom and security on the other" (p. 9). Thus, Tannenbaum's focus was the unions' shared governance of the work place with the employer, a part, but only a part of their internal philosophy. This goal and the Old Unionism's actions to implement it are embodied in the collective bargaining agreement negotiated with the employer and in public policy. At the time of Tannenbaum's study (1951), the principal governmental policies incorporated in labor's effort to "bridge the gap" between the insecurity of employment under a capitalist system and "freedom and security" were the Federal Anti-Injunction Act, the National Labor Relations Act, the Railway Labor Act and court decisions. These public policies shielded workers from the pressures of the market, contributed to the Old Unionism's goal of redistributing income between employers and workers and to share in the governance of labor relations. Theoretically, this is about as far as Tannenbaum went in analyzing the meaning and practice of the philosophy of the Old Unionism.

Other leading industrial relations specialists, notably Commons (1946) and Slichter, took a similar tack and concentrated on the governance aspect of the philosophy of the Old Unionism. They interpreted the Old Unionism's collective bargaining agreements as the foundation of "industrial government" intended to safeguard the worker as wage earner and "industrial citizen" under a market system.

However, Slichter also went well beyond governance and introduced a new dimension to the unions' philosophy, one applicable to their external philosophy: He forecast the emergence of a New Society in the U.S., paralleling Laski's expectations for Britain (Chapter I), but one far different in concept and structure. From the perspective of the early post-World War II years (the same time perspective as Professor Laski), Slichter forecast that the union movement in the U.S. would alter the country's social and economic system. He wrote: "Many kinds of employees are organizing themselves into trade unions, and these unions are the most powerful economic organizations of the time [and for that reason a] laboristic society is succeeding a capitalist one" (Slichter, 1948, p. 5). His outline of the New (Laboristic) Society were vague; it was not a blueprint of the new social order comparable to Laski's. However, it logically meant that the laboristic (union dominated) society would significantly redistribute income from employers to unionized workers through collective bargaining, not public ownership of the means of production. In contrast to Laski, Slichter's forecast of the future society was based on empirical observation, not a social theory. It would come about from what Slichter thought was happening to the private labor market at that time (increased unionization), rather than any hypothetical role unions would play under a re-structure society as laid out by a social theorist. Slichter's central point was that labor's practice of collective bargaining would change the social order. Unions, by their actions, not by theories, would create the laboristic society.

However, Slichter's extrapolation of contemporary events proved to be wide of the mark, just as were Laski's. He evidently believed that the Old Unionism was on the brink of new and wider expansion. Actually, the centers of union power, the Old Unionism, which Slichter expected would generate the new "laboristic society" were at or near their peak strength and already poised for decline. Coal and steel, two of the industries he mentioned as the new centers of union power (in the late 1940s), began to decline shortly after he wrote. Indeed, were it not for the Korean War, the unions' decline in these industries would have commenced sooner. As a matter of fact, analysts began to describe the Old Unionism as stagnant within a half-dozen years of Slichter's forecast; they referred to their analysis as the "stagnation hypothesis." Since then, market forces have demolished the potential of a "laboristic" economy – at least in the private sector of the economy. Although Slichter's expectations that the Old Unionism would give rise to a New (Laboristic) Society, went awry, his insight has relevance to the public sector. If we update his term "laboristic society" to mean the New Unionism's goal and power to redistribute income from the private to the public sector, instead of the redistribution of income from employers to union members, we have a revised, viable and updated version of Slichter's "laboristic society," a New Society characterized by the socialization of income.

Subsequent analysts stuck to the theme of the Old Unionism's sharing of governance in the work place. In their celebrated study, *What Do Unions Do?*, Freeman and Medoff (1984) did not directly discuss the philosophy of the Old Unionism. Indeed, there is not even an index reference to the topic, especially surprising in light of the book's title. However, in answer to the question of their book, they replied that one thing the Old Unionism did was to offer an alternative to unilateral managerial authority, what they called an "exit-voice." Drawing on the work of Albert O. Hirschman, they depicted the union as offering a collective voice – a sharing of governance in the work place – as the alternative to quits or discharge, that is, an exit from employment. Fundamentally, there is no discernible difference between "exit-voice" and Tannenbaum's theory that unions bridged the gap between the insecurity of employment and workers' job security under a capitalist system.

On the other hand, Freeman and Medoff's analysis of the Old Unionism's levelling effect on wage differentials did update the governance philosophy of at least one branch of the Old Unionism, those engaged in industrial bargaining (Freeman and Medoff, 1984, Chapter 11). Because industrial bargaining (which ensued with the rise of the CIO) covers both skilled and unskilled workers, the Old Unionism in some manufacturing industries began to produce a more egalitarian wage structure, that is, they narrowed the differential between skilled and less skilled occupations. This was the result partly of internal union political policy, catering to the more numerous less skilled at the expense of the more skilled members and partly a haphazard consequence of industrial bargaining. The process was also greatly stimulated by the awards of the National War Labor Board of World War II. Perhaps, industrial bargaining and its egalitarian wage effects could be regarded as a special case of a "Laboristic New Society," or an example of the philosophy of "more" gone awry.

Even though the Old Unionism's economic objective of "more" is thought to unite members, its application in industrial bargaining also causes discord when it when it promotes wage egalitarianism. Thus, Freeman and Medoff applauded the Old Unionism for reducing wage differentials among blue collar workers as an economic and social achievement. Gregg Lewis, after recalculation of Freeman's estimates for blue collar workers in manufacturing confirmed that, indeed, "for these workers unionism had made wage dispersion smaller for unionized status than for nonunion status." While wage egalitarianism may suit some academic tastes, it did not suit the preferences of higher paid unionized workers. Insofar as they were concerned, the levelling effects which industrial unions imposed on their more skilled members provoked resistance. In the case of the Auto Workers in the mid-1950s, a skilled workers revolt nearly led to them to withdraw from the UAW and the formation of their own union. To conciliate them, the UAW amended its constitution to set up a skilled trades department with the authority to veto future agreements. Other industrial unions fell into step. Evidently reducing wage inequalities, egalitarianism, may please some academics, but it does not please those whose relative loss of wages are the wherewithal producing intellectually satisfying egalitarian results. It substitutes a perverse inequality for a market (including human capital) determined differential. Two generations ago, the Webbs, whose socialism ought to have made them believers in wage egalitarianism, put their finger on the expected worker reaction to wage egalitarianism: "[E]xperience seems to show that in no trade will a well-paid and well-organised but numerically weak section [of skilled workers] permanently consent to remain in the subordination to inferior operatives, which any amalgamation of all sections of a large and varied industry must usually involve" (the Webbs, 1920, p. 129).

All of the foregoing views of Old Unionism's philosophy of governance in industrial relations share an important preconception: They mistrust the market as a protector of the worker as a wage earner and as an "industrial citizen." Instead, they regard the market as biased against, if not an exploiter of the wage earner. Although unions and government have, indeed, played significant and constructive roles in relations between employees and employers, markets have also contributed a substantial, probably the largest share, of the forces protecting working standards (the Friedmans, 1980, Chapter 8). Irrespective of the shares of protection afforded the worker by unions, government and markets, the philosophy of the Old Unionism encompassed in "industrial government," "voice," or work rules intended "to bridge the gap between labor on the one hand and freedom and security on the other" assumes that the philosophy of governance can abridge the market. However, as the decline of the Old Unionism has demonstrated that can only be partially successful. At the same time, governance issues are but a part of the philosophical issues with which the Old Unionism was concerned.

External Philosophy: Organizing the Unorganized

Like its internal philosophy, the Old Unionism's external philosophy also underwent change, change which arose from experience with government policies in organizing the unorganized and the economy. While the government policy of exclusive representation settled, more or less, the inter-union rivalry over which organization would represent organized workers, the larger issue of organizing the unorganized private labor market remained unresolved. Currently over 90% of the private civilian labor force is outside the union movement, just to sketch the challenge which the Old Unionism's faces in organizing.

To date, the Old Unionism has not found a solution to its central problem of sharply reduced membership and market share (Chapter II). The absorption of some public sector workers by several of the Old Unions is so marginal that it has had little impact on the size of the movement as a whole.

Is there any adaptation in its philosophy which would enable the Old Unionism to reverse it long term slide? Does it lie in a more interventionist public policy on labor relations? At first blush, history would indicate such a course. Under the influence of government policy embodied in the National Labor Relations Act of 1935, the Old Unionism experienced major extensions of its membership, power and influence in the private labor market. That success caused the Old Unionism to shift its policy from the invisible hand of government (more or less) in organizing the unorganized to the visible hand of government. However, the effectiveness of government's visible hand to assist in organizing workers eventually waned and the Old Unionism began losing market share after 1953 and rank and file members after 1970 (Chapter II). The Old Unionism's natural response has been to seek a stronger dose of the same medicine, an even more visible governmental hand in organizing the unorganized. Typically, the AFL-CIO abetted by the conventional intellectual wisdom has turned to government to succor its sagging strength. Specifically, their proposals embrace a series of public policy changes which would, they believe, redress the balance of power between unionism and private employers. In market terms, they seek government intervention to overwhelm the competitive forces which have unremittingly undermined the Old Unionism. A Democratic President and Congress would give a major boost toward this goal.

But would a more interventionist policy work? The laboratory example is Canada (Troy, 1991). Canada's labor relations policies have been advocated as a model for the U.S. to emulate because, it is claimed, these policies enabled the Canadian labor movement to escape "the American disease," decline in membership and percentage organized (density), over the last two decades. If the "British disease" was unionism run amuck and the "American disease" union decline, the Canadian virtue was said to be a thriving labor movement. As the writer of a 1991 Labor Day Op Ed article in the *New York Times*, bemoaning the fate of the American labor movement put it, "Well, I could sneak across the border into Canada. They have a labor movement there" (Geoghegan, 1991, p. A19).

According to the conventional wisdom, the "American disease" is the result of a labor policy subverted by the Reagan-Bush Administrations coupled with employer opposition to unions. However, this analysis misdiagnoses "the American disease," recommends the wrong remedy (assuming there is one) and misrepresents the condition of the Canadian labor movement. In both countries, public sector unionism, the New Unionism, has prospered; in both countries, the Old Unionism, private sector unionism, has declined, and rather sharply by the standard measures of union robustness. Thus, the "American disease" of union decline in the private sector is not unique to the U.S., but has been occurring in Canada and, for that matter, across all advanced capitalist countries (Troy, 1990).

Paradoxically, the peak union participation rate of the Old Unionism in Canada never matched that of the U.S.. The U.S. peak was 36% in 1953 and the Canadian 34% in 1958. Thus, Canadian policy, as interventionist as it is, was unable to push the penetration rate above the highest U.S. level, although it contributed to the ability of Canadian rate to remain above the U.S. beginning in the 1960s. However, Canada's lag behind the U.S. in economic changes in labor markets and a more protectionist trade policy, not differences in policy, are responsible for the differences in levels of union penetration rates between the two countries private labor markets. The key point is not that Canadian rates of union penetration are currently higher than American since the 1960s, but that in both countries, the trend is in the same direction, decline (Troy, 1992). Therefore, since the proposed treatment for "the American disease," Canadian labor policy, has been unable to prevent the ebb of the Old Unionism in Canada, why should it even be considered as a policy model for the U.S.? Nevertheless, a more interventionist policy will continue to be the Old Unionism's favored means of recuperation.

A new and even more interventionist policy has been urged by Professor Paul Weiler of Harvard. Perhaps recognizing that market forces may be too great for even a revised NLRA to revive the Old Unionism, a policy he has advocated for a decade, he has now switched to championing legislatively mandated works councils, what he calls his "Constitutive Model:" "... it is necessary," he says, "to take away from the employees (and also the employer) the choice about whether such a participatory mechanism will be present" (1990, p. 282). Unlike reforming the NLRA, which he recognized could be treated as special interest legislation (the ghost of Roscoe Pound's legal immunities of unions!), Weiler would compel representation, and representation with the right "of internal participation in a specified range of decisions in all enterprises." In one way or another workers – for their own good – must have some form of "industrial democracy," or "exit-voice," even if it has to be forced down their throats.

External Philosophy:
Business Unionism and Neo-Mercantilism

Since its inception (the establishment of the AFL in 1886 and the CIO in 1937), the Old Unionism's basic economic philosophy has been to redistribute income from employers to the organized workers. It is best known as the philosophy of "more," or "business unionism." Business unionism was an expression of the Old Unionism's acceptance of capitalism and rejection of socialism. From Samuel Gompers to Lane Kirkland the message has been the same. In 1914 Gompers stated: "In improving conditions from day to day the organized labor movement has no 'fixed program' for human progress.... We do not set an particular standard, but work for the best possible conditions immediately obtainable for workers.

When they are obtained then we strive for better" (Gompers, 1919, pp. 21–22).

In 1980 Lane Kirkland, president of the AFL-CIO, wrote: "In creating their domestic trade unions, American workers cast aside all parties, conspiracies and secret societies whose aim was to create any sort of 'dictatorship of the proletariat.' They committed themselves to work within the system, acknowledging the rights of others while asserting their own. They seek no more today, and they will settle for nothing less" (Kirkland, 1980, p. 4).

Selig Perlman summarized the trade unionists' own assessment of the philosophy of the Old Unionism this way:

> The philosophy which these ... leaders developed might be termed a philosophy of pure wage-consciousness. It signified a labour movement reduced to an opportunistic basis, accepting the existence of capitalism and having for its object the enlarging of the bargaining power of the wage earner in the sale of his labour. It implied an attitude of aloofness from all those movements which aspire to replace the wage system by cooperation, whether voluntary or subsidized by government, whether greenbackism, socialism, or anarchism (Perlman, 1966, p. 308).

When the CIO came on the scene in the 1930s it, too, adopted the "philosophy of wage consciousness," of business unionism. As Perlman noted, it was extended to "the outer boundaries of the wage-earning class as a whole" (Troy, 1982, p. 5). During the formative years of the CIO the Communist Party gained control of several important unions affiliated with the new Federation, but even these hewed to business unionism, although combining it with their sectarian goals. Eventually, these organizations were expelled from the CIO with the bulk of their membership recaptured by other CIO and AFL unions.

Business unionism also expressed the Old Unionism's general acceptance of the invisible hand of government. To paraphrase Perlman's observation, 'the labor movement's objective was to enlarge the bargaining power of the wage earner *in the sale of his labor.*' Although this approach was micro-economic in its application at the workplace, on the macro-economic level it was also the Old Unionism's general strategy in response to the question of how to improve the standard of living of (organized) workers. "More," or business unionism, was the substitute for "cooperation ... socialism or anarchism," in Perlman's words.

So complete has been the Old Unionism's acceptance of capitalism, that one commentator, Professor Joseph Shister wrote that "American unionism has [so] fully accepted private enterprise ... that more than a few union leaders have patterned themselves after the successful corporate executives with whom they deal – in speech, dress, style of living, etc." (Shister, 1966, p. 601). Few, if any, patterned their living styles after apocryphal leaders of the "toiling masses."

The philosophy of "more," or "business unionism," stemmed from the Old Unionism's experience with exclusive jurisdiction. Just as that principle answered the question of how to stay organized, it also addressed the question of how to maintain and improve wages and related matters. Its answer was simply "more," or the phrase, "more, more now" (Carroll, 1923, p. 179), albeit only for those enrolled in the trade union. "More" focused on the distribution of income between employers and union members, and ignored economic growth.

"More" is not meant here as a pejorative term implying greed, but as an expression of self-interest, as dictated by a belief in markets, a belief which the Old Unionism has always held. It is on a par with the self-interest which Adam Smith noted when he pointed out that we owe our bread to the baker's self-interest not his altruism. "More" has played as pragmatic and successful a role for the Old Unionism as it has for businessmen: "The test of truth for the American trade unionist is *what works*" (Tyler, 1959, p.4; emphasis in the original).

Exclusive jurisdiction was also the manifestation of the Old Unionism's bargaining power in a market economy. This experienced-based economic policy drew upon micro-economic theory of the market, knowingly or not. Economic theory had concluded that unions of skilled workers would exert the most power to raise members's wages. Coincidentally, that economic theory arose at the end of the 19th century just as unions were developing their practice of exclusive jurisdiction. Subsequently, exclusive representation, the legal substitution and supplement to the economic power of unions, made its contribution to unions' power to raise the wages relative to comparable groups of unorganized workers.

Although this characterization of the philosophy of the Old Unionism served well during the period from the founding of the AFL in 1886 to the era of the New Deal, thereafter it fell short as a description of the philosophy of the Old Unionism. Leaving it at simply "business unionism," or "more," fails to take into account the Old Unionism's experience under the New Deal, and the influence of Keynesianism, the experience which generated what I call neo-mercantilism. By neo-mercantilism I mean a revival of the policy of government regulation of the economy which Adam Smith attacked so brilliantly in his *Wealth of Nations* two centuries ago. Although contemporary neo-mercantilism differs from its antecedent in some important ways, they share the same statist bent, that the government knows the interests of individuals better than do the individuals themselves and increasingly shifts the economy's total expenditures from the individual to the state.

The modern and historical versions of mercantilism differ in some ways. For example, labor was regulated to keep it cheap; now regulation is intended to raise wages, even at the cost of unemployment. Instead of price ceilings of the old mercantilism, the new imposes price floors. Meantime, the original and current versions share nationalism as a goal, building the power of the nation state.

The various exegeses on the Old Unionism's philosophy never got beyond "exit-voice," "industrial government" or "business unionism." They did not take into account the continuing evolution of union philosophy, that it did not begin and end with "more." Developments in economics and politics which began under the New Deal radically enlarged and altered the Old Unionism's philosophy, but that experience has yet to be recognized in analyses of what motivates the Old Unionism, what it does and why. To date, scholarly assessments have not incorporated these changes in the Old Unionism's philosophy. Instead contemporary analyses of private unions' philosophy, to the limited extent they even recognize that unions do have a philosophy, continue to describe that philosophy simply as "business unionism" or "more." Socialist critics, such as Harold Laski, also missed the transition of the Old Unionism's philosophy from a philosophy of "more" to a philosophy of "more government intervention in the economy and society." Labor leaders, too, are not aware or ignore the "structural break" in the philosophy of the Old Unionism. Lane Kirkland has been quoted above on organized labor's commitment to working within the capitalist system. However, the AFL-CIO's social proposals fail to recommend policies consistent with free markets, other than enforcement of the anti-trust laws, so long as organized labor remains essentially exempt from them. To the contrary, its proposals would subordinate private enterprise to an expanding sweep of government regulation. The most recent extension of its move toward a philosophy of "more government intervention" is advocacy of an industrial policy. The policy is directed toward protectionism in international trade, government direction of industrial development and increased regulation of labor relations. Industrial policy ranges from specifics such as a favorable balance of merchandise trade (which harks back to the mercantilism of the 15–18th centuries), minimum domestic content, regulation of plant closure, minimum wage legislation to grand concept proposals to virtual economic planning. Some business groups, like their counterparts in organized labor distrust the market and so share the notion of an industrial policy. They believe that coordinating "the formulation of economic policy – including trade, regulatory, fiscal, monetary and tax policy – [will] enhance capital formation by U.S. businesses [and would have] vast potential for creating new, productive jobs for Americans" (Walsh, 1985, p. 62). The AFL-CIO's industrial policy would set up a tri-partite official body to issue decrees which would apply tax policy, subsidies and credits to selected businesses. It would abrogate market allocation of resources to turn the job over to government. These policies would be supplemented with an agenda of politically correct investments to which business would be expected to adhere.

Advocacy of an industrial policy has been sparked by the merchandise trade deficits, especially with Japan, the success of Japanese industrial policy and the false charge that America was losing its industrial (manufacturing) base – deindustrializing. What was called deindustrialization was in fact the secular change in the composition of industry, a development characteristic of modern economies since the industrial revolution began. Short term forces, the high value of the dollar in foreign exchange from 1979 to 1985 and deregulation spurred industrial change as well. As a result of these forces, employment in older industries, notably in manufacturing, and the union membership in them fell sharply. However, employment in high-tech, mostly nonunion manufacturing grew, so the trend in over-all manufacturing employment over the past quarter century in the U.S. has remained stable. Meanwhile, the proportion of white collar employment within manufacturing rose while blue collar production worker declined. Another even more important indicator that deindustrialization is a false charge is the stability of manufacturing's share of real gross domestic product. It has remained virtually unchanged over the past two decades and longer. Thus, instead of deindustrialization, long run changes coupled with intense international competition stimulated a shift in the composition of manufacturing employment, and with reference to the Old Unionism, has traded unionized for nonunion employment.

The defining experiences which initiated the change in the philosophy of the Old Unionism to more government intervention were the

Great Depression of 1929, the economic policies of the New Deal and the economic theories of John Meynard Keynes. Under the impact of these developments, the Old Unionism's philosophy evolved from "more," to include "more government intervention" in the economy and society, the philosophy of "neo-mercantilism."

Neo-mercantilism does not replace the philosophy of business unionism, but rather complements it. Together they make up the current external philosophy of the Old Unionism. Today, the Old Unionism combines its acceptance of capitalism with government intervention in the economy and society on a large and ever increasing scale, as befits the doctrine of Fairness.

Neo-mercantilism transfers private responsibility to public bureaucracies and seeks to transfer income from consumers to private sector union members. Regulation also satisfies the goal of the caring society, of Fairness. Furthermore, regulation grows by what it feeds upon: When public policy fails, the policy itself is seldom if ever faulted; instead, insufficient resources (as in the failed public system of education), or inadequate enforcement or regulatory power are held responsible. Thereby, public administration has the remarkable facility of never, or seldom ever of erring and from that premise demands more resources to enforce its will.

The arrested development of the philosophy of private sector unions in current literature is illustrated in text books. Most do not even mention that the Old Unionism has a philosophy, while others limit their discussion to American unions' preference for "more," or "business unionism," and their rejection of socialism. None make any distinction between the philosophies of Old and the New Unionism and there is no discussion of neo-mercantilism.

One of the few texts which does address the unions' philosophy is that of Professor D. Quinn Mills of the Harvard Business School. In this leading text, Professor Mills identifies "more," or "business unionism," as the current philosophy of organized labor in the U.S. He does not identify a separate philosophy for public sector unions (the New Unionism), apparently leaving the reader to infer that the philosophy of business unionism applies to the entire union movement. Professor Mills also reiterates the difference in philosophies between American and European union movements: American unions are concerned only with the improvement of members' standard of living through the precepts of business unionism, while European movements "have sought to advance the entire working class by transforming total society" (Mills, 1986, p. 46).

The contrast between the goals of American and foreign union movements accurately portrays the era prior to the New Deal. However, that has changed. The Old Unionism's updated philosophy of neo-mercantilism does intend to transform the economy and social organization, but not through the antiquated methods of public ownership still held by many European unions. Instead, neo-mercantilism relies on indirect government intervention in the economy, macro-economic policies, to manage the economy and direct government intervention in specific areas of the labor market covering such matters as health and safety, minimum wages, pensions and, of course, labor relations. Neo-mercantilism also favors an industrial policy: Government intervention, euphemistically called a partnership with the Old Unionism and management, in the planning of what is to be produced and how. It would cartelize important segments of American industry and include the Old Unionism as part of the cartel. Another dimension of it is protectionism in international trade.

The CIO led in the change in philosophical move to neo-mercantilism, although the AFL was not far behind. Again, an empirical approach became an "informed by a body of long-term principles," to update the philosophy of the Old Unionism, to supplement business with neo-mercantilism. However, in contrast to business unionism, which it derived from its experience in the marketplace, the Old Unionism derived its philosophy of neo-mercantilism from its experience with government interference in the economy and society under the New Deal. The derivation is a manifestation of the Old Unionism's shift from the invisible to the visible hand of government. For the AFL the shift was pronounced because it had historically accepted the invisible hand strategy in maintaining and improving members' standards of living. In fact, the Federation believed it achieved the fulfillment of its view of laissez-faire in the labor market just on the eve of the New Deal, when Congress and the Hoover administration adopted the Norris-Laguardia Act (the Federal Anti-Injunction Act) of 1932. That law closely circumscribed the issuance of court orders in labor disputes, a goal long sought by the AFL in the belief that it was the major obstacle in its organizational path. In contrast to its senior partner, the CIO was born in the midst of the changeover from reliance on the invisible to the visible hand of government and for that reason led the way in the Old Unionism's acceptance of neo-mercan-tilism.

Another impetus to the Old Unionism's acceptance of more government intervention in society was its ongoing experience with organizing the unorganized. As the visible hand of government began to pay rich dividends in organizing the unorganized (to both the AFL and the CIO) with the enactment of the National Labor Relations Act in 1935, it took no great leap of imagination to seek extension of government intervention more broadly in the economy and society.

The new external philosophy, neo-mercantilism, like business unionism also accepts capitalism, but seeks fundamental modifications in the system. In the economic realm, it theorizes that government economic policies are required to maintain a high level of employment under a market system. Its economics are the economics of one this century's outstanding economists, the late Lord Keynes. Its essence is that the market system by itself is unable to generate sufficient aggregate demand to achieve and maintain full employment, so government demand (spending from borrowing) is required to make up the deficiency. Until recent years, this would have meant reliance primarily on fiscal policy, the taxing and spending power of government. More recently, government intervention has come to also encompass monetary policy as well. Together, the two, fiscal and monetary policies, are identified as macro-economic policies.

The impact of Keynes' ideas on the economic aspect of neo-mercantilism may be gauged by quoting Keynes' description of the power of ideas on policy:

> ... the ideas of economists and political philosophers, both when they are right and when they are wrong, are more powerful than is commonly understood. Indeed the world is ruled by little else. Practical men, who believe themselves to be quite exempt from any intellectual influences, are usually the slaves of some defunct economist, Madmen in authority, who hear voices in the air, are distilling their frenzy from some academic scribbler of a few years back (Keynes, 1935, p. 383).

Keynes' ideas captured the thinking of the Old Unionism (the AFL and the CIO) where historically other intellectuals failed and for good reason. Pre-Keynesian intellectuals advocated the replacement of capitalism with socialism, while Keynesianism accepted, but modified capitalism. Indeed, to doctrinaire socialists, Keynesianism was anathema because it undercut socialist theory and "saved" capitalism. For the Old

Unionism, the transition to Keynesianism was easy to make. It could readily support macro-management of the economy as consistent with its belief in the capitalist system. Moreover, Keynesian intervention was indirect, not direct as required by socialism and the ownership of the means of production; the indirect intervention was the visible hand was covered by a velvet glove.

Neo-mercantilism also means an activist role for government on health, safety, minimum wages, pensions and labor relations. These social concerns coupled with its New Deal economic experience also led organized labor to become even more active in politics as well, reaching its climax in the role it played in gaining the Democratic Party's nomination of Walter Mondale as the candidate for President in 1984. Hitherto, the literature on unionism have treated these aspects of organized labor's activities as the Old Unionism's concern for the wider interests of workers, including those not in unions. Put in the perspective of neo-mercantilism, these activities amount to much more – an effort to transform society according to the canons of Fairness.

A leading example often cited as Labor's concern for the wider interests of workers is its support of the minimum wage law and increases in that rate. Since probably none of the members of the Old Unionism benefit directly from minimum, wages, are they acting out of altruism, as claimed? Or are they acting in the interests of their members when they support minimum wage legislation?

First, one has to look, again, to history. Until the New Deal, the AFL *opposed* minimum wage legislation, and for several reasons. The Gompers's tradition was that government intervention on the behalf of workers to improve their working conditions diminished the appeal of unions because governmental programs would become a substitute for unionism and bargaining. Interestingly, a recent study of the decline of unions reached this conclusion (Neuman and Reisman, 1984). The Gompers' tradition also considered government intervention in the labor market a potential "instrument of oppression [of] the workers (Tyler, 1959, p. 5). Thus, Gompers argued that in times of labor shortages, the minimum could become a maximum (Carroll, 1923, p.57), an interpretation consistent with his support of capitalism and the market system.

The AFL reversed its position on the minimum wage, perhaps because it did indeed wish to portray itself as interested in the welfare of low paid workers. Orthodox economists do not find the law beneficial. To paraphrase Milton Friedman, it escapes one's logic why it is better for some earning less than the minimum wage to become unemployed and earn nothing because of the minimum. But whether the Federation and its successor AFL-CIO will admit it or not, supporting the minimum exerts pressure on employers to raise union rates (and nonunion rates), if only to restore the wages of unionized workers relative to the minimum wage workers. To the extent this upward pressing effect leads to the unemployment of some union members, the unions can hardly have served the interests of their members.

There is also a direct benefit from the maximum hour portion of the law The *Garcia* case (1985) was economically significant to the unionized bus drivers. Although they would not benefit from the wage provisions of the Fair Labor Standards Act of 1938, they would benefit from its over-time provisions. The employer transit authority (the San Antonio Metro-politan Transit Authority (SAMTA) contended that as a local public entity it was exempt from coverage. However, the Supreme Court rejected the claim and compelled the public transit authority to pay overtime rates to public employees and employees of public instrumenta-lities. It was the assertion of federal jurisdiction under the Fair Labor Standards Act of 1938 (the minimum wage, maximum hour law) which lays the foundation for Congressional authority to regulate labor rela-tions as the state and local level (Appendix A).

Neo-mercantilism and the social philosophy of the New Unionism underlie the Old and the New Unionism's alliance with other special in-terest groups. While this makes these philosophies open ended, and therefore ideally suited to the transformation of society, the alliances they engender can be counter-productive. This is suggested by the history of failed efforts to practice a 19th century version of such alliances. The short-lived National Labor Union, an association founded in 1866, and which disappeared in 1872, illustrates the fate which befell unions which joined forces with other special interest groups of that time. As Norman Ware, a labor historian described it:

> The National Labor Union at no time in its career had the slightest resem-
> blance to the American Federation of Labor which followed it fourteen
> years later. It was a typical American politico-reform organization, led by
> labor leaders without organizations, politicians without parties, women
> without husbands, and cranks, visionaries, and agitators without jobs (Ware,
> 1964, p. 10).

To some extent, this experience was replicated by the meteoric rise and fall of the Knights of Labor at the end of the 19th century. It, too, had a grand scheme for transforming American society, from capitalism to Cooperation, and failed. Those failures demonstrated that alliances with other special interest groups contributed to the instability of private sector unionism in the U.S. The founding of the American Federation of Labor in 1886 repudiated schemes of social transformation in favor of business unionism, and thrived.

In the current era, alliances with other special interest groups have been revived as a policy for both the New and the Old Unionism. For the Old Unionism, such alliances are a confession of weakness. As union membership and penetration of private labor markets has slipped drastically over the past two decades, the last century's panaceas for the working man are being revived by alliances between the Old Unionism and other special interest groups. Like the earlier attempts, these alliances hold out the promise of "solidarity" with other special and often disaffected groups, but instead of solidarity, the Old Unionism is more likely to find division among its own ranks over some of the goals of the groups with it has been urged to ally itself. As Carroll's study of labor and politics early in this century pointed out, while unionists could be united around economic objectives, the diversity of union members' backgrounds and beliefs on social issues could easily rend the organization (Carroll, Chapter IX, 1923). An current egregious example is abortion rights. Given that Catholics are a significant if not a majority group within the Old Unionism, it would be inviting internal dissension on a massive scale for the AFL-CIO to take a position, as it has been urged, especially at a time when it is very much on the defensive.

Neo-mercantilism, an update of past policies of government interference dating from the 18th century and earlier, puts the Old Unionism at odds with the re-invigorated world market system, the New Age of Adam Smith which has ensued over the past two decades. From an historical perspective, the Old Unionism had adjusted to the conditions and ideas of the past half century, but not to the conditions of the late 20th and oncoming 21st century. And I believe the lag to be unbridgeable. This perspective helps to explain why the Old Unionism has been unsuccessful in adapting to the new information age as we head into the 21st century. John Dunlop once characterized the lag of the Old Unionism's adjustment to new conditions this way:

> American labor organizations today reflect primarily the influence of long-term continuities with gradual changes and adaptations to evolving

problems and opportunities. They are shaped more by events of the past century than by forces of the last fifteen years (Dunlop, 1978, P. 79).

I believe that the Old Unionism is unlikely to be able to adjust to the New Age of Adam Smith. The most convincing evidence of this inability to adjust to the New Age of Adam Smith has been the cataclysmic decline of its membership and market share over the past two decades.

CHAPTER V.

The Philosophy of the New Unionism and Its Consequences

What unions are, what they do and why touches upon all aspects of labor organization, but none more than their philosophy. The consequences of the application of that philosophy was captured by the quotation from Professor Charles Lindbloom cited previously and repeated here: "Little wonder that it is rarely perceived that unionism in the United States now is as revolutionary in consequence as it is conservative in intention" (p. 20). When these words were written over a half-century ago he had in mind the Old Unionism; the New Unionism lay in the future. However, his assessment proved to be largely misplaced because the Old Unionism has met the market place and its revolutionary consequences for the economy have been largely blunted. Not so for the New Unionism, however. As its meteoric rise and durability demonstrate, it has prospered as the Old Unionism has foundered and waned in power (Chapter II). Consequently, Lindbloom's words, mis-timed as to the Old Unionism, apply to the New Unionism. In this chapter, I examine the intentions, the external philosophical objectives of the New Unionism. I begin with a review of the New Unionism's internal philosophy.

Internal Philosophy

The New Unionism's internal philosophy which defines union structure, inter-union and employer relations was borrowed from the Old Unionism. The transfer was natural since unionism originated in the private labor market and because the Old Unionism dominated the labor movement from its formative years to the present. Also, many of the predecessor organizations of the New Unionism affiliated with the main federations of the Old Unionism, the AFL and the CIO, bringing them into close association with the Old Unionism and its practices.

The New Unionism (and its predecessors) retained intact the Old Unionism's approach to structure and inter-union relations. Like the Old

Unionism, the New structured itself to reflect philosophy and practices of exclusive jurisdiction which originated with the Old Unionism. The New Unionism also, like the Old, was shaped by the geography of the country. Finally, the federal form of government also played a decisive role in shaping the structure of the New Unionism. The public and professional associations of government employees which became the keystone of the New Unionism, also had established structures parallel to those of the Old Unionism. In appearance, therefore, the structure of the New Unionism and inter-union relations differs not at all from the Old.

However, the forces which underlay the similarity of structure, inter-union relations and relations with employers between the New and the Old Unionism differ significantly. The structure of the New Unionism is derived from its *political* market, in contrast to the *economic* market which prescribed the structure of the Old Unionism. The major consequence of the difference is the relationship with the employer. While nominally and at times actually adversarial, the relationship between the New Unionism and its governmental employer is more cooperative than combative: Both want a larger budget and managerial attitudes and practices differ significantly from those in the private sector (Chapter III).

At the same time, the jurisdictional disputes which troubled the Old Unionism have also affected the New Unionism. The bottom line in both movements is membership, money and the power and influence which comes from numbers. Those organizations of the New Unionism affiliated with the AFL-CIO attempted to avoid jurisdictional disputes by having an arbitrator appointed by the Federation determine which union should seek representation rights (Stern, 1988, p. 81–82).

The New Unionism's practice of exclusive jurisdiction is reflected in their jurisdictional claims and their organizational titles. Their jurisdictional claims are both occupational (or functional) and industrial. The Teachers, Fire Fighters, Letter Carriers, Postal Clerks exhibit the occupational or functional form; the Government Employees, and the State, County and Municipal Employees, the industrial. Although similar in jurisdictional form, the occupations embraced by the New Unionism differ from the Old Unionism. Occupationally, the New Unionism represents predominantly white collar occupations, while the Old Unionism enrolls mostly blue collar workers (Chapter II). Most members of the New Unionism are professionals, in particular, teachers. The professional make-up of the New Unionism is a distinction with a major difference from the Old Unionism: The professionals, especially the teachers, have a greater propensity to accept and advocate the social and economic transformation embodied in the New Society. In a social paradox, the preconception that militant blue collar unions are more likely to challenge the social structure is refuted by the current experience with the New Unionism and the New Society. When the Old Socialism referred to the workers who would lead the way to the brave new world, they had in mind downtrodden factory hands. In an ironic twist of history, the New Socialism depends upon middle class white collar members of the New Unionism to bring about the New Society.

In practicing the Old Unionism's demand for a share in the governance of the workplace, the New Unionism has greatly altered the consequence of workplace governance. Because it deals with the sovereign employer, the New Unionism alters government by introducing an unelected body into the making of public policy. Governance in the public labor market is not the same as union encroachment on managerial prerogatives in the private labor market; these are relations between private parties, not between the state and private groups (Chapter III). A corollary has been the New Unionism's impact on civil service. Over time the New Unionism has steadily eroded the civil service system of personnel relations, changing the nature of government employment, just as it is changing the nature of public governance. Again, this is not parallel to collective bargaining's impact on personnel relations in the private sector.

A New External Philosophy: Social Unionism

The most important dimension of the New Unionism's philosophical differences with the Old lie not in the internal philosophy of each, but in their external philosophies. Superficially, it would appear that the New shares the Old Unionism's external philosophy of "more." However, form belies substance. In fact, as practiced by the Old Unionism, "more" modified but did not imply the transformation of the market system and capitalism. To the contrary, "more" or business unionism accepted these institutions, albeit with modifications which made the competitive system more difficult to operate. Indeed, this was the core idea behind Lindbloom's apprehension a half-century ago that the Old Unionism and the market system were incompatible. However, the New Age of Adam Smith has since greatly reduced the power of the Old Unionism to interfere with markets.

On the other hand, "more" as practiced by the New Unionism does transform the economy and society because the public employer is also the sovereign state. "More" as practiced by the New Unionism redistributes income between the State and private parties; it socializes income, the keystone of the New Socialism and the New Society (Chapter I). As Professor Friedman has noted, government now exercises ownership over a major share of the income produced by economy's factors of production. In this fundamental way, the economy and society have steadily been transformed, one which does not require the ownership of the factors themselves, but of the income which they produce. Government monopoly over the furnishing of some services, most notably the postal service, and its near monopoly over elementary and secondary education, greatly enlarge the scope of the New Socialism. And the New Unionism is a major factor in the continuing evolution of this New Society.

The New Unionism's version of "more" is, therefore, an external philosophy distinct from the Old Unionism. I term the New Unionism's version "social unionism." The term, like the term New Unionism, is not new, but like the distinction I have drawn between the New Unionism and the Old, as well as between the New Unionism and its predecessor organizations ("proto-unions"), I argue that my use of the term differs in content and comprehensiveness from earlier usage. Moreover, when the term was used, it was applied to the Old Unionism. For example, Professor Joseph Shister wrote of a philosophy of social unionism which he said encompassed " under that rubric more vigorous and innovative organizing and political activity" (Shister, 1966, p. 600). He envisioned it as in conflict with the older philosophy of "more" and bearing the potential of splitting the AFL-CIO, then only a decade old. However, not only did his version of social unionism as re-invigorated organizing and political activity not split the federation, but actually never got off the ground. Moreover, Shister, like others whose views on the philosophy of the Old Unionism I have summarized never saw the extension of "more" into "more government intervention," what I have called neo-mercantilism (Chapter IV).

Social unionism, like the Old Unionism's updated philosophy of neo-mercantilism, requires increasing government intervention in the economy. However, the two differ in the goals of that interference. Social unionism would bring about a new society based on the socialization of income; it is the New Socialism. An active role for the New Unionism in "nationalizing" income has been advocated by the leader of one of the largest of the New Unions. Gerald McEntee, president of the American Federation of State, County and Municipal Employees, AFL-CIO has recently put forth these demands: "We want to get involved in what happens to pension money, how they work out the ratings. We want to get involved in making decisions in terms of tax base, in terms of priorities. We want to play a larger role in the formation of public policy, the formation of national policy, as it affects our people" (*Forbes*, May 13, 1991, p. 86).

On the other hand, neo-mercantilism rejects socialization of income, the New Socialism, and is in conflict with it. Neo-mercantilism at the macro-level seeks high or full employment and an industrial policy (like Japan's), and at the micro-level plans to regulate labor markets on matters of health, safety, pensions and employment at will (Chapter IV).

The New and the Old Unionisms' goals are in conflict over who should receive the national income. The New Unionism focuses on the distribution of income between the private and public economys. In contrast, the Old Unionism focuses on redistributing income between private parties, employers and union members. The Old Unionism, or at least its members if not its leaders, resist policies intended to transfer an increasing share of the national income from the private to the public sector, notwithstanding benefits it brings to their union brothers and sisters in the New Unionism. They oppose it because it costs them higher taxes, like all other citizens. Parenthetically, this is but one of the issues which belie the notion of the solidarity of Labor's interests; it is also one of the most important. This chasm is not bridged by a sharing of other goals, or practices such as affiliation with a common federation, common forms of structure and administration or claims of "solidarity."

The chasm exists and divides the New from the Old Unionism not only philosophically, but in practical affairs as well, most notably in the voting behavior of their respective memberships. As demonstrated by the voting record of private blue collar workers in the election of President Reagan in 1980 and 1984, and President Bush in 1988, in contrast to the voting support given candidates Mondale and Dukakis by the public sector leaders and membership.

The fact that the Old and the New Unionism do have different external philosophies raises the question of why: Why should the New Unionism have its own philosophy (social unionism)? The conditions requisite for the New Unionism to have its own philosophy are its origins, the labor market in which it functions, the industrial relations system, and its sovereign employer. Another necessary condition for the New Unionism to have its own is that it had to attain a "critical mass" in membership and market penetration in order to constitute a distinction with a difference from the Old. Once across the threshold of becoming a movement, analytically it became necessary to treat the contemporary public sector labor movement as a movement apart from the collection of labor organizations in the public sector which preceded, as well as the contemporaneous Old Unionism (Chapter II). As reported in Chapter II, currently, the New Unionism represents over three times an many workers in its labor market as the Old and constitutes about 40% of the total membership of the nation's union movement. Early in the next century the New Unionism will also become the senior member of the American labor movement. By these measures the New Unionism has certainly achieved the "critical mass" necessary to generate a philosophy, the philosophy which I call social unionism. As Professor Kovacs wrote in his analysis of the philosophy of the Canadian private sector (Old) union movement nearly three decades ago:

> The philosophy of the labour movement cannot be examined in isolation without reference to its historical evolution, for the labour movement is a dynamic institution which passes through various stages of development. Thus in order to discover the philosophy behind the movement it is necessary to look at its pattern of growth. [sic] by the social and political structure in which it is allowed to grow, as a social force it, too, is influential in shaping the environment, directly or indirectly, through its collective activities and policies (Kovacs, 1964, pp. 25–26).

The development of the New Unionism's philosophy was not planned but, in keeping with the development of union philosophy in general, was the result of "the turning and twisting," of its experience in the public labor market and with a sovereign employer. Like the development of the philosophy of the Old Unionism, social unionism came about through its distinct experience in the economy and society.

That public sector unions should pursue increased government intervention in the economy and society is consistent with their development. Indeed, their origin, formation and expansion owe much to public policy (Chapter II). To make further gains in membership, influence and power, public sector unions would naturally return to that wellspring and demand more government intervention on their behalf. Their demand for government intervention is well grounded in economics, the concept of derived demand: Increased demand for public service, typically means gains in public employment and, in turn, increased public sector union membership. Even though the correlation is not perfect, there is a high degree of association between increased public expenditure and public employment. Such a conclusion is certainly warranted by the experience of public sector unionism under the Great Society programs of President Johnson and the theories of Adolph Wagner on the growth of public spending (Chapter III).

The Great Society programs were the defining experience of social unionism, just as the economic catastrophe of the Great Depression reshaped the character and philosophy of the Old Unionism. The Great Society programs and their counterparts by state and local governments also demonstrate how the New Unionism can influence the size and nature of the demand for their services, a capability virtually unavailable to the Old Unionism. As political organizations with impressive wealth and income and with ever growing membership who are also voters, the New Unionism can influence the amount of public expenditure and the demand for the services of its members. In the process, the New Union- ism also encounters a cooperative employer which shares the unions' interest in ever increasing public budgets. One notable result of this pro- cess has been the phenomenal growth of expenditures and employment in public education, an achievement all the more remarkable considering the continuing failures of public education.

A comparable scenario is not present in the private sector. In the private sector, the employer is adversarial and concerned with minimiz- ing labor costs per unit of output, while the Old Unionism can do little to increase consumer demand for its services. The union label and more recently TV advertisements are the Old Unionism's principal methods to stimulate demand for union-made products and their results have been negligible. Indeed, the differential effect of the Old and the New Union- ism on the demand for their services brings to light another clash in eco- nomic function between the two. The Old Unionism's effect on costs (through higher compensation) may lead to a decline in demand for the input (labor) because of a reduction in the quantity of the output demanded, a decline in demand, or a substitution of capital for labor. In turn, the reduction in employment implies a reduction in union member- ship. Such is rarely the case in the public sector. Higher costs generated by increased compensation costs seldom leads to a reduction of employ- ment, the output of services, and to a limited substitution of capital for labor. Productivity gains so frequently touted as part of recurring agreements in the public sector are most conspicuous by the absence of fulfill-ment. In the public sector additional costs (induced by higher compensation) typically lead to demands for additional funds (new taxes) to maintain services, with the affected unions in the forefront demanding increased taxation. Public employers typically join them in the demand for increased revenues to maintain and expand public services. More-over, lacking a market mechanism to signal that a given service is not in demand or is falling in demand, governments seldom withdraw a service, once it has been provided irrespective of costs. The writer can only recall the abolition of one federal agency, the Civil Aeronautics Board, during the 1980s, despite an Administration dedicated to the reduction of the federal bureaucracy. How many state and local agencies have disap-peared, irrespective of need?

Public sector unions, together with other groups drawing from the public bursary, have been remarkably successful in re-allocating income from the private to the public sector. Indeed, their success is all the more striking when one considers that as many other countries are apparently rediscovering the economic and political merits of free market allocation of resources and a political system focused on the individual, public poli-cies in this country are steadily moving the economy and society toward more public control of economic resources and therefore more public interference in the decision making by individuals. Despite efforts of the Reagan Administration, which only slowed the shift, policy makers in this country at all levels of government, federal, state and local, have belied their words in favor of the market system with the deeds favoring a system of socialization of decision making through increased public spending.

Some figures on the increased share of resources now expended by the public bursary demonstrate the shift in resources and decision mak-ing from the individual to society. Over the last three decades (1960–1989), government expenditures (federal, state and local) as a share of the national income have increased by 30 percent (from 32.1 to 41.7 percent of the national income). By way of reference, in 1929, gov-ernment expenditures accounted for 12 percent of national income (*Economic Report of the President, 1990*, Tables C23 and C79, pp. 319 and 387). Defense expenditures as a share of National Income were actually larger in 1960 than 1990 (*Economic Report of the President, 1990*, Table C81, p. 389 and *Historical Statistics of the United States*, Part 2, Series Y472- 487, p. 1116), so the growth of total government in this period is owed more to the gains in social expenditures. While public sector unions are not noted for their advocacy of increased military expenditures, they nevertheless benefit from a larger military to the extent that civilian employment associated with defense is a fertile area of membership growth. Moreover, the gains in the New Unionism often come in sections of the country where the Old Unionism is weak. For example, while civilian employment is well organized in military installations in Southern states, the same states rank low in the country in the degree of union share of the private labor market.

Except for some federal government unions, the New Unionism prefers social spending. I believe this preference is for ideological as well as for empirical reasons. The teachers' unions are foremost in the demand for social spending. On the other hand, at the federal level, unions like the American Federation of Government Employees, AFL-CIO, support defense expenditures because of the associated civilian employment. The Old Unionism, those employed by the federal government in arsenals, shipyards and military installations and those in the defense industry, also support military expenditures for empirical reasons. This generality holds even in the eccentric case of the International Association of Machinists, AFL-CIO, whose former president steadily opposed increased the military build-up of the 1980s, despite the fact that the membership and financial well-being of many affiliated local unions and members were so closely tied to the defense of the country. While segments of both the New and the Old Unionism benefit from defense expenditures, defense outlays will generate more jobs and members for the private than the public sector of the labor market. On the other hand, social programs generate more employment to administer social welfare expenditures. If there is an military-industrial complex in the private sector (including unions from both the Old and the New Unionism) to push for defense expenditures, it is currently over-matched by the social-welfare complex in the public economy; the latter has far more money to spend. Wagner's law on the propensity for increased government spending has demonstrated its long run viability!

In current dollars, social welfare spending by federal, state and local governments rose from $52.3 billion in 1960 to $834.4 billion in 1987 (*Statistical Abstract of the United States, 1990*, Table No. 575, p. 350). This constituted a 16 fold gain in less than three decades! In per capita constant dollar values, social welfare expenditures grew most during the decade, 1960–1970, when it rose 6.5% annually (*Statistical Abstract, 1990*, p. 350). As a share of the Gross National Product Social Welfare spending nearly doubled, 1960–1987. It jumped from just over one-tenth of the GNP in 1960 to just under one-fifth of the GNP by 1987. As a proportion of all government outlays (federal, state and local), it rose from just over 38% to more than half, 53.5% (*Statistical Abstract, 1990*, p. 352).

The growth of federal grants and allocations to state and local governments and federal standards on social expenditures have amplified state and local government employment, explaining in part its more rapid gain over federal employment. At the same time, state and local governments' more favorable policies toward unionization generate more union members and unionization than if the funds were administered directly by federal employees.

Pragmatic Basis of Social Unionism

Historical examples demonstrate that it is unnecessary for the New Unionism to be ideologically committed to socialism in order to pursue the New Socialism. While private sector unions and union leaders did not accept an ideological basis for public ownership, they could and did advocate public ownership of some industries – for pragmatic reasons. As early as 1886, the American Federation of Labor approved a convention resolution in favor of public ownership of telecommunications, telephone and telegraph (Henle, 805), although the nascent Federation opposed socialism. Later, John L. Lewis, president of the United Mineworkers of America (and a Republican), in a challenge to Samuel Gompers for the presidency of the American Federation of Labor in 1921, declared just prior to the Federation's convention:

> I stand for Government ownership of the railroads, nationalization of the mines, and other progressive legislation that would give the workers and toilers of America the freedom and justice in industry they deserve (Henle, July, 1965, p. 805).

While this statement was an opportunistic effort by Lewis to gain the support of socialists and other opponents of Gompers in the AFL in Lewis' effort to replace Gompers, who opposed nationalization, it also reflected a widely held view of the time: "The years from 1919 through 1921 saw the issue of Government ownership reach its high water mark in the history of the [private] trade union movement." (Henle, p. 805).

The reasons that unions wanted the railroads and mines to be nationalized at that time were pragmatic, not ideological. Specifically, the unions involved advocated nationalization of the rails and mines because they wished to protect and extend the favorable position which they had gained with little effort under government policies during World War I. Unions anticipated that a return to private ownership of the rails would undo the status and the gains in membership and penetration of employment won under government auspices. For these reasons, the philosophy of "business unionism" was shelved in favor of government ownership of the railways. However, nothing came of the railway unions' plan to nationalize the roads and in 1920, the carriers were returned to private ownership. Subsequent legislation culminating in an enactment of 1951 restored the power the railway unions had achieved under *de facto* government ownership 1918–1920.

From this and other historical examples, it is evident that unions can practice the socialization or nationalization of income without having to become socialists. Indeed, by disposing of the ideological baggage which comes with doctrinaire socialism, the pragmatic approach is more likely to gain adherents and succeed. Moreover, packaged as "Fairness," it becomes very marketable in a country with a long history of nominal opposition to socialism.

While the new collectivism rejects the role of the state as the owner of the instruments of production, it, too, relies on the state as the center-piece for wielding policy, the policy of redistributing income. The redistribution would be far more comprehensive and sweeping in concept, scope and impact than the old collectivism. It would preserve the goose (not only by permitting, but encouraging private ownership of enterprise) while taking an increasingly larger share of the golden eggs. Through the taxing, borrowing and spending power of government the contemporary new socialists intend to transfer income from individuals in the private economy to managers, or more properly, social engineers in the public economy. Their leading example is Sweden. Far from being the "middle way," the Swedish model exemplifies the policy of socializing income in an advanced state of development. It is worth noting that left wing ideologues, confronted by the failure of socialism in Eastern Europe and elsewhere, now assert that these countries do not wish to opt for the more market (less socialist) economies exemplified by the U.S., but for the Swedish "middle way." The phrase disarms the unwary into thinking that this is a happy "average" between market and government controlled economy. Actually, of course, the Swedish "middle way" exemplifies an advanced stage in the "socializing of income," with a debilitating effect on individual enterprise.

The tilting of the axis of union power from the private toward the public sector makes the New Socialism and the New Society attainable. The New Unionism is both the creature and one of the architects of that society. It has firm theoretical and political bases for a more durable and decisive impact on achieving its goals than the Old Unionism. In contrast to the Old Unionism whose very success in establishing any monopoly power provokes incentives for the undoing of that power, the New Unionism can go on from strength to strength. Privatization has only limited potential, if only because the New Unionism, aided and abetted by political allies, can thwart the competitive alternative. This difference in the power potential between the New and the Old Unionism caused a commentator on the British public union movement to point out a decade ago: "... that it is now the unwritten Treasury view that Britain does not have a trade union problem, what we have is a trade union problem in the public sector" (Burton, 1982, p. 54).

In lieu of privatization, the major market response will have to come from budgetary restraint. But is that feasible? Given the prospect of a major increase in public spending on health there this is doubtful. Meanwhile, the political alliance between organized labor, both the New and the Old wings, and the Democratic Party grows. Those Republicans dubbed by the *Wall Street Journal* as Depublicans share in the steady expansion of government ownership of the national income.

Within organized labor as a whole, the common goal of more government intervention in the interests of a Fair society checks the disagreements of the Old and the New Unionism over their conflicts on what that intervention should accomplish. In 1981 the AFL-CIO mandated a share of its per capita receipts be allocated to its Committee on Public Eduction (COPE). The enhanced funding of COPE led a writer from the *New York Times* to comment that "the unions of the AFL-CIO are becoming the most dependable financial resource of the Democratic Party" (Troy, 1982, p. 7).

The overt political intervention of the Federation, which began with the New Deal, marked a new departure in its political as well as its philosophy. Historically, organized labor, notably the Old Unionism, described its political activities as "rewarding its friends and punishing its enemies." Historically, that was treated by many analysts as evidence of the lack of political action by the Old Unionism prior to the New Deal. However, as Professor Taft wrote: "The existence and importance of the state federations of labor and their activities in winning concessions from the legislature as well as in shaping the political tactics of American labor has largely been ignored by students of labor and politics" (Taft, 1962, p. 306).

While "rewarding friends an punishing enemies" is still true, its political friends are almost always Democrats and its political enemies Republicans. In 1984 the Federation was the key to Walter Mondale's winning of the Democratic Party's nomination. Ironically, it appears that the majority of members of the Old Unionism voted for Reagan, while most members of the New Unionism voted for Mondale, the candidate who promised the voters to raise their taxes. The average worked out to a plurality of union households voting for Mondale, but one well below the showing of organized labor historically on behalf of Democratic presidential candidates. Subsequently, organized labor's candidate, in particular the Old Unionism's candidate for the 1988 nomination, Richard Gephart, did not receive the nomination.

The New Unionism's commitment to the New Socialism would at last achieve intellectuals' long frustrated goal of getting the American union movement, or at least its public movement, to behave more like European unions. And they have good cause to be optimistic. Paradoxically, the continued decline of private sector unions will boost the prospects of the New Unionism pursuing the goal of a New Society. The weakening of the Old Unionism will increasingly make the New Unionism appear to the public and to politicians as the representative voice of all organized labor.

Privatization

Two potential checks to the New Unionism and the New Socialism are limitations on public budgets and privatization. Resistance to public expenditures has occurred at various times and states, such as California's proposition 13 and Massachusetts' proposition 2 1/2. Referenda may be another obstacle to continued expansion of public spending. A constitutional requirement for a balanced federal budget would be the most serious impediment to unrestrained spending. At one point, some conservatives came to the questionable conclusion if the federal debt had any benefit, it was its potential as a brake on government spending. Likewise, it was thought that indexation of income tax rates by cutting off inflationary increases in federal tax receipts would retard federal expenditures. Events have shown how illusory these have been. At the state level the threat of a lowered rating on state bonds may slow expenditures, but that is uncertain. Adolph Wagner's Law continues to function without any serious impairment.

The other potential check to the New Unionism and the "nationalization" of income, the New Socialism, is to privatize or contract out many services now offered by government. The most important of these would be education, which would affect state and local governments most, and the federally operated postal service. To protect their monopoly grip on primary and secondary education, the core of the New Unionism, organized teachers have opposed parental choice in education. Politically, this has led both the National Education Association, and the American Federation of Teachers, AFL-CIO, to support the candidacy of Governor Clinton, the Democratic candidate for the presidency. He, of course, has assured the unions of his opposition to free choice in this vital market, the education market.

Education along with health services are among the most rapidly growing areas of employment and public investment, so the impact of the New Unionism on the public economy will necessarily also expand. Between 1990 and 2005, state and local government employment is expected to increase as rapidly as over-all nonfarm employment, but over one-half of the increase is likely to be in education (Carey and Franklin, 1991, p. 57). Only a competitive, private education system could restrain both the monopoly position enjoyed by educational unionism and curtail "staff activism and involvement in public affairs" in this vital and failing area of service. Hence, privatization should not be analyzed solely in financial cost/benefit terms, or even only on the basis of the quality of service, but also as a check to the clipping of sovereignty.

The U.S. Postal Service operates the oldest monopoly because it has the corner on first class mail conferred on it by the Constitution. As a result, that "monopoly has preserved large flows of revenue and high wage rates despite studies showing that private companies could carry the mail more efficiently and at lower cost" (Barro, 1991, p. A 12). Because it is an inefficient monopoly, the USPS has seen its market control eroded by competitive delivery of packages and express mail by private carriers (Federal Express, United Parcel) and technological change, especially the fax machine. The failure of the USPS, the postal unions and their Congressional allies to have fax transmissions officially classified a form of first class mail delivery and therefore under the exclusive control of the USPS has opened a wide competitive gap in the monopoly power of the Service. However, it is premature to believe that the USPS is on the verge of decay. It has used its formidable monopoly position to compete with its private rivals in express mail and package delivery.

Sanitation is another service which will attract privatization. A classic example from Britain illustrates the issue. The governing council of the city of Liverpool, controlled by the Labor Party, faced with bankruptcy, finally decided to hire a French company to collect the garbage. Under municipal "management" it cost the taxpayers $13.4 million annually to pick-up the garbage which the French firm contracted to pick-up for less than half the amount, $6.3 million. The organized municipal workers struck as a 'matter of principle' leaving Liverpudlians (the citizens of Liverpool) with mountains of garbage ("Tale of the Bin Men," Editorial, *Wall Street Journal*, June 26, 1991, p. A 8).

Contracting out is not a trouble free alternative to government provision of services. Strikes, which might be illegal in the government sector, are legal in the private labor market. However, that ought to be given little weight as the record of unions in sanitation, fire air traffic and postal services reveals. Perhaps a more important drawback would be political influence in letting out contracts. Under political influence the costs of government could even go up.

The New Unionism also opposes the sale of public assets such as airports, mass transit, ports, and hospitals (PED, Spring 1992). As the Public Employees Department, AFL-CIO, candidly wrote: "The AFL-CIO called on Congress and state and local officials to guard against the sale of vital public facilities and warned against the dangerous trends represented by privatization, contracting out, prison labor, and any policies that threaten public workers" (PED, Spring 1992). The value of likely federal candidates for privatization may exceed $300 billion and includes among it major items Amtrak, the air traffic control system, the National and Dulles airports, the Naval Petroleum Reserve, surplus military bases, the Postal Service, the Tennessee Valley Authority, the Bonneville marketing administration and others like it, government owned timber and grazing land, and not to forget the huge holdings in failed savings and loan institutions (Bleiberg, p. 10).

The New Unionism's opposition to privatization extends to school lunches. Thus, the PED reported (happily) that "organized employees of the Dearborn, Mich. schools waged a successful campaign to privatizing school lunches." One wonders if students were given a taste test?

At the local level of government, "examples of privatization in virtually every type of municipal government function" have been identified.

These include sports, cultural, and recreational facilities; jails and prisons; fleet maintenance; and transit systems (Reason Foundation, 1991, p. 10).

Privatization, like the New Unionism itself, has become an international phenomenon. Likewise, the New Unionism's opposition is also international. A summary statement of opposition from an organization of European unions illustrates the point:

> The European trade union organisations reject any policy of privatisation of the public services, whether affecting collective services on national interest such as telecommunications and public transport, or those supplied by local authorities and the national health service at decentralised level. This type of privatisation has been unequivocally condemned in the general resolution adopted by the European Trade Union Confederation (ETUC) at is 5th Statutory Congress held in Milan in 1985 (European Trade Union Institute, 1988, p. 98).

To ward off privatization, the European trade unions "do believe, nonetheless, that there is in many cases a need to embark on reform of the management of these services, in order to bring them closer into line with the requirements of consumers, the local community and the workers themselves, via the appropriate forms of industrial democracy (European Trade Union Institute, 1988, p. 98). Presumably the "appropriate forms of industrial democracy" are the unions, whose record in public enterprise contributed so mightily to the demand for privatization in the first place.

The heat from privatization has been felt in the U.S. as well. The Public Employees Department, AFL-CIO, has recognized that "[t]here is an urgent need to improve the effectiveness and efficiency of our public programs" and, like their European counterparts, have called for union participation in to bring about "the revitalization of our public services" (PED, March 1992, p. 6). Acknowledgement that problems exist is a step forward; recommendations which would further involve the New Unionism's participation in the management of public services is a prescription of the same remedy but with heightened adverse consequences.

On the other hand, when privatization occurs, the industrial relations environment changes. It is transformed from the protective security of limited competition or monopoly to the world of competition. In a study of British experience, which has the most to draw upon to date, the changeover entailed a switch from a political to a business environment. The switch was hardly welcomed by the former public employees, or for sympathetic academics either (Ferner and Collins, Sept. 1991). It is poetic justice that some of first, if not the first, evaluations of the effects of privatization on industrial relations should emanate from Britain, for, after all, it was also home to the beginnings of trade unions.

The Consequences of Social Unionism: Municipal Insolvency

Strategically, the New Unionism's attack point to gain convergence in industrial relations is the sovereign employer (Chapter III). One of the consequences of that attack is municipal insolvency. Municipal insolvency demonstrates one the leading consequences of social unionism.

The increasing incidence of governmental deficits and bankruptcies are tied, in great part, to bargaining and arbitration and are a telling indicator of the New Unionism's encroachment on the sovereignty of governmental bodies, particularly those at the local level. Yes, the heart of the matter (sovereignty) is money, the power of the New Unionism to influence the size and distribution of public finance. While the New Unionism's power to influence the demand for their services has been recognized, the connection to clipping sovereignty with its consequences for deficits and bankruptcies has not.

The most obvious breach of sovereignty by the New Unionism has been through its contribution to the insolvency of local governments. Insolvency and its resolution necessarily invade the sovereign power of the government jurisdictions affected. Government is a labor intensive industry, so personnel costs are a major fraction of total costs, measuring from 60% to 75% of municipal budgets (Spiotto, 1991, p. 15). And the New Unionism has pushed up wages and fringe benefits, probably far more than statisticians have measured (Freeman, 1986). Wages in the public sector are less subject to competitive forces and capital-for-labor substitution than in the private sector. These factors make it difficult for local governments to contain wage increases and have contributed to pushing them into insolvency.

While the New Unionism has directly curtailed sovereignty by its contribution to insolvencies, it has also altered the process of governance. In the legal process of resolving insolvencies, the New Unionism and collective bargaining have brought about a shift in sovereign powers from elected officials in local government to the judicial branch of the federal government, or to *ad hoc* authorities such as that set up to rescue New York City from bankruptcy in 1977.

The New York City rescue from bankruptcy was designed to avert judicial oversight. Judicial oversight of bankruptcy of local governmental bodies is derived from federal bankruptcy law; it injects federal authority into local matters. Federal judicial oversight may come about either through the municipality's agreement in the proceeding, or by the assertion of court authority. Either way, there is a change in how government operates.

Theoretically, the Federal Bankruptcy Code does not give the court the authority to act as an executive and legislative body. Actually, it does. Section 904, Chapter 9 of the Code permits the insolvent municipality to give the bankruptcy court the authority to interfere with the governmental powers of the debtor municipality, its property or revenues and the municipality's use of any income-producing property (Spiotto, 1991, p. 27). In the absence of the municipality's consent, the court may not interfere with the choices a municipality makes on the services it provides, but *de facto* as well as *de jure* it can and indeed it must. In reconciling the demands of debtors and citizens, the court must balance the taxpayers' need for services against the demands of creditors for tax revenues to pay debts. The bankruptcy reorganization plan which the court must approve to reconcile these competing demands is the equivalent of legislative action taken by a municipal executive and legislative bodies, despite mandates for judicial restraint by the Bankruptcy Code and the Constitution. Since Chapter 9 "is not a vehicle for elimination of debt but rather for debt adjustment (Spiotto, 1991, p. 17), in the process of adjustment, the court must apportion the municipality's revenues among expenditures, that is, it must make administrative and legislative choices for the municipality.

The City of New York's *de facto* bankruptcy case exemplifies avoidance of federal judicial intervention under the bankruptcy code, while the case of the San Jose (California) School District illustrates that intervention. The City of New York went bankrupt *de facto* in 1975 when it was unable to market its debt. It was decided that legal bankruptcy had to be avoided because under Chapter 9, a proposed plan of adjustment must show that 51% of the amount had been accepted by creditors. At the time, it was estimated that 160 thousand individuals or families held nearly $5 billion of the City's debt, about 2/3 of the amount in outstanding bonds, and that, in addition, many registered bonds were held in nominee names. Since it would be manifestly very difficult, if not impossible, to gain acceptance of a reorganization plan because of the dispersion of the debt among so many holders, an alternative to the Bankruptcy Court was devised and found, the State of New York (Spiotto, 1991 (a), p. 10). Beside the administrative problems, the avoidance of bankruptcy was also a high political priority since the political costs would be even higher.

Among the major contributors to the City's fiscal debacle were its unions. Of this there is little if any dispute. Nevertheless, two analysts of the City's financial debacle, one a leading politician, could not muster the resolution to identify the unions' role. Instead, they euphemistically identified only "groups" to whom "New York's elected officials ... found it difficult to say no" and from whom they could not obtain a *"quid pro quo"* (Shalala and Bellamy, 1976, p. 1122). In their explanation of the City's difficulties, Shalala and Bellamy never identified the "groups" to whom the City could not say 'no' and from whom they could not demand a *"quid pro quo."* Since the word "union" never appears in their analysis of New York City's fiscal crisis, a visitor from outer space would think that New York was a nonunion City and could only speculate on the identity of these mysterious "groups." Most of Shalala and Bellamy's analysis focused on the sources of revenue loss and little on steadily increasing demands from the unidentified groups, another insight into the ideology of those committed to ever-increasing government. Nevertheless, the unions were clearly among the leading "groups" to whom the politicians could not say no, indeed, did not want to refuse and from whom increased productivity (one aspect of a *quid pro quo*) failed to materialize despite repeated assurances to the electorate. (The theme of increased productivity from City employees remains an enduring element in bargaining, with results yet to be seen).

To avoid a *de jure* bankruptcy and federal court oversight, the State of New York was brought in as a surrogate for a bankruptcy court to resolve the financial debacle of the City. In general, most, if not all states have authority to permit the appointment by state courts of a receiver or statutes providing the appointment of a state agency to deal with a default on public debt. Such arrangements are surrogates for bankruptcy and in political terms mean that an appointed body supplants the duly elected or legislatively established authority in the execution of public responsibilities.

In the case of the New York City bankruptcy this step illustrated how the New Unionism contributes to changing sovereignty by its contribution to local government bankruptcy: Instead of a bankruptcy court (itself an abridgement of sovereignty), the State of New York oversaw the adjustment of the City's debt. The State's first step as surrogate for a court was to create a new body with the authority to commandeer fiscal and governing powers normally vested by the electorate in City officials. Even Shalala and Bellamy described this as a "program of governance" which "eliminated the last vestiges of fiscal home rule of the City" (p. 1128). Governance of the City of New York's finances shifted from the elected officials of the City, excepting the Mayor, to state officials (not elected for that purpose) and to state appointee experts, not elected at all. The new authority was titled the Emergency Financial Control Board (Control Board). Necessarily and actually, the Mayor's authority was more nominal than actual. Decisions on the finances New York City, a political entity with one the largest budgets of any political jurisdictions in the U.S. after the federal government, would now be decided mainly by individuals never elected by the people of the City! Although legal the procedure should not obscure the real transfer of political power from the people to an administrative panel. If these developments are not serious reductions in the sovereign powers of the people and a change in representative democracy, what then are? And if the New Unionism was not a major factor, first in clipping sovereign power by its contribution to the bankruptcy and second in shifting elective authority to a *de facto* non-elective panel, then how else are these remarkable shocks to sovereignty to be understood?

The body created by the State, the Emergency Financial Control Board (Control Board), was made up of the Governor of New York, the Mayor, the City and State Comptrollers and three members appointed by the Governor. It was to be assisted by a Special Deputy State Comptroller. The Emergency Board's powers included the authority to approve a three year financial plan for the City from 1975 to 1978. To do so it was empowered "to estimate revenues and expenditures, to approve major contracts [including labor agreements] and all borrowing, and to extend (if necessary) the freeze on the number of City employees through fiscal year 1978, and to disburse City revenues only after it is satisfied that the expenditures are consistent with the Financial Plan" (Shalala and Bellamy, p. 1129). Although the Mayor was vested with the authority to decide spending priorities, it was clearly circumscribed by the Emergency Board's powers. In addition, the Control Board's authority extended to the City's "semi-independent" agencies, the public school system, higher education, hospitals and other services.

To finance this revolutionary change in the sovereignty of New York City, several drastic steps were taken to administer the finances of the City. First was the creation by the State of the Municipal Assistance Corporation for the City of New York (MAC) to convert the City's short term to long term debt by means of new bond issuance. MAC was upheld as constitutional by the courts. MAC's bonds were backed by a four percent City sales tax and a stock transfer tax, both heretofore paid to the City, marking another aspect of the change in the political process. The bonds also carried the "moral obligation" of the State of New York, reinforcing the Control Board's authority over major aspects of the City's finances. Major purchases of MAC and City bonds were committed by the City's five pension plans. Ironically, in this way, the unions which had contributed so substantially to the City's financial plight, were now to use some of the financial largesse to which the City could not say "no," to help rescue the City. Needless to say, the same unions claimed great civic virtue for this act. However, this claim is akin to a person, who after executing his parents, begs the court for mercy because he is an orphan!

The rescue plan also brought judicial intervention in the procedures, marking yet another departure from the processes of elected government. The State enacted special default legislation shielding the City from creditors for ninety days coupled with the filing of a financial plan for repayment with a state supreme court. The state court had to approve the plan, as would a federal court under Chapter 9 of federal law, thus injecting the unelected judiciary into the resolution of what is inherently executive and legislative domain. Federal intervention in local finance was also a part of the change in the governance of the City. The U.S. Congress enacted legislation which would enable the City to meet its seasonal financial needs. Under an agreement between the U.S., the City, the State and the Control Board, the Secretary of the Treasury was authorized to make short term loans to the City not to exceed $2.3 billion at any one time (Shalala and Bellamy, 1131).

A re-run of this situation faced New York City in 1991–92 and on this occasion the City again teeters on the edge of losing control of its finances to the Control Board. The 1991 example also revealed a shift in the City's personnel management to the Municipal Assistance Corporation. The Chairman, Felix Rohatyn, rejected the Mayor's proposed five year budget plan because the City's demand for $1 billion in MAC bonds as a substitute for a real estate tax increase would also substitute long term indebtedness to meet current expenditures. The MAC chairman criticized the City's five year plan because it did not grapple with a long term solution to its fiscal woes. To that end, he recommended that the City must cut personnel more deeply: "In the end, Mr. Rohatyn, the Mayor, the Governor and the State Financial Control Board which oversee the city's books and could impose binding powers on its spending if the budget fell out of balance, will have to thrash out their differences" (Purdum, Nov. 1991, p. 8). Thus, the Emergency Control Board has become an arbiter between the Municipal Assistance Corporation and the City. The device marks a step to shroud responsibility for fiscal responsibility and yet another step away from representative democracy. As King Louis XIV said, "Apres moi, le deluge." Or as another French expression has it, the more things change, the more they remain the same.

Of interest, too, are the unions' response to these unfolding developments in New York City. One leader commenting on the Mayor's plan to abandon a one-half billion dollar tax increase to meet the deficit said: "This effectively destroys the social programs we elected Dinkins to deliver" (*New York Times*, Sunday, Nov. 10, 1991, "News of the Week in Review," p. 8).

While New York City is the outstanding example of bankruptcy avoidance, through use of an alternative, the San Jose School District became the most significant example of bankruptcy among local government agencies over the past decade (Spiotto, 1991 and 1991a). In 1983 the School District was unable to meet its debt to telephone and water utilities for unpaid services, and unpaid wage increases to its employees. Most of its creditors were teachers, a situation arising out of promised salary increases which the District could not meet, especially after the State of California adopted Proposition 13. The School District did not challenge its obligation to pay bondholders. The reason it did not was to avoid the stigma of repudiation and undermine its future ability to borrow. Under the existing 1937 bankruptcy code, the School District could have gone into bankruptcy and the bondholders would have had to line up like all other creditors to receive any payment. Furthermore, 51% of the creditors would have to approve the move into Chapter 9. Once the move into Chapter 9 occurred, revenues dedicated to the payment of bondholders could have been allocated for any purpose, thereby changing bondholders into general creditors. Furthermore, like corporate bankruptcy, interest paid on the municipalities bonds could have been reclaimed within 90 days of the filing of bankruptcy (Mysak, Feb. 11, 1991,

p. 12). In 1988, the Bankruptcy code was amended to adopt the practice which the San Jose (and other bankrupt jurisdictions followed) to protect bondholders. In this manner, the credit worthiness of the jurisdiction is maintained. Moreover, unlike corporate bankruptcy creditors cannot put the municipality into bankruptcy, irrespective of the mismanagement of its financial affairs. Municipal bankruptcy is voluntary. In fact the municipality may not proceed without the authorization of the state government.

In the San Jose case, the bankruptcy plan was agreed under the terms of the Federal Bankruptcy Code and by a Federal Court. It secured the claims of the bondholders, as noted. However, the School District challenged its obligations to pay its nonbonded debts, in particular the claims of the School District's teachers. In the plan adjusting the non-bonded debt, the court ruled that the School District could reject the contracts it had previously signed with its employees and roll back wages. About a half year after the School District resolved its dispute with the teachers and other employees by an agreement to fund about 60% of the promised increases.

The San Jose case paralleled a Supreme Court ruling upholding contract rejection in the private sector (*NLRB v. Bildisco and Bildisco*, 465 US 513, 91984). As a result, "given the fact that labor obligations are among the most burdensome problems faced by municipalities, as evidenced by the San Jose School District bankruptcy," the Bankruptcy Court's power to void collective bargaining agreements became very attractive to local governments (Spiotto, 1991a, p. 21). However, also given the stiffer standards which must be applied in private sector bargaining agreements in the aftermath of the *Bildisco*, the option of voiding agreements in the public sector are probably also more difficult now than at the time of the San Jose case.

Another approach to municipal bankruptcy occurred in Scranton, Pennsylvania. Already in default, the city, the fifth largest in the State, petitioned the State for designation as a "distressed municipality." If approved, the State of Pennsylvania will appoint an administrator with power to dictate new labor agreements and reorganize city agencies. The root of the problem are an oversized municipal work force, high wages and an arbitration award to members of the fire fighters union (de Courcy Hinds, 1991, p. A18).

More is yet to be heard of the New Unionism and local government bankruptcies, such as in the case of the city of Bridgeport, Connecticut, but the underlying themes are clear. As James Spiotto, the leading authority on municipal bankruptcy said, "... labor obligations are among the most burdensome problems faced by municipalities" and in Bridgeport, the municipality's 14 union contracts accounted for 60% of the budget. In Philadelphia, another metropolis with severe fiscal woes, labor costs account for over half of its budget (Mysak, 1991, p. 12).

The New Unionism's, specifically the PED's, response to the Bridgeport insolvency was to call for federal legislation which would bar bankrupt municipalities from invalidating their collective bargaining agreements: "the PED supports enactment of legislation to assure protection to preserve existing collective bargaining agreements to protect public sector employees' wages and benefits, including pension funds and the contribution commitment by employers to those funds" (PED, *Adopted Resolutions*, Oct. 3–4, 1991 p. 18).

Coupled with its role which contributes, if not underlies completely, municipal insolvency, the New Unionism is an ardent opponent of a constitutional amendment requiring a federal balanced budget. A balanced budget is described as an "economic catastrophe" which would also "undermine the decision-making process of Congress" (PED, *Forum*, Spring, 1992, p. 3). The PED announced its opposition in conjunction with other groups "concerned about domestic programs." It identified as political allies such groups as seniors, parents, child welfare, civil rights and health care advocates, all "working to defeat the legislation." The core of the New Unionism's opposition are jobs. Although not providing a figure of the total loss in nonfarm jobs (which would include public sector jobs), the PED reported estimates ranging from over 220 thousand in Texas to one thousand jobs in Montana and Delaware. Offsetting increases in employment by permitting individuals to spend rather than government were not offered by the PED (PED, 1992, p. 3).

Congressional "flexibility" to respond to changing social and economic need would be curtailed, the PED announced. It called for sharp reductions in defense spending and the re-allocation of those funds "to viable conversion programs, education, health care, infrastructure and gradual deficit reduction."

It is evident that collective bargaining does diminish and redistribute sovereignty through its impact on local government insolvency. This is one of the major consequences of social unionism. By shifting authority to control boards, courts and administrators, collective bargaining in the public sector has "will nilly" fostered a new authority which will take over bargaining from elected public officials. Paradoxically, the New Unionism and public sector bargaining have engendered limitations on their power and on convergence: Governmental bankruptcy has become a surrogate for market forces as a check to the New Unionism and the New Industrial Relations system.

Comparable Worth

Social unionism has generated a new concept of wage payment, comparable worth, conspicuously absent (or nearly so) in the private labor market, organized and unorganized, at least as yet. Comparable worth means that diverse occupations having the same "worth" in job evaluation will receive the same wage. Considerations of demand and supply are set aside by the procedures of job evaluation. Comparable worth represents not only a comparative advantages of the public over the private system of organized industrial relations (Chapter III), but also a major threat to market and collective bargained wage determination in the private sector. In effect, it is also another issue which divides the New from the Old Unionism and puts them at odds.

It is no accident that comparable worth emerged in the public, the socialized sector of the economy. Comparable worth is a prime example of the application of Fairness in the New Society. Like entitlements, it, too, echoes medieval times, the practice of the "just wage." In the middle ages, wage rates were set by ecclesiastical authorities according to the doctrine of what was "just," the then current form of societal regulation in quest of Fairness.

Comparable worth in the public labor market is analogous to the goal of the Old Unionism to "take wages out of competition" in the private labor market. In attempting the goal of taking wages out of competition, a non-sense idea, given that wages and salaries comprise over 4/5ths of the national income, some theorists worried that the monopoly power of the Old Unionism would pose unresolvable problems for capitalism: "Unionism is destroying the competitive price system ... [i]t sabotages the competitive order, not because of work stoppages but because it cannot produce high output and employment at union wage rates" (Lindbloom, pp. 4, 5). While the monopoly power of unions to raise wages is a theoretical and empirical fact, Lindbloom's gloomy assessment overlooked the long-run power of markets to undermine the short term effect of unions on wages and output in the private sector. The union effect on wages is important, but exaggerated (Friedman, 1951).

Are matters different in the public labor market? Extensive immunity to competition may enable the New Unionism to convert the short into long-run effects which preserve advantages in compensation. According to many empirical studies, the union impact on wages in the public sector is smaller than in the private sector. However, I agree with Richard Freeman that these studies have probably understated the true measure of the New Unionism's impact (Freeman, 1986). One insight into that issue are the findings on the comparable cost of privatized and publicly furnished services. These have demonstrated that public production ranges from 10% to 40% above comparable private production (*New York Times*, Sunday, July 7, 1991, p. 1). Since the public sector is labor intensive, it seems unlikely that the wage studies concluding that the New Unionism raises wages less than the Old have captured all or the right variables. To reiterate Lindbloom's description of the Old Unionism, a description which is really more applicable to the New Unionism of our time: "Little wonder that it is rarely perceived that unionism in the United States now is as revolutionary in consequence as it is conservative in intention" (p. 20).

CHAPTER VI.

Conclusions

Just 30 years ago President Kennedy released the genie of the New Unionism. Instead of being merely an extension of unionism into the public labor market, that development marked a break in the historical record of labor organization. Instead of exemplifying a new spurt in labor organization, the New Unionism constitutes something new in the labor market. It is, in fact, a new labor movement. It differed from the Old Unionism of the private labor market in its origins, make-up and most importantly its goals, its philosophy.

Labor markets and ideas also underwent a structural break. Almost a decade prior the emergence of the New Unionism, the labor market switched from a goods to a service dominated labor market. Part of that transformation was the increase in public employment, a growth which facilitated the unfolding New Unionism. Today, public employment exceeds employment of manufacturing.

The ideological change was the emergence of the New Socialism. The New Socialism is pragmatic, has no pre-determined logic or ideologues and is not explicitly acknowledged by the New Unionism. It is not the socialism of the proletariat, but of the middle class. Under the precepts of the New Socialism an increasing share of the national income is to be spent by government. Ownership of the means of production, the discredited and failed core of the Old Socialism has been displaced by increased public ownership of the income produced by the factors of production. Currently, government spends close to 45% of the national income. The New Socialism is more durable than the Old and has steadily revolutionized society and the economy, and without a rush to the barricades.

The New Unionism is part and parcel of the New Socialism. Together they are essential ingredients of the New Society. The New Unionism is incapable of bringing about the New Society, but is an active partner with political allies, notably the Democratic Party, in socializing (redistributing) income.

The future of the New Unionism seems assured. Its record of expansion since the 1960s has been an almost uninterrupted one of expansion in membership and market share. The New Unionism is virtually exempt from the rigors of competition, in contrast to the Old. As a result, while the New has flourished, the Old has waned. Moreover, this disparate record is characteristic of most advanced industrial countries.

Currently, the New Unionism is larger than the CIO ever was and exceeded the membership of the old AFL throughout most years of its years. Moreover, like the social and economic revolution of which it is a part, it achieved its present status with little opposition from its public employer; indeed, it received active support from its political employers. As history moves into the next century, it is evident that early in the 21st century, the New Unionism will become the center of union power in this country, as it already has in Canada, Britain, France and other countries.

Since the inception of the New Unionism it has steadfastly worked to forge a new system of industrial relations. Much has already been achieved in the fulfillment of that goal, a goal which I have called convergence. To the New Unionism, convergence means full rights of collective bargaining, that is, the removal of most if not all limitations on bargaining matters and strikes. This would establish a system virtually indistinguishable from that in which the Old Unionism functions.

The most significant advance toward convergence has been the curtailment of sovereignty, most dramatically at the local level of government. Municipal insolvencies have dramatized the power of the New Unionism to diminish sovereignty in the fiscal domain. The New Unionism has also altered representative democracy, again most effectively at the local level, notably in education.

The most important step which would bring about convergence in the industrial relations systems would be the enactment of a federal law which would "nationalize" labor relations in the public labor market. The constitutional feasibility of such legislation has been present since 1985 under the Supreme Court's decision in *Garcia*. Election of a Democratic president and Congress could bring this into the reach of the New Unionism.

Under the impact of changes in ideology, labor markets and the intensification of world competition, the philosophy of the Old Unionism underwent change, but is in conflict with the philosophy of the New.

From one of simply "more," that is a redistribution of income within the private economy, from employers to organized workers, the Old Unionism has added a philosophy of what I call neo-mercantilism. Neo-mercantilism traces its theoretical origins to Keynesian economics and its empiricism to the New Deal. It demands active government intervention in the economy to maintain high levels of employment. Its most recent policy addition is an industrial policy, protectionism in foreign trade.

While the Old Unionism favors government intervention to stimulate the economy, it opposes the socialization of income. It opposes the policies of the New Unionism to redistribute income from the private to the public economy. The New Unionism has yet to see a tax it doesn't like.

The application of the philosophy of the New Unionism fulfills expectations which social engineers once held out for the Old Unionism. While the Old Unionism fell by the way-side as a vital ingredient of the New Society dreamed of by the Old Socialists, the New Unionism, together with is political allies, has already achieved a substantial measure of success in erecting a New Society.

References

Aaron, Benjamin. "The Future of Collective Bargaining in the Public Sector," in B. Aaron, J.M. Najita, and J.L. Stern, *Public Sector Bargaining* (Bureau of National Affairs: Washington, DC: 2d Ed., 1988).

Abood v. Detroit Board of Education, 431 *U.S.* 209, 1977.

AFL-CIO. "The Changing Situation of Workers and Their Unions," *A Report by the AFL-CIO Committee on the Evolution of Work*, Feb. 1983.

Ashenfelter, Orley. "The Effect of Unionization on Wages in the Public Sector: The Case of Fire Fighters," *Industrial and Labor Relations Review*, Vol. 24, No. 2, January 1971.

Bain, George S. and Robert Price. *Profiles of Union Growth, A Comparative Statistical Portrait of Eight Countries*, (Oxford: Basil Blackwell, 1980).

Barro, Robert J. "Let's Play Monopoly," *Wall Street Journal*, Tues., Aug. 17, 1991.

Battista, Andrew. "Labor, Politics, and Public Policy: A Discussion," *Proceedings of the 1991 Spring Meeting*, Industrial Relations Research Association, Aug. 25–27, 1991.

Birnbaum, Jeffrey H. "Congressional Democrats Choose Tax Fairness, Health Care as Issues on Which to Make a Stand, *Wall Street Journal*, July 31, 1991.

Bleiberg, Robert M. "Socialists, Get Lost: Privatization Has Triumphed Nearly Everywhere in the World," *Barron's*, Oct. 14, 1991

Brown, Henry Phelps, "The Counter Revolution of Our Time," *Industrial Relations*, Vol 29, No. 1 (Winter 1990).

Bureau of Census. "Labor-Management Relations in States and Local Governments," *1982 Census of Governments*, Vol.3, No. 3.

———. 1987 Census of Government. Public Employment. Number 2. *Compendium of Public Employment*, Vol. 2. GC87(3)–2.

———. 1987 Census of Government. Public Employment. Number 3. *Labor-Management Relations*, GC87(3)–3.

Bureau of National Affairs. *Public Sector Overtime Pay: The Impact of 'Garcia' On State & Local Governments*, A BNA Special Report, GERR NO. 1117–Part II.

Burton, John. "Public Sector Unions in Britain and the United States," *Government Union Review*, Special Edition, 1982.

Burton, John and Thomason, Terry. "The Extent of Collective Bargaining in the Public Sector," in B. Aaron, J.M. Najita, and J.L. Stern, *Public Sector Bargaining* (Bureau of National Affairs: Washington, DC: 2d Ed., 1988).

Canadian Auto Workers. "Statement of Principles," Undated broadsheet.

Carroll, Mollie Ray. *Labor and Politics*, (Boston and New York: The Riverside Press, 1923).

Carey, Max L and James C. Franklin, "Industry Output, Job Growth Slowdown Continues," *Monthly Labor Review*, Vol. 114, No. ii, Nov. 1991.

Cohen, Sanford. "Does Public Employee Unionism Diminish Democracy?" *Industrial and Labor Relations Review*, Vol 32, NO. 2, Jan. 1979.

Cook, James, "Collision Course," *Forbes*, May 13, 1991.

Commons, John R. *The History of Labour in the United States*, (New York: MacMillan, 1946), Vol I.

———. *Labor and Administration*, "Unions of Public Employees," and "Labor and Municipal Politics," (New York: Macmillan, 1913).

Crovitz, Gordon L., "Stretching the Davis-Bacon," *Barron's*, April 15, 1991.

de Courcy Hinds, Michael. "Short of Cash, Scranton Is Reorganizing," *New York Times*, Thursday, Dec. 26, 1991.

Derber, Milton. "Management Organization for Collective Bargaining in the Public Sector," in B. Aaron, J.M. Najita, and J.L. Stern, *Public Sector Bargaining* (Bureau of National Affairs: Washington, DC: 2d Ed., 1988).

Donovan, Raymond J. Secretary of Labor, Appellant v. San Antonio Metropolitan Transit Authority, et al., No. 82–1951 *Brief For The Secretary Of Labor*, In the Supreme Court of the United States, October Term, 1983.

Duncan, Greg J. and Frank P. Stafford. "Do Union Members Receive Compensating Wage Differentials?" *American Economic Review*, June 1980; and "Do Union Members Receive Compensating Wage Differentials? Reply," *American Economic Review*, Sept. 1982.

Dunlop, John T. "The Development of Labor Organization," in Richard A. Lester and Joseph Shister, eds., *Insight into Labor Issues*, (New York: Macmillan, 1948).

———. "Past and Future Tendencies in American Labor Organizations," *Daedalus*, Vol. 1, Winter 1978.

———. "Structural Changes in the American Labor Movement," in *Labor and Trade Unionism: An Interdisciplinary Reader*, (New York: Wiley, 1960).

Ellis, Lisa. "Unions' Long-Term Rivalry Boils Over," *Philadelphia Inquirer*, Sept. 15, 1991.

Ehrenberg, Ronald G. "Municipal Government Structure, Unionization, and the Wages of Fire Fighters," *Industrial and Labor Relations Review*, Vol. 27, No. 1, October 1973.

European Trade Union Institute, *Privatisation in Western Europe*, Brussels, April 1988.

Ferner, Anthony and Trevor Collins. "Privatization, Regulation and Industrial Relations," *British Journal of Industrial Relations*, Vol. 29, No. 3, Sept. 1991.

Freeman, Richard B. "Unionism Comes to the Public Sector," *Journal of Economic Literature*, Vol. 24, No. 1, 1986.

———. "American Public Employment," in Clark Kerr and Paul D. Staudohar, Eds., *Industrial Relations in a New Age*, (San Francisco: 1986).

Freeman, Richard B. and Casey Ichniowski, eds. *When Public Sector Workers Unionize*, (National Bureau of Economic Research; Univ. of Chicago Press, 1988)

Freeman, Richard B. and James L. Medoff. *What Do Unions Do?* (New York: Basic Books, 1984).

Friedman, Milton. "Some Comments on the Significance of Labor Unions for Economic Policy," in David McCord Wright, ed., *The Impact of the Union*, (New York: 1951).

———. "We Have Socialism, Q.E.D.," *New York Times*, Sunday, Dec. 31, 1989, p. E. 11.

Friedman, Milton and Schwartz, *A Monetary History of the United States, 1867–1960*, (National Bureau of Economic Research, Princeton Univ. Press, Princeton: 1963).

Friedman, Milton and Rose. *Free to Choose*, (New York: Harcourt, 1980).

Fuchs, Victor. *The Service Economy*, New York: National Bureau of Economic Research, 1968.

Geisert, Gene. "The Impact of Collective Bargaining: The Effect on Curriculum," *Government Union Review*, Winter 1984.

Gompers, Samuel. *Labor and the Common Welfare*, (New York: E.P. Dutton, 1919), compiled and edited by Hayes Robbins.

Heckscher, Charles C. *The New Unionism: Employee Involvement in the Changing Corporation*, Twentieth Century Fund, (New York: Basic Books, 1988.

Henle, Peter. "A Chronicle of Trade Union Positions on Government Ownership," *Monthly Labor Review*, July 1965.

Hines, Walker D. *War History of American Railroads* (New Haven: Yale Univ. Press, 1928).

Hirsch, Barry, T. *Labor Unions and the Economic Performance of Firms*, W.E. Upjohn Institute for Employment Research, Kalamazoo, MI 1991.

Ichniowski, Casey. "Economic Effects of the Firefighters' Union," *Industrial and Labor Relations Review*, Vol. 33, No. 2, Jan. 1980.

Kirkland, Lane. "Labor's Outlook – Building Strength," *The AFL-CIO American Federationist*, Vol 87, No. 3, March 1980.

Laski, Harold J. *Trade Unions in the New Society*, (New York: Viking, 1949).

Keddy, John. "Econometric Analyses of American Traded Union Growth: New Evidence, Mimeograph, April 1988.

Keynes, John Meynard. *The General Theory of Employment, Interest and Money*. (New York: Harcourt, 1935)

Kochan, Thomas A., Katz, Harry C. and McKersie, Robert B., *The Transformation of American Industrial Relations*, (New York: Basic Books, 1986).

Kovacs, Aranka E. "A Tentative Framework for the Philosophy of the Canadian Labour Movement," *Industrial Relations*, Vol. 20, No. 1, Jan. 1965.

Krislov, Joseph. "The Independent Public Employee Association," *Industrial and Labor Relations Review*, Vol. 15, July 1962.

Kristol, Irving. "Understanding Trade Unionism," *Wall Street Journal*, Monday,

Oct. 23, 1978).

———. "The Tragedy of Multiculturalism," *Wall Street Journal*, Wednesday, July 31, 1991.

Lindbloom, Charles. *Unions and Capitalism*, (New Haven: Yale University Press, 1949).

Lou Harris & Associates, "A Study on the Outlook For Trade Union Organizing," (New York: Louis Harris and Associates, Inc., Nov. 1984, mimeo.

Mantoux, Paul. *The Industrial Revolution in the Eighteenth Century*, (London: Jonathan Cape, 1961).

Meltzer, Bernard D. and Cass R. Sunstein. "Public Employee Strikes, Executive Discretion, and the Air Traffic Controllers," *University of Chicago Law Review*, Vol 50, No. 73.

Mills, Daniel Quinn. *Labor-Management Relations* (New York: McGraw-Hill, 1986, Third Edition).

Mitchell, Daniel J., "Bring Back Gramm-Rudman-It Worked," *Wall Street Journal*, Monday, Aug. 12, 1991.

Mitchell, Daniel J.B. "Collective Bargaining and Compensation in the Public Sector," in B. Aaron, J.M. Najita, and J.L. Stern, *Public Sector Bargaining* (Bureau of National Affairs: Washington, DC: 2d Ed., 1988).

Mysak, Joe. "Bridgeport or Bust?, *Barron's*, Feb. 11, 1991.

New York Times, "Unions Are Expanding Their Role to Survive in the 90's," Sunday, Aug. 19, 1990, Business Section, p. 19.

Neumann, George R., and Rissman, Ellen R. "Where Have All the Union Members Gone?" *Journal of Labor Economics*, Vol 2, No. 2, April 1984, pp 175–192.

Novak, Michael, "Socialism's Last Stand," *Forbes*, Oct. 28, 1991.

Olson, "Dispute Resolution in the Public Sector," in B. Aaron, J.M. Najita, and J.L. Stern, *Public Sector Bargaining* (Bureau of National Affairs: Washington, DC: 2d Ed., 1988).

Perlman, Selig. "The Cigar Makers," in *The History of Labour in the United States*, Vol II, (New York: Augustus Kelley, 1966).

Polanyi, Karl. *The Great Transformation*, (Boston: Beacon Press, 1971).

Public Employees Department, AFL-CIO (PED). *Privatization Update*, Spring 1992.

———. Reinvigorating The Public Service: Union Innovations To Improve Government, *March 1992*.

———. *Forum*, Vol. No. 2, Spring 1992.

———. *Issues and Answers*, March 1991.

———. "Adopted Resolutions," PED Constitutional Convention, Oct. 3–4, 1991.

Pound, Roscoe. *Labor Unions And The Concept of Public Service*, American Enterprise Association, (Washington, D.C.: 1959).

Purdum, Todd S. "Dinkins Has a 5-Year Plan: Critics Say It Doesn't Add Up," *News of The Week in Review, New York Times*, Sunday, Nov. 10, 1991.

Reason Foundation. *Privatization 1991*, Fifth Annual Report on Privatization, (Santa Monica, CA, 1991).

Shalala, Donna E. and Carrol Bellamy, "A State Saves a City: The New York Case," *Duke Law Journal*, Vol. 1976.

Sheflin, Neil. "Transition Function Estimation of Structural Shifts in Models of American Trade Union Growth," *Applied Economics*, Vol. 16, Feb. 1984.

Sheflin, Neil, Leo Troy and C. Timothy Koeller. "Structural Change in Models of American Trade Union Growth, *Quarterly Journal of Economics*, Vol. 96, No. 1, Feb. 1981.

Shister, Joseph. "The Direction of Unionism 1947–1967: Thrust Or Drift?" *Industrial and Labor Relations Review*, 1966.

Slichter, Sumner. *Trade Unions in a Free Society*, (Cambridge: Harvard Univ., 1948 Press).

Spero, Sterling D. *Government as Employer*, (Carbondale and Edwardsville: Southern Illinois Press, 1972).

Spiotto, James E. *Chapter 13*, "Municipal Insolvency: Bankruptcy, Receivership, Workouts and Alternative Remedies," from a Manuscript, 1991.

———. "Strategies For Communities In Crisis: Is There Life After A Budget Deficit?" Paper prepared for the Government Finance Officers' Association, June 3, 1991 (a).

Steiber, Jack. *Public Employee Unionism: Structure, Growth, Policy*, (Washington, DC., Brookings Institution, 1973).

Stern, James L. "Unionism in the Public Sector," in B. Aaron, J.M. Najita, and J.L. Stern, *Public Sector Bargaining* (Bureau of National Affairs: Washington, DC: 2d Ed., 1988).

Summers, Robert S. *Collective Bargaining and Public Benefit Conferral: A Jurisprudential Critique*, (Ithaca: New York Institute of Public Employment, N.Y. State School of Industrial and Labor Relations, 1976).

Taft, Philip. "Labor History and the Labor Issues of Today," in the *Proceedings of the American Philosophical Society*, Vol. 106, No. 4, Aug. 1962.

———. *The A.F. of L. in the Time of Gompers*, (New York: Harpers, 1957).

Taylor, Philip E., *The Economics of Public Finance*, (Macmillan, Third Ed., 1961).

Troy, Leo. "Market Forces and Union Decline: A Response to Paul Weiler," *The University of Chicago Law Review*, Vol. 59, No. 2, Spring 1992.

Troy, Leo. "Can Canada's Labor Policies Be A Model For the U.S?" Paper presented at the annual meeting of the Canadian Industrial Relations Association, June 1991 (a).

——. "Convergence in International Unionism Et Cetera: The Case of Canada and the U.S.," Queen's University, School of Industrial Relations, Working Paper, 1991 (b); forthcoming in the *British Journal of Industrial Relations*, March, 1992.

——. "Is the U.S. Unique in the Decline of Private Sector Unionism," *Journal of Labor Research*, Vol. XI, No.2 Spring 1990 (a).

——. (b) "Will A More Interventionist NLRA Revive Organized Labor?" *Harvard Law School Journal of Law and Public Policy*, 1990.

——. "Public Sector Unionism: The Rising Power Center of Organized Labor," *Government Union Review, Summer, 1988.*

——. "State and Local Government Employee Relations After Garcia," *Government Union Review*, Summer 1986.

——. "The Convergence of Public and Private Sector Industrial Relations Systems in the United States," *Government Union Review*, Summer 1984.

——. "The Impact of Public Employee Unionism on the Philosophy and Policies of Organized Labor," *Government Union Review*, Spring 1982.

Troy, Leo and Sheflin, Neil. *Union Sourcebook Membership, Structure, Finance, Directory* (West Orange: Industrial Relations Data and Information Services, Aug. 1985).

Tyler, Gus. "A New Philosophy For Labor," The Fund for the Republic, New York, 1959.

U.S. Department of Commerce, Bureau of Census, *Historical Statistics of the United States*, Colonial Times to 1970, Bicentennial Edition, Sept. 1975.

U.S. Department of Labor, *Employment and Earnings*, Jan. 1992.

U.S. President. *Economic Report of the President*, (Feb. 1990).

Ullman, Joseph C. and James P. Begin. "The Structure and Scope of Appeals Procedures For Public Employees," *Industrial and Labor Relations Review*, Oct. 1977.

Von Mises, Ludwig. *Socialism*, (New Haven: Yale Univ. Press, 1951).

Visser, Jelle. "Trends in Trade Union Membership," OECD, *Employment Outlook 1991*, Chapter 4, July 1991.

Walsh, Edward. "White Paper: Organized Labor," *Government Union Review*, Fall, 1985.

Webb, Sidney and Beatrice. *The History of Trade Unionism*, (London: Longmans 1950).

——. *Industrial Democracy* (London: Longmans, Green & Co., 1920).

Weiler, Paul C. *Governing The Workplace: The Future of Labor and Employment*, (Cambridge: Harvard Univ Press, 1990).

Wellington Henry H. and Ralph K. Winter. "The Limits of Collective Bargaining in the Public Sector," *Yale Law Journal*, Vol 78, NO. 7 June 1969.

——. *The Unions and the Cities*, (Washington: DC, Brookings Institution, 1972).

Westbrook, James E. "The Use of the Nondelegation Doctrine in Public Sector Labor Law: Lessons From Cases That Have Perpetuated An Anachronism," *St.Louis University Law Journal*, Vol 30, March 1986.

Whalen, Christopher. "Unholy Alliance: Global Bureaucrats Must Break the Socialist Ties That Bind," *Barron's*, July 22, 1991.

Wildman, Wesley A. "Teachers and Collective Negotiations," in Albert A. Blum, ed., *White Collar Workers*, (New York: Random House, 1971).

Williams, C. Brian, *Canadian Trade Union Philosophy: The Philosophy of the English Speaking Trade Union Movement, 1935–1967*, Draft Study prepared for the Task Force on Labor Relations (Privy Council), Project No. 18, July 1969.

Wolman, Leo. *Ebb and Flow in Trade Unionism*, (New York: National Bureau of Economic Research, 1936).

Zax, Jeffrey S. and Casey Ichniowski. "Bargaining Laws and Unionization in the Local Public Sector," *Industrial and Labor Relations Review*, Vol 43, No. 4, April, 1990.

Ziskind, David. *One Thousand Strikes of Government Employees*, (New York: Columbia Univ. Press, 1949).

APPENDIX A

State and Local Government Employee Relations After Garcia

I. Federalism and State and Local Government Employee Relations

The Supreme Court's decision in *Garcia v. San Antonio Metropolitan Transit Authority, et al*[1] in 1985 over-ruled the decision which had been acclaimed as a watershed in the federal-state relationship, *National League of Cities v. Usery*, 1976.[2] By apposite reasoning, *Garcia* was one of the most important decisions in recent years of the Supreme Court bearing on public sector labor relations and therefore on the future of the New Unionism.

A less dramatic view of the importance of these cases has been put forward by the Advisory Commission on Intergovernmental Relations, among others. According to ACIR, "the dispute in *Garcia*, while carried on in the profound tones of Constitutional doctrine and grand political theory, is really quite minor [because] [t]he range of state actions amenable to protection under the *NLC* doctrine were very limited".[3] Of the limited range of such actions ACIR noted were issues of state employment. Given the size of state and local government employment and their payroll, it is puzzling as to why these issues should be regarded as "limited" or "narrow".

The hinge of *Garcia* is that the Supreme Court majority of five to four ruled that the Tenth Amendment did not preclude the application of the federal minimum wage and maximum hour law, the Fair Labor Standards Act of 1938, as amended, to employees of state and local governments. Although the case involved only employees of a publicly owned transit system, the decision applies to employees of state and local governments generally.

A decade earlier the *NLC*, or *Usery*, decision had apparently stemmed the tide of federal regulation and intrusion into state and local activities which began with the New Deal, nearly forty years earlier.

Garcia removed any restraints imposed by *National League* and reopened the opportunity for Congress to extend its governance of relations between state and local governments and their approximately 14 million employees. The future of employee relations at the state and local level of government is linked to the changing constitutional relations implied by *Garcia*. Clearly, the *Garcia* decision, should it stand future tests, will significantly affect the way state and local governments carry out their responsibilities and the burdens which taxpayers will shoulder.

The potential significance of public policy for labor organization in general is evident in the light of the declining position of organized labor. The significance for the New Unionism is paramount. Congressional implementation of *Garcia* will propel an already expanding union movement not only to greater heights, but to the leadership in the union movement as a whole.

The history of the rise of public sector unionism clearly demonstrates the vital importance of public policy encouraging organizing and bargaining. In the span of a relatively few years, from 1962 to 1976, a union movement much larger than the former Congress of Industrial Organizations was quickly established and with little cost to organized labor. Policies favorable to organization and bargaining were adopted by the federal government and by many state and local authorities. Were Congress to enact and apply a comparable and uniform policy to state and local governments, unionization and collective bargaining would receive its most substantial boost from public policy. Given the higher level of existing unionization in the public labor – about four times that in the private sector – coupled with a favorable labor relations policy uniformly applicable to state and local governments, the potential of the *Garcia* decision to the future of organized labor cannot be easily exaggerated.

II.　Summary of Legislative Background of Garcia.

The central question in *Garcia* was whether a publicly owned and operated mass transit system was subject to the Fair Labor Standards Act of 1938, the federal minimum wage and maximum hour law? The FLSA requires employers to pay their employees the statutory minimum hourly wage and to pay them time and one-half for hours worked in excess of 40 hours during the work week.

States and their political subdivisions were exempted from the original provisions of the Act. However, in 1966, Congress extended coverage of the Act to include most employees of hospitals, institutions and schools operated by states and their subdivisions, irrespective of whether these were operated for profit.[4] Labor conditions in public schools and hospitals were deemed able to affect commerce and so were regulated. Congress defined the activities of public agencies as enterprises engaged in commerce or in the production of goods for commerce and thus within the ambit of the commerce clause of the Constitution and federal enactment.

Previously, in 1961, Congress had amended the FLSA to extend the coverage of the Act to enterprises instead of employees in the private sector; the extensions of 1966 embraced public enterprises within the scope of the minimum wage and maximum hour law. The enterprise concept takes into consideration the nature and size of an employer's business and extends to all employees including those performing only local duties, if the business is an enterprise engaged in commerce or in the production of goods for commerce. The constitution ality of the "enterprise" concept embracing publicly operated hospitals, schools and other institutions was sustained in *Maryland v. Wirtz*.[5] In *Wirtz*, the Supreme Court affirmed that Congress had the authority to regulate intrastate commerce which substantially affects interstate commerce, as long as Congress has a rational basis for subjecting a particular activity to its authority and uses means reasonably related to its goals. As Justice Harlan put it, if Congress has "a rational basis for finding a chosen regulatory scheme necessary to the protection of commerce, our investigation is an end".[6]

Congress justified its interference with state functions on the ground that it only subjects a state to the same minimum wage and overtime pay requirements applicable to other employers whose activities affect commerce. When states engages in the kind of economic activity Congress regulates in the private sector, Congress asserted that it had the constitutional right to compel states to conform to federal regulation.

Specifically apropos *Garcia*, the 1966 amendments to the FLSA also included all transit employees, excepting operating employees (drivers, operators and conductors), of all transit companies engaged in commerce whether publicly or privately owned, so long as the enterprise was subject to state or local regulation. In *Wirtz*, Maryland did not challenge the public transit employees provisions of the 1966 amendments to the FLSA and the Supreme Court did not consider its validity in upholding the application of the amended FLSA to the states and their political subdivisions.

Eight years later, in 1974, Congress further extended the coverage of the FLSA, on this occasion broadening its coverage to virtually all state and local public agencies and their employees, and it included a schedule for phasing out the special exclusion from overtime coverage of the operating personnel of the transit systems previously excluded under the amendments of 1966.

III. The Tenth Amendment Resurrected.

Enter now the *National League of Cities v. Usery*.[7] In 1976, the National League of Cities and others challenged the constitutionality of the newly amended FLSA and on this occasion a somewhat revamped Supreme Court held that the Congress' extension of the FLSA to the states and their subdivisions was unconstitutional and in a 5 to 4 vote reversed *Wirtz*. More important, *National League* – at least at this point – appeared to have arrested forty years of encroachment of the federal commerce clause of the Constitution over areas traditionally regulated by the states. In effect, the Court resurrected the Tenth Amendment to reassert the existence of some state sovereignty and dual federalism which had decayed so extensively since the Court upheld the constitutionality of the National Labor Relations Act in 1937.[8] As one critic of *National League* put it, "proponents maintained that the role of the states in our federal system requires a recognition of states' rights to autonomy beyond rights granted individuals and businesses, and that indeed a mistake of the last forty years had been the blurring of the line between federal regulation of states and of individuals".[9]

The Court declared that Congress had affirmative limits, in this case, the Tenth Amendment, which barred an otherwise permissible extension of the commerce clause. Further, the Court distinguished between Congressional regulation of private individuals and business (the private sector) and the regulation of states *qua* states, that is, as "sovereign" entities. And, then finding that the states' power to determine employee compensation was an "undoubted attribute" of state sovereignty, the Court declared that compliance with the amended FLSA would "operate to directly displace the States' freedom to structure integral operations in areas of traditional governmental functions[10] it recognized a domain for the exercise of state sovereignty which would be resistant to an expansive federal authority. Necessarily, the ruling and its explication also became central to the *Garcia* decision and are essential to evaluating that decision's potential impact on future relations between state and local governments and their employees.

There were four decisions intervening between *National League* and *Garcia* in which the applicability of *National League* was the central issue. In all four, the decisions nibbled away at the content of state sovereignty: "During its short life, the *National League of Cities* doctrine seemed more symbol than substance".[11] The last two foreshadowed the demise of *National League*. Two dealt directly with matters involving employee relations; two did not.

In its reviewing process the Court evolved four standards from its *National League* decision to evaluate the areas of state activity which might be shielded from the sweep of the commerce clause under the revived federalism so I shall recapitulate each of them.

The standards devised to evaluate exempt and nonexempt areas of state activity under the Tenth Amendment were, first, that the challenged statute regulates states as states. Second, the federal legislation must address matters that are indisputably attributes of state sovereignty. Third, that it must be apparent that compliance with the federal law would directly impair states' ability to structure integral operations in areas of traditional governmental functions.[12] In order for a challenge to a Congressional exercise of its application of the commerce power to states to succeed, all three had to be met. Even so, the challenge based on the Tenth Amendment could fail because the nature of the federal interest may outweigh the states' and so require state submission. This, the fourth standard, stemmed from Justice Blackmun's concurring decision in *NLC* and was re-stated in *Hodel*, thus posited a balancing of interests such that there may be situations in which the federal interests must over-ride those of states justifying state submission to federal authority. In her dissenting opinion in *Garcia*, Justice O'Connor elaborated on the meaning of the balancing of interests. She wrote that in determining whether an asserted federal interest justifies state submission, the Court must consider "not only the weight of the asserted federal interest", but also " the necessity of vindicating [it] in a manner that intrudes upon state authority."[13]

In the first of the quartet of cases between *NLC* and *Garcia*, *Hodel*, in 1981, the issue was whether the Surface Mining and Reclamation Act of 1977, as amended, regulating private mining operators violated the Tenth Amendment. The Court unanimously ruled in this case that the Surface Mining and Reclamation Act of 1977 as amended, touched individual businesses not states as states. Therefore the standards of the *NLC* decision did not apply here. Instead, the Court found that the Act created a program of 'cooperative federalism' which did not compel states to enforce federal standards, spend state funds, or to join a federal program.[14] For the challenge to have succeeded, the Court stated it had to meet all three standards set forth in *NLC*, which it failed to do. Hence, in this case the Court found no Tenth Amendment obstacle, so that in principle, the revived dual federalism re-established under *NLC* apparently remained intact. But did it?

In characterizing the Surface Mining and Reclamation Act as a program of 'cooperative federalism' the Court covered the *NLC* with what some have termed a "fig leaf", meaning that it hid the absence of any real content to the Tenth Amendment.[15]

One year after *Hodel*, in 1982, in *United Transportation Union v. Long Island Railroad Company*, the Supreme Court applied its standards and again unanimously ruled that Congress had not exceeded its authority. The case had arisen from a breakdown in negotiations between the State of New York and its commuter railway employees on the Long Island Railroad and the attempt of the state to apply state law barring strikes by public employees. In weighing the balance between federal and state interests, the federal interests prevailed because of the long standing federal regulation of the railways.

In this instance, the Court found that the operation of the Long Island Railroad by the State of New York was not an integral part of traditional state functions and therefore was not covered by the standards of *NLC*. Although the Court said it did not intend to impose a static historical concept of state functions, it noted that the railway system in this country had been subject to pervasive federal regulation under the Interstate Commerce Act for nearly a century and that the State of New York could not be unaware of this when it acquired the Long Island. The Court indicated that this uniform and long-standing regulation of the railways was essential to the transportation system and the national economy, which could be harmed by strikes, if federal law were inapplicable.[16] The fact that the commuter line had passed from private to public control did not change the historical reality that the operation of railways was not among the traditional functions of state and local governments. (Indeed, under *NLC* the Court had already stated that railways were excluded from the list of traditional governmental functions[17]). To permit states to acquire private property and then seek exemption from federal regulation on the basis of the Tenth Amendment would erode federal system as surely as federal usurpation of state authority, the Court noted. Thus the Court found that federal regulation of state-owned railways did not impair a state's ability to function as a state. Therefore, the case failed to pass the third standard the Court had laid down under *NLC*, whether states' compliance with federal law would directly impair their ability to structure integral operations in areas of traditional functions.

In the third of the "progeny" of *National League*, the *Federal Energy Regulatory Commission v. Mississippi*, the Court divided 5 to 4, with the four dissenters in *NLC* now joined by Justice Blackmun, to create a new majority which continued through to *Garcia* and the final overthrow of *NLC* by *Garcia*.

In *FERC*, the issue was whether the Public Utility Regulatory Policies Act (PURPA) of 1978, which regulated state public utilities, violated the Tenth Amendment under the rules prescribed by *National League*. PURPA would require state public utility commissions to implement federal goals, to "consider" the use of six different rate designs, adopt standards relating to the terms and conditions of service, and to promulgate "lifeline rates" for service which would meet essential needs of consumers. The state agencies could reject the federal proposals after public hearings, but were required to submit a written account setting forth the reasons for their rejection.

In this case the federal legislation's use of state regulatory bodies to further federal goals was a novel aspect of Tenth Amendment issue apparently not faced hitherto by the Court. The Court majority approached this novel issue by reviewing the legislation under the congressional power of preemption (Article VI of the Constitution), rather than applying the criteria developed under *NLC* and *Hodel*. It concluded that preemption of state regulation was permissible under the traditional concept of federal preemption. It saw no additional burden imposed on state regulatory bodies, since they would have been enforcing state rules similar to those prescribed by the federal legislation. Thus, the Court stated that "each State regulatory authority shall, after notice and opportunity for public hearing, implement such [federal] rule (or revised rule) for each electric utility for which it has rate making authority,"[18] and concluded that such procedures were the customary activities performed by the Mississippi Public Service Commission. On the other hand, the Court opined, if states were permitted to avoid enforcement of the federally established rules, avoidance would defeat the preemption doctrine.

When it reviewed the provision of the statute requiring **mandatory** consideration by state regulatory bodies of federal standards, the Court majority acknowledged that their authority to make decisions was perhaps the "quintessential" aspect of state sovereignty. However, it circumvented the issue by pointing out that Congress could have completely preempted the authority to regulate utilities, at least insofar as private rather than state activity was concerned, and that out of deference to state authority, PURPA permits the states to continue regulating, provided only that they only consider suggested federal standards. There was nothing in PURPA compelling the states to enact a legislative program. States had the choice of either abandoning regulation altogether or meeting the requirements in considering federal standards. In effect, the Court majority argued that PURPA extended the 'cooperative federalism' enunciated in *Hodel* which allows states, within limits set by federal standards, to legislate and administer programs which meet their own needs. Likewise the majority found that the procedural requirements imposed on the state regulatory bodies did not compel the exercise of the State of Mississippi's sovereign powers.

In *FERC* the Court majority added yet another case in which the apparent revived federalism in *NLC* did not apply, but it did not yet attack the revival head-on. Indeed, it evaluated the issue raised in terms of the standards emanating from *NLC*. However, Justice Powell, one of the dissenters wrote that the pre-emption of federal over state authority upheld by the majority in this case could enable Congress to "reduce the States to federal provinces," and that the procedural provisions of the Act violated a state's sovereignty as guaranteed by the Tenth Amendment.[19]

Justice O'Connor in her dissent asserted that the majority decision in this case would conscript the state utility commissions into the national bureaucratic army and violated the principles laid down in *NLC*. Applying the first three principles laid down in *Hodel*, she concluded first, that PURPA regulated the states as states, noting that the Act addresses its commands to the States even though its ultimate aim was the regulation of private utility companies. Second, Justice O'Connor concluded, the power to make decisions and set policy for state agencies, which the even the Court majority recognized as an attribute of state sovereignty, embraced more than the power to enact laws; that it also included the power to evaluate and decide which proposals are most worthy of consideration, the order in which they should be taken up, and the precise form in which they should be debated. PURPA, she declared, intruded on all these functions of sovereignty. Next (third), she pointed out, the Act directly impaired the states' ability to structure integral operations in publicly regulated utilities, an area of traditional government function. Utility regulation is a traditional function of state government and the regulatory commission, integral to the performance of that function, was burdened by PURPA. Federal requirements were so burdensome that they impaired state commissions ability do deal with local regulatory problems. Over-all, the majority decision, she wrote, was not only contrary to the principles of *NLC*, but to the values of federalism and inconsistent with constitutional history.

Equal Employment Opportunity Commission v. Wyoming[20] decided in 1983 was the fourth and final case preceding the momentous decision in *Garcia* in 1985. Of the quartet of cases between *National League* and *Garcia*, *EEOC v. Wyoming* has the closest bearing on employee relations.

Like its predecessor, *FERC*, *EEOC* was decided by a five to four majority. The issue in this case was whether the state of Wyoming, in mandating the retirement of a game warden at age 55, violated the Age Discrimination in Employment Act of 1967, as amended (ADEA)? Put another way, did Congress act constitutionally when it extended the definition of employer to include state and local governments? When the Act was originally adopted in 1967 it did not apply to the states, paralleling the history of the incremental extension of minimum wage and maximum hour law to eventually include state and local governments.

ADEA was amended in 1974 (as Section 28 of the FLSA amendments) in the wake of *Wirtz* to embrace the states. In its report on the legislation, the House of Representatives stated, "[t]he amendment is a logical extension of the committee's decision to extend FLSA coverage to Federal, State and Local government employees".[21]

ADEA makes it unlawful for an employer to discriminate against an employee or potential employee between the ages of 40 and 70 on the basis of age, except "where age is a bona fide qualification reasonably necessary to the normal operation of the particular business, or where the differentiation is based on reasonable factors of age".[22]

The Wyoming statute required that "[a]n employee may continue in service on a year-to year basis after age ... fifty five (55), with the approval of the employer and under conditions as the employer may prescribe." After a supervisor for the Wyoming Game and Fish Department was involuntarily retired at age 55 pursuant to the statute, he filed a complaint with the Equal Employment Opportunity Commission alleging a violation of the ADEA. The State of Wyoming responded by arguing that the ADEA challenged its sovereignty under the Tenth Amendment.[23]

In deciding the case the Court continued to apply the criteria of *NLC* and *Hodel* and applied the four standards to this case. It concluded that the State's challenge did not pass all four, a necessary requirement to succeed. Justice Brennan writing for the majority began by emphasizing that "the principle of immunity articulated in *National League of Cities* does not create 'a sacred province of state autonomy,' but instead is a 'functional doctrine' tailored to ensure that the unique benefits of a federal system in which the States enjoy a 'separate and independent existence' ... not be lost through undue federal interference in certain core state functions"[24] first criterion in that it regulated the States as States. It bypassed the second, whether an attribute of state sovereignty had been violated by the ADEA's prohibition discrimination by states based on age. The State had argued in its brief that the establishment of terms of employment for state employees was "indisputably" an attribute of state sovereignty.

The Court commented that matching the second criterion to the case posed significantly more difficulties, but determined that it did not have to consider the criterion because the Act did not impair Wyoming's ability to structure integral operations of traditional functions, the third leg in the test: "We conclude that the degree of federal intrusion in this case is sufficiently less serious than it was in *National League of Cities* so as to make it unnecessary for us to override Congress' express choice to extend its regulatory authority to the States".[25] In addition, the Court implied that the amended ADEA could prevail over the Wyoming's statute either under the balancing test or, for that matter, section five of the Fourteenth Amendment.

With respect to issue of possible discrimination based on age, Wyoming did not argue that arbitrarily discriminating against employees because of age was an attribute of state sovereignty. It denied "a prerogative to be arbitrary ... but rather, asserts a prerogative to exercise the same attributes of sovereignty that the United States exercises in matters of employment relations."[26] The State asserted that its law mandating the retirement at age 55 of full time game wardens who are full time law enforcement officers was reasonable. Further, the State pointed out that the state law's reasonableness was demonstrable by comparison with both the entire public employee retirement system in Wyoming and with the federal system.

Thus, the actuarial basis for the patrol/warden plan of retirement by age 55 provided for a contribution rate about double that for the general retirement system of public employees in Wyoming. Further, if the EEOC charge of discrimination prevailed it would construe and apply ADEA usurping the power of the state legislature to set reasonable qualifications for state employees and thus dilute if not strip states of their power to govern themselves. The issue simply put, was whether the legislature of Wyoming has the authority to set what it believed were appropriate employment standards for those it employs to carry out the duties the State has prescribed.[27] The Supreme Court answered, no.

As for comparison to federal law governing early retirement of federal law enforcement officers, Congress in 1974 enacted legislation which reduced the mandatory retirement age from 70 to 55 for virtually all federal enforcement officers and fire fighters. Moreover, like the Wyoming statute these employees could continue in employment with the approval of the employer. The justification Congress gave for the early retirement of these employees was also akin to that of Wyoming. Congress noted "that certain mental and physical capabilities may decline with age and in some jobs with unusually high demands, age may be considered a factor in hiring and retaining workers. For example, jobs such as some of those in air traffic control and in law enforcement and fire fighting have strict physical requirements on which the public safety depends."[28] In effect, the State of Wyoming asked no less for itself in setting employment standards for comparable type employees.

When it came to state finance, the Court majority also found no conclus ive evidence that compliance with ADEA would drain Wyoming's budget. While the most tangible consequential effect of federal intrusion identified in *NLC* was financial, the application of ADEA to the states would not have a direct or obvious effect on state finances, the Court concluded.[29] The financial reasoning went like this: Although older workers with seniority could be expected to earn more than younger workers and accrue increased benefits upon retirement, these costs could be offset by increased employee contributions to the pension fund coupled with smaller pension payouts because of actuarial experience.

A second effect identified in *NLC* would be impairment of the states' ability to use their employment policies to further social and economic goals. However, Wyoming claimed no such purpose and the Court ruled that even if such could be imagined for the Wyoming statute, it would not be outside the bounds indicated in *NLC.*[30]

Justice Stevens' concurrence with the Court majority went well beyond their findings. Instead of continuing to recognize the viability of *NLC* and the application of its standards on a case by case approach, he rejected *National League* outright, foreshadowing the approach which the majority would take in *Garcia*.

Justice Stevens reasoned that the main purpose of the Constitution was to solve commercial problems and that the Court had construed the commerce clause so as to give Congress the power to meet the needs of a changing economy. It was the intent of the Constitution as interpreted by the Court to give Congress the power needed under the Commerce Clause to discharge its central mission, meeting the needs of a dynamic and constantly expanding national economy.[31] **"Today", he wrote, "there should be universal agreement on the proposition that Congress has ample power to regulate the terms and conditions of employment throughout the economy."**[32] (Emphasis added).

As for the public sector labor market, Justice Stevens had this to say: **"Because of the interdependence of the segments of the economy and the importance and magnitude of government employment, a comprehensive congressional policy to regulate the labor market may require coverage of both public and private sectors to be effective."**[33] (Emphasis added).

Justice Stevens also saw no restraint put on the Commerce Clause by the Tenth Amendment or the Court: "Neither the Tenth Amendment, nor any other provision of the Constitution, affords any support for that judicially constructed limitation on the scope of the federal power granted to Congress by the Commerce Clause."[34]

Foreshadowing the majority view to come in *Garcia*, he stated th at *NLC* was not only incorrectly decided, but also inconsistent with the central purpose of the Constitution and not entitled to the deference which the doctrine of *stare decisis* (once a question has been decided, that decision should be followed) ordinarily commands for the Court's precedents.

Chief Justice Burger in dissent argued that the Constitution did not authorize the federal government to establish detailed standards for the selection of state employees, and that, the State's statute had indeed met all four standards developed under *Hodel*. In his judgment, the Age Discrimination in Employment Act was unconstitutional as applied to the states.

Chief Justice Burger agreed with the majority that ADEA did regulate the States as States. As for the second standard, he disagreed with the majority by finding that the selection of state employees and control over state parks were in fact attributes of State sovereignty: Choosing who is to be part of state government, subject only to **constitutional** limits is surely an attribute of state sovereignty. Chief Justice Burger found that Wyoming also met the third standard, in that compliance with the federal law impaired the its freedom to structure integral operations in a traditional area of state government, state park management. In effect, he pointed out that the ADEA impaired Wyoming's administration of employees' conditions of employment.

As for state finances, Chief Justice Burger wrote that older employees earn more than younger ones, so that the decision could be expected to increase the state's labor costs. He argued that older workers cost more because their wages are higher and benefit costs linked to the wage must therefore also increase. Medical costs could be expected to increase because of older work force imposed on the states by compliance with ADEA.

Adding to increased labor costs would be less state flexibility to prom ote and limit its ability to hire more physically fit younger workers. Non-economic costs will further the state's ability to manage its work force, since older workers will ordinarily be at the higher ranges of the work force thereby barring or impeding the advancement of younger employees. As a result, younger workers' incentive to excel would be dampened reducing productivity. With respect to the balancing test, the Chief Justice contended that the state's interest in structuring its employment to meet local needs outweighed any federal interest.

Justice Powell also dissented and in his separate dissent he directly attacked Justice Stevens' claim that the central function of the Constitution was commercial. Instead, he argued that its principle purpose was to establish a government based a federal union of 'sovereign states.' State sovereignty was an essential ingredient to the federal system and the Tenth Amendment was adopted to insure that the federal government did not usurp state authority. Under Justice Stevens' analysis, he pointed out, it would be difficult to point to any state function which could be exempted from federal exemption. Federalism even under current economic circumstances is not totally subservient to the Commerce Clause, he commented.

Reviewing the powers delegated to the federal government under the Constitution, Justice Powell contradicted Justice Stevens' claim of the centrality of the Commerce Clause by noting that it followed the delegated powers of taxation, paying the debts of the country, providing for the defense and common welfare, and to borrow money on the credit of the United States. The power to regulate commerce, which is next, is only one among many other delegated powers which follow.

As for state sovereignty, Justice Powell recalled that in the previous term, the Court had recognized state sovereignty in exempting them from antitrust proceedings. Other examples are available, but under the view put forth in Justice Stevens' concurring opinion, "it is not easy to think of any state function – however sovereign – that could not be pre-empted.[35]

IV. *Garcia* – The Message.

Garcia overruled *National League of Cities* discarding the standards which had been set up to evaluate and identify those state and local government activities which would escape the sweep of Congressional power under the commerce clause. Justice Blackmun, who had previously expressed some uneasiness in his concurrence with the majority in *NLC* and who had broken with the majority in both *Federal Energy Regulatory Commission v. Mississippi* and *Equal Employment Opportunity v. Wyoming*, wrote the majority decision in the overrule.

The case began in September 1979 when the U.S. Department of Labor, Wage and Hour Administration, issued an opinion that San Antonio's publicly owned and operated transit system, operated by the San Antonio Metropolitan Transit Authority (SAMTA), was not subject to the exemption of *National League*, and therefore was not immune to the overtime requirements of the Fair Labor Standards Act, as amended.[36] Because wage levels at SAMTA were well above minimum wage levels, the Authority did not challenge the minimum wage provisions of FLSA, as amended.

For its part, SAMTA and its predecessor public agency, the San Antonio Transit System, which operated the mass transit system since the City acquired it in 1959, informed its employees four months after *National League* in 1976 that the decision relieved the Agency from the overtime pay requirements of the FLSA. These payments would be substantial since the unionized employees earned rates well above the minimum.

Such was the situation until the opinion handed down by the Labor Department asserting application of the overtime provisions to SAMTA in September 1979. SAMTA filed action against the Secretary of Labor seeking a declaratory judgment setting aside the Department's claimed jurisdiction of the FLSA. The Secretary counterclaimed. On the same day that SAMTA filed its action, Garcia and some other employees sued the Authority for payment of overtime as provided under FLSA. After lower Court litigation, which ruled in favor of SAMTA under the *NLC* doctrine, the case was appealed and went to the Supreme Court.

The Court found that SAMTA did not argue that it was exempt by virtue of operating an intrastate rather than and interstate transit system, because it had been long recognized that the Commerce clause extended to intrastate commerce which affects interstate commerce. Instead, Justice Blackmun pointed to the four fold standards promulgated under *Hodel* as the possible basis for SAMTA's claim to immunity from federal overtime regulation. In particular, the third condition was the focus of the case: That the imposition of federal standards must directly impair the States' ability to structure integral operations in areas of traditional government functions.

A review of the "troublesome" problems of the lower courts to match state and local governmental activities with the third standard showed a diversity of experience. For example, activities found to be protected under *National League of Cities* included regulation of ambulance services, licensing automobile drivers, operating a municipal airport, performing solid waste disposal, and operating a highway authority. On the other hand, federal courts ruled that the issuance of industrial development bonds, regulation of intrastate natural gas sales, regulation of traffic on public roads, regulation of air transportation, operation of a telephone system, leasing and sale of natural gas, operation of a mental health facility and the provision of in-house domestic services for the aged and handicapped were not exempt under *National League of Cities*.

After reviewing these cases, the Court declared that it found "it diffi cult, if not impossible, to identify an organizing principle that places each of the cases in the first group on one side of the line and each of the cases in the second group on the other side.[37] In the *Long Island Railroad* case, the Court had recognized the difficulties in determining workable standards for traditional governmental functions. To some extent the Court relied on historical standards, but "disclaimed a rigid reliance on the historical pedigree of state involvement in a particular area."[38] At the same time, it was asserted that the Court did not rely on an unchanging or static historical view of what constituted state functions immune to federal regulation.

Standards for separating governmental functions between those which would be immune and those which would not under *National League* could not be faithful to the role of federalism in a democratic society, according to the Court. The reason for the problem, it continued, was that within the context of federalism, states must be free to undertake any activity their citizens choose for the common weal. Otherwise, states would be unable to function as laboratories for social and economic experiment,[39] if they must pay the additional price of uncertainty as the application of *NLC* standards when they undertake public control and ownership of what once had been privately operated production of goods or services.

Given this problem, Justice Blackmun: "We therefore now reject, as unsound in principle and unworkable in practice, a rule of state immunity from federal regulation that turns on a judicial appraisal of whether a particular government function is 'integral' or 'traditional.'" Any such rule leads to inconsistent results at the same time that disserves principles of democratic self-governance, and it breeds inconsistency precisely because it is divorced from those principles."[40]

Did this mean that there were no limits to Congressional power to interfere with state functions? No, according to Justice Blackmun, so the opinion turned to the same consideration which underlay *National League*, how the Constitution insulates the states from Congressional exercise of the commerce power.

One approach would be to identify elements of state sovereignty regarded as essential to states' separate and independent existence. However, this would be akin to the Court's search for traditional state functions, something already rejected, so it, too, would be unworkable and unsound in principle. Even more compelling is the fact that a variety of sovereignty powers were withdrawn from the states under the Constitution, thereby limiting state sovereignty. So what remains to the states?

In one of the most telling conclusions of *Garcia*, the Court majority answered that although the states do "unquestionably" retain a significant measure of sovereign authority, "[t]hey do so, however, only to the extent that the Constitution has not divested them of their original powers and transferred those powers to the Federal Government."[41]

Perhaps another way of putting this is that the states retain whatever power Congress chooses to leave them.

As for the Tenth Amendment it is found to be only a truism: "...the fact that the States remain sovereign as to all powers not vested in Congress or denied them by the Constitution offers no guidance about where the frontier between state and federal power lies."[42] And so the Court declared "we have no license to employ freestanding conceptions of state authority when measuring congressional authority under the Commerce Clause."

The power of the federal political process, the Court continued, preserved states' interests. Indeed, in the final analysis, the Court reasoned that "the fundamental limitation that the constitutional scheme imposes on the Commerce Clause to protect the "States as States" in one of process."[43] Indeed, "the principal and basic limit" pointed to by the Court is the political process which will prevent the enactment of laws "unduly" burdensome on the states. Since this process has worked as intended, according to Justice Blackmun, it was unnecessary for the Court to define or identify the affirmative limits which the constitutional structure, that is the Tenth Amendment, might impose on congressional use of the commerce clause.

Evidence of the effectiveness of the political process cited by the Court was federal revenue disbursed to states to support general and specific programs, growing in the previous quarter century from $7 to $96 billion, so that federal grants accounted for about one-fifth of state and local government expenditures. The Court pointed to federal funds which the states have received for such varied services or facilities as police, fire protection, education, public health, hospitals, parks, recreation and sanitation.

One cannot fail to comment on these federal grants of monies to the states: The taxes funding all this "federal money" comes from taxpayers in the individual states and given the extent of the federal bursary's financial claims on the taxpayer, it is small wonder that states often find it necessary to turn to the federal treasury for revenue.

Addressing the case at hand specifically, the Court argued that SAMTA had been the beneficiary of such federal bounty, indeed, to the amount of $12 million during its first two fiscal years. Thus, even though Congress may have imposed some financial burden on the states and their subdivisions by subjecting them to the FLSA, it also provided "substantial countervailing financial assistance as well." Indeed, this financial assistance may have improved the condition of public mass transit beyond what would have been the case had Congress never intervened at all. Again, this was cited by the Court as evidence that the political process "systematically protects States from the risk of having their functions in that area [mass transit] handicapped by Commerce Clause regulation." One cannot wonder if this really does not constitute of catch 22 situation.

In addition to wringing "federal money" from the national government, the Court called attention to the fact that states have been exempted (to date) expressly or by implication from the obligations of the National Labor Relations Act, the Labor Management Reporting and Disclosure Act, the Occupational Safety and Health Act, the Employee Retirement Insurance Security Act, the Federal Power Act, and the Sherman Act. The fact that states are subject to the FLSA, as well as other federal statutes, should not obscure the extent to which states have been able to minimize their obligations under the Commerce clause, according to the Court.

On the other hand, the Court saw its role to render due respect for the reach of congressional power within the federal system and on that basis overruled *National League*. In so doing the Court also ignored the principle of *stare decisis*, a doctrine which states that once a question has been decided, that decision should be followed.

Dissent from the majority opinion was expressed by Justices Powell and O'Connor. Justice Powell began by attacking the decision as a substantial alteration of the federal system as provided for by the Constitution. In ignoring the doctrine of *stare decisis* the majority was charged with ignoring repeated acceptance of *National League* and the standards which evolved from it, even though the decision and its derivative standards had not been found applicable in *Hodel, FERC, Long Island Railroad* and *EEOC*. He pointed to the finding in *National League* and repeated in *FERC* that states' regulation of its relationship with its employees was an'undoubted attribute' of state sovereignty. Also noted was the "key prong" in *National League*, repeated and reformulated in *Hodel*, which examined whether the states' compliance with the federal law would directly impair their ability to structure integral operations in areas of traditional functions. While acknowledging that defining the meaning of the that standard, was difficult, difficulties of this nature had been met by the Court many times in its history. Perhaps, like pornography, it may not be susceptible to legal definition, but it can be recognized when it is seen. Even though all standards were met, the Court still ruled that "[t]here are situations in which the nature of the federal interest advanced may be such that it justifies state submission."[44]

Despite this record, the majority departed from the doctrine of *stare decisis*, a matter greatly deplored by Justice Powell, but less important, he commented, than what the majority decision did to the Constitution: "Despite some genuflecting in [the] Court's opinion to the concept of federalism,....[the] decision effectively reduces the Tenth Amendment to meaningless rhetoric when Congress acts pursuant to the Commerce Clause."[45] At the same time, the majority position was to withdraw the unelected federal judiciary from making decisions on state policies. The majority opinion left to the decision of the federal government the extent of authority which states may exercise.

While this majority view sounds like conservative constitutional doctrine aimed at limiting the Court's role to interpreting, not making the law, it appears to me that this is a case of the wolf wearing sheep's clothing.

Justice Powell went on to point out that the majority concern over what one might term "judicial activism" flew in the face of nearly two centuries of judicial review in the constitutional system, and in this case its recognition of the Tenth Amendment and the federal system. Since *Marbury v. Madison* it has been the settled role of the judiciary to say what the law is with respect to the constitutionality of Congressional enactments. Henceforth, the states' role in the federal system, by virtue of the majority decision, "may depend upon the grace of elected federal officials, rather than on the Constitution as interpreted by this Court."[46] In effect, Congress would be the judge of its own cause.

As for the states' ability to obtain federal funds for state and local activities, cited by the majority as evidence of the vitality of the political process, Powell wrote that political success is irrelevant; what counts is whether the political processes are the proper means for safeguarding the constitutional position of the states within the federal system: "The States' role in our system of government is a matter of constitutional law, not of legislative grace".

Extension of the Commerce Clause to SAMTA by the majority opinion could result in further emasculation of the powers of the states. This indication was indicated by the Court's redistributing the division of power laid out in the Tenth Amendment, if not indeed standing the amendment on its head. The majority decision would shift the relationship from one in which powers not delegated to the United States ... are reserved to the states, to one in which "only to the extent that the Constitution has not divested [the States] of their original powers and transferred those powers to the Federal Government", do the states retain sovereign authority.

Specifically, the extension of the FLSA to SAMTA would logically permit federal control under the Commerce Clause **"over the terms and conditions of employment of all state and local government employees [t]hus, for purposes of federal regulation, ... [rejecting] the distinction between public and private employers that had been drawn carefully in *National League of Cities"*.[47] (Emphasis added).

When the majority trod upon the balancing test, it did not find the federal interest outweighing the state's, because according to Justice Powell, it couldn't, since the reverse was true. In fact, the financial impact on the states and localities of "displacing their control over wages, hours, overtime regulations, pensions, and **labor relations with their employees** could have serious, as well as unanticipated effects on state and local planning, budgeting, and the levying of taxes."[48] (Emphasis added).

Justice O'Connor wrote a separate and biting dissent to the majority opinion, characterizing their concept of federalism as a "weak essence". Declaring that there is more to federalism, that the issue is "whether any area remains in which a State may act free of federal interference." Conceptually, "the essence of federalism is that the States have legitimate interests which the National Government is bound to respect even though its laws are supreme."[49] And, that it was the duty and responsibility of the Court to oversee that the national government respected the legitimate interests of the states.

Garcia, Justice O'Connor wrote, reflected a conflict between federalism and an "effective use of the commerce power" and in the face of that conflict, the Court majority's opinion retreated from rather than seeking a reconciliation of the difference: "The Court today surveys the battle scene of federalism and sounds a retreat [but] [l]ike Justice Powell, I would prefer to hold the field and, at the very least, render a little aid to the wounded."[50]

She noted the Court recognized the need for Congress to deal with an expanding and nationally integrated economy through the use of the commerce power. In recognition of this economic development, the Court had adopted a "generous" interpretation of the commerce power to enable Congress to deal with national economic problems. In so doing the Court had validated congressional regulations dealing with intrastate activities which substantially impacted interstate commerce. Congress needed only a rational basis identifying that intrastate activity which substantially affected interstate commerce for its enactments to gain Court approval. However, *Garcia* now eased the Congressional burden: all that is required is a showing that the regulated intrastate activity need only "affect" interstate commerce.

Accompanying the historic expansion of congressional use of the commerce power in the private sector she noted a steady extension of that power to *state* activities and in way which worried her: "As far as the Constitution is concerned, a State should not be equated with any private litigant."[51] Yet this is what Congress has done steadily, particularly over the past two decades as it expanded federal regulatory actions. For example (after Court validation) the ADEA enabled the federal government to tell states the age at which they can retire their enforcement officers and PURPA set the regulatory standards for public utilities, procedures and even the agenda which public utility commissions must consider and follow. The political process which had been advanced by the majority as the means for warding off undue federal interference in state activities failed to function in these instances. All that remains between what is left of state sovereignty and Congress after *Garcia*, Justice O'Connor wrote, "is the latter's underdeveloped capacity for self–restraint."[52]

Justice O'Connor's prescription for maintaining a vital federalism "lies in weighing state autonomy as a factor in the balance when interpreting the means by which Congress can exercise its authority on States as States."[53] Insofar as identifying those state actions which would be immune to federal regulation, she argued that while there are definitional problems, it is the Court's duty to resolve such matters, not to shun them.

V. Conclusions

Garcia has opened the door for federal legislation to nationalize labor relations. This can either be done by a new law, or by subjecting all public employees, federal, state and local to the National Labor Relations Act, private sector labor law. The latter is probably more efficient and has the precedent of the transference of the postal workers to its jurisdiction. Special limitations would no doubt be added, such as on strikes by certain essential services, such as police and fire. Other restrictions would also be applied, no doubt, but over time could expected to be repealed or undermined by administrative or judicial decisions.

Another approach would be to write a separate law. An example of this approach is reported in Appendix B. Either way the New Unionism's goal of convergence in industrial relations would be realized. Finally, it should be noted that *Garcia* also undermined the concept of the state as a sovereign employer, a major feature of the New Unionism's drive for convergence in industrial relations systems.

End Notes

[1]105 *S.CT.* 1005 (1985)

[2]426 *U.S.* 833 (1976)

[3]Advisory Commission on Intergovernmental Relations, *Reflections On Garcia And Its Implications For Federalism*, (Wash. D.C., Feb. 1986), M-147, p. 12.

[4]The following discussion covering the extension of the FLSA to states is from Raymond J. Donovan, Secretary of Labor, Appellant v. San Antonio Metropolitan Transit Authority, Et Al., No. 82-1951 *Brief For The Secretary Of Labor*, In the Supreme Court of the United States, October Term, 1983.

[5]392 *US* 183

[6]Bureau of National Affairs, *Public Sector Overtime Pay: The Impact of 'Garcia' On State & Local Governments*, A BNA Special Report, GERR NO. 1117-Part II, June 10,1985, p.4.

[7]426 *US* 833 (1976).

[8]N.L.R.B. v. Jones and Laughlin Steel Corp. 301 *US* 1 (1937).

[9]Martha A. Field, "Garcia v.San Antonio Metropolitan Transit Authority: The Demise of A Misguided Doctrine", *Harvard Law Review*, Vol. 99, 1985, p. 90.

[10]426 *US* 833, at 852.

[11]Martha A. Field, *Op.Cit.*, p.106.

[12]*Hodel v Virginia Surface Mining and Reclamation, Association Inc.* 452 *US* 264 (1981) at 287-288.

[13]Lawrence R. Velvel and Elaine Kaplan, *Supplemental Brief of the National League of Cities*, et al., in the Supreme Court of the United States, October Term, 1984, Nos. 82-1913 and 82-1951, p.2. quoting 456 *U.S.* at 781, n.7.

[14]For much of this discussion and some of what follows I am indebted to Sheldon Mills Rodgers III, "Garcia v. Samta" *Mercer Law Review*, Vol.37, pp.532-549.

[15]Advisory Commission On Intergovernmental Affairs, *Op.Cit.*

[16]*Brief for the National League of Cities, the National Governors' Association, the National Association of Counties, the National Conference of State Legislatures, the Council of State Governments, the International City Management Association* As Amici Curiae in Support of Appellees (San Antonio Metropolitan Transit Authority et al), In the Supreme Court of the United States, October Term 1983, pp.23-24.

[17]455 *US 678* (1982), at 684–685.

[18]William B. Lockhart, Yale Kamisar and Jesse H. Choper, *1982 Supplement to Fifth Edition, Constitutional Law, The American Constitution, Constitutional Rights and Liberties* (St.Paul: West Publishing, 1982), quoting *FERC*, p. 7.

[19]456 *US* 742 (1982), at 773 and 775.

[20]460 *US* 226 (1983)

[21]Steven F. Freudenthal and Bruce A. Salzburg, *Brief For The State of Wyoming, Et Al.*, in the Supreme Court of the United States, October Term, 1981, No. 81–554, p. 10.

[22]*EEOC v. Wyoming*, 460 U.S.226, at 226, Syllabus.

[23]The Wyoming State Highway Patrol and Game and Fish Warden Retirement Act, Wyoming Statute # 31-3-107 (c) (1977) & Supp.1984.

[24]Raymond J. Donovan, Secretary of Labor, *Op.Cit.*, pp.15–16.

[25]460 *U.S.* 226, at 239.

[26]Steven F. Freudenthal and Bruce A. Salzburg, *Op.Cit.*, p.15.

[27]Steven F. Freudenthal and Bruce A. Salzburg, *Op.Cit.*,pp.17,19, 28.

[28]*Ibid.*, p. 13, n.6.

[29]*Ibid.*, at 240–241.

[30]*Ibid.*, at 242.

[31]*Ibid.*, at 246–247.

[32]*Ibid.*, at 248.

[33]*Loc.Cit.*

[34]*Loc.Cit.*

[35]*Ibid,*, at 275.

[36]The discussion which follows on the *Garcia* case comes principally from the full text of the Supreme Court's decision reported in full in the Bureau of National Affairs, *Op.Cit.*, pp.37–69.

[37]*Ibid.*, p.40.

[38]*Ibid.*, p.41.

[39]*Ibid.*,p. 43, citing *New State Ice Co. v. Liebman 285 U.S. 262*, 311 (1932) (Brandeis, J. dissenting).

[40]*Ibid.*, p.43.

[41]*Ibid.*, p.44.

[42]*Loc.Cit.*

[43]*Ibid.*, p.46.

[44]*Ibid.*, p.48, citing *Hodel*, 452 *US*, at 288, n.29

[45]*Ibid.*, p.48.

[46]*Ibid.*, p. 48.

[47]*Ibid.*, p.55.
[48]*Ibid.*, p.58.
[49]*Ibid.*, p.56.
[50]*Loc.Cit.*
[51]*Ibid.*, p.59.
[52]*Ibid,*, p.58.
[53]*Loc.Cit.*

APPENDIX B

A Model of Convergence:
The Aftermath of *Garcia*

I. Background

In Appendix A, I reported that the Supreme Court's decision in *Garcia* opened the way for congressional regulation of employee relations at the state and local level. Two years afterward, the first effort to act on that opportunity was undertaken, the introduction of proposed legislation to enact a labor law governing fire fighters. Perhaps the reasons the fire fighters were selected as the trial balloon were, paradoxically, the existing high degree of organization of the function (see below), the small size of employment compared to total public employment, and because of the essential which they perform. According to the U.S. Bureau of Census, in 1987 there were just over 230 thousand employees employed in fire protection and nearly 2/3 of these were already unionized. Thus, the Bill's provisions would have applied only to a third of all fire fighters and only a tiny fraction of the total state and local public employment of some 15.5 million.

While the approach was limited, it was doubtless regarded as a viable alternative to legislation establishing a new system of industrial relations for public sector (the New) unionism in general. The proposed law is also instructive because it indicates that separate legislation for the New Unionism would go much further in entrenching an already powerful union movement than incorporating the New Unionism under private sector labor law. Indeed, based on an examination of the fire fighters bill, a separate approach would more than fulfill the New Unionism's goals of convergence (Chapter III).

The goal of any public sector legislation is to give the New Unionism "full rights of collective bargaining," or what in Chapter III is identified as convergence in the industrial relations systems of the public and private labor markets. Convergence, I pointed out in that chapter, has gained steadily over the years, and a "nationalized" labor law would fulfill the ultimate goal of convergence.

Convergence will also further reduce state and local government sovereignty as it adds additional stress to their finances. Of course, convergence will increase the substitution of collective bargaining for political decision making at the state and local level.

The first legislative step after *Garcia* probably should be regarded more as a trial balloon in the direction of convergence. However, it is a useful gauge by which to evaluate how convergence would be treated legislatively. The bill introduced in the U.S. House of Representatives was H.R. 1201, the Fire Fighter National Labor-Management Relations Act (FNLMRA), in the First Session of the 100th Congress, on February 24, 1987. It was introduced by Representative William Clay (D. Mo), the same Congressmen who some years earlier had played what can only be described as an irresponsible role in inciting the strike by the Professional Air Traffic Controllers in 1981 (Chapter III). It is worth noting that the AFL-CIO's Committee on Political Education (COPE) has rated Representative Clay at 100% in his voting record on labor issues. In analyzing this first post-*Garcia* model of convergence, I will cross-reference it with the National Labor Relations Act of 1935, as amended after which it is so closely modelled, and other relevant materials.

II.   Findings and Purpose of the Proposed FNLMRA of 1987

The findings offered as justification of the proposed Act were as follows: First, that the interruption of essential services provided by fire fighters caused turmoil for local and municipal governments and unsafe conditions for public. On the affirmative side, it states that a national policy would have positive effect by contributing to a process enabling fire fighters to participate in the procedures affecting their careers, contribute to the resolution of disputes and prevent the disruption of services.

The purpose of the bill was to "guarantee the right of professional fire fighters [of state and local governments] to organize and bargain collectively." These purposes tracked the NLRA, but omit references to denial by some employers (in this case, state and local governments) of employees (fire fighters') right to organize and bargain. In contrast, the NLRA justified government intervention to prevent the denial of employees' right to organize by some employers, and in the Amended (Taft-Hartley) Act a parallel denial of employee rights by unions. These interferences, according to the NLRA, led to strikes and other forms of industrial unrest which, in turn, burdened commerce. Among the unfavorable affects on commerce was the diminution of employment and wages. Furthermore, the NLRA found that the inequality of bargaining power between large aggregations of capital and employees not possessing the full freedom of association, or liberty of contract, depressed wages and thereby aggravated business conditions.

Putting aside the accuracy of some of the Congressional findings in the NLRA, it becomes immediately clear that the rationale for the proposed fire fighter's statute as expressed in its findings soft pedals the right to organize and gives more weight to dispute resolution. It makes no mention of public employers' denial of their employees' right to organize, **the "raison d' etre** for the NLRA, as a cause of disputes. The omission initially strikes one as odd, because not only do most state and local governments have no legislation or policies legally guaranteeing and protecting the right to organize, but also because some disputes and strikes arose from the issue.[1] Perhaps the Bill's reference to interruption of services due to a "breakdown" in employee – management relations is an oblique reference to the issue.

Compelling reasons for the absence of any reference to the denial of the right to organize was the already the high degree of union penetration of local fire protection. This would make it difficult for the Bill to refer to the denial of the right by public employers as a reason for enacting the Bill in its statement of findings. For the country as a whole, the U.S. Bureau of the Census reported that in 1987, 65 percent of all full-time employees in fire protection were organized. The lowest degree of union penetration at that time for an identifiable function nation-wide among state and local governments was 35 percent in public hospital services. This puts union penetration in fire protection nearly 7 times that in the private economy, currently down to an estimated under 10 percent.

The degree of union penetration of fire protection among full-time employees by state, including the District of Columbia, the need for further protection becomes even more paradoxical. The penetration rate ranged from nearly complete unionization in the District of Columbia (93%) and New York (87%) to 9% in South Carolina and 5% in North Carolina. Many other states showed high union penetration rates among fire fighters including Pennsylvania, Minnesota and Hawaii. These data indicate that it would be indeed difficult to claim that public employers were denying fire fighters the right to organize! A better case could have been made for hospital workers, but even these were more than four times as unionized as workers in the private labor market. Indeed, the statistics on fire fighters question the necessity of a federal law governing labor relations in fire protection. If anything, the underlying goals of the FNLMRA would appear to have been an effort to organize the states in the south and southwest and to assist the growth and power of the dominant union in the field, the International Association of Fire Fighters.

Another significant difference between the statement of findings in the FNLMRA and the NLRA is the absence in the proposed fire fighters' bill of any reference to the wages of fire fighters. The NLRA contended that the inequality of unorganized workers and employers depressed wages. As for wages, econometric studies show that fire fighters's wages are well above levels which would prevail in the absence of unions and that the fire fighters' union is more effective in raising wages than others in the New Unionism.[2]

Actually, the effect of the IAFF on wages and total compensation may be underestimated. Most notable is the underestimation of pension values at current employer costs, not the actuarial value to the employee. Since the union impact on fringes exceeds its effect on wages, this can result in a significantly biased underestimate. Another potential source of understatement is that the data for the quantitative studies do not include other extra compensation as additional income (days worked at overtime are one example). Over all estimates "suggest union wage effects are roughly twice as large as the 5-to percent of the standard cross-section analysis."[3]

It seems evident from the foregoing summary of wage and employment conditions among fire fighters that there is no similarity between the proposed FNLMRA and the NLRA when it came to justifying the enactment of the FNLMRA because of compensation, and for good reason. Fire fighters' compensation can hardly be classified as depressed.

III. Policy

The FNLMRA proposed to grant rights both to employees and to employee organizations, a significant departure from the NLRA. Under the NLRA, the rights protected are those of employees covered by the Act; rights of employee organizations are not included.

Employee organizations' rights are: (1) Unions' access to the work place (at reasonable times), use of employer's bulletin boards, mailboxes *and other communication media* (subject to reasonable regulation) and to use the employer's facilities at reasonable times for the purpose of meetings concerned with rights guaranteed by the Act, except that where an exclusive representative has been chosen, such rights are denied other employee organization. (2) The check-off of dues, subject only to submission of an authorization of the employee; again, this right limited to exclusive representative only. (3) Where exclusive representation prevails, non-members shall be mandatorily required to pay the equivalent of the dues, fees, assessments paid by a member. In other words, the Bill would require the agency shop. Failure to pay the agency shop fee would be grounds for lawful dismissal. (4) Employee organizations would have the right to be present at a grievance procedure, although an individual employee or a group has a right to present grievances and have them adjusted without the intervention of the bargaining representative. This procedure parallels that under the NLRA.

The open access of unions to the public employers work place and access to the public employer's means of communications will enormously facilitate the organization and strength of already powerful unions. Under the NLRA, solicitation of employees to enroll in the union is subject to determination by the National Labor Relations Board. In general, companies may prohibit union activity on company time; such may not be the case under the FNLMRA.

As for bulletin boards, in the private sector, these are left to negotiation between the parties and while the private employer may accede to them, contract language would ordinarily proscribe any material of a political, religious or derogatory nature from being placed on the bulletin board. No limitations are set forth in the proposed fire fighters' law. Doubtless, such access would greatly strengthen the unions' political effectiveness and with access supplied by the taxpayer.

Guaranteeing fire fighters' unions access to the public employer's communication media would require public employers (and therefore taxpayers) to subsidize newsletters, announcements and magazines which surely should be the unions' own responsibility. It would leave public management with no separate means of communicating with employees.

The dues check off is left to the determination of the individual employee under the NLRA and is not a right of a labor organization as it would be under the proposed FNLMRA. Doubtless, unions would use the legislation to impress union members that the law intends that each individual should agree to a check-off. Membership of 100% would be virtually guaranteed.

As for the agency shop fee, again there is nothing in the NLRA requiring non-members to pay the union a representation fee. Indeed, the NLRA presumes the possibility of non-members to be represented under the concept of exclusive representation. Under the NLRA, agency shop fees may be collected, if the parties agree to it through negotiations and if the place of employment is not in a state banning agency shop fees, that is, a right-to-work state. Whether the proposed FNLMRA would violate right-to-work prohibitions is questionable. The legislation makes no provision for the application of such laws, as does the NLRA under its section 14 (b). Under that section of the Act, state policy on union shops and, by judicial interpretation, on agency shop fees, take precedence over federal policy which permit both. Since the FNLMRA has not equivalent to 14 (b), it certainly intends no exception. Whether the courts will also see it that way would remain to be seen. However, since union shops and agency shop fees are legal under the Railway Labor Act even in right-to-work states, it is possible that the agency shop fee under the FNLMRA would pass judicial scrutiny in these states.

It is not surprising that the agency shop fee is not left to negotiations between the parties under the FNLMRA and that non-payment of fees are grounds for dismissal. It is not surprising in view of the very high degree of unionization among professional fire fighters and because many states and localities have set the precedent. However, it is surprising that the proposed law fails to mandate that the fee not be used for political purposes or impose procedures on unions which would require return to non-members (and members) who object to the expenditure of their fees or dues for political purposes. The Supreme Court has so found more than once and even those states which mandate agency shop fees in the public sector also require some procedures and adjustments to those objecting to the political use of their agency fees. Any limitations of this nature would presumably be left to the Commission which would administer the Act. By its provisions, the Act enables the Commission to prescribe rules and regulations governing the **payment** of the agency shop fees. However, it is silent on their **expenditure,** so the outlook is dubious, in my judgment. For there to be any limitations on the expenditure of agency shop fees, judicial intervention would probably be necessary.

A related omission in the proposed Act is the absence of any reference to standards of conduct for employee organizations as required of unions under the Labor Management Reporting and Disclosure Act of 1959. Although the International Fire Fighters and a handful of its subordinate bodies do fulfill these obligations under that Act, most of its local organizations do not. This is also true of independent unions of fire fighters.

IV. Employee Rights

The employee rights protected are (1) to form, join, or assist employee organizations. (2) To participate in collective bargaining with employers through representatives of their own choosing. (3) And to engage in other activities, individually or in concert, for the purpose of establishing, maintaining, or improving terms and conditions of employment and other matters of mutual concern.

Although the FNLRMA's extension of federal legal protection to fire fighters' rights to organize and bargain collectively over the terms and conditions of employment and other matters parallels the policy of the NLRA, the policy of the proposed FNLMRA also differs significantly from the NLRA on employee rights. In contrast to the NLRA, significantly there is no language protecting the right of fire fighters to refrain from exercising those rights. Indeed, as just pointed out, the agency shop fee would be imposed by the law and there would be no exceptions for states which have right-to-work laws. Furthermore, the Bill would permit the negotiation of the union shop, but there is nothing similar to the NLRA's requirement that unions may not deny membership in the organization for any reason other than the non-payment of dues. Thus, the Bill would restore the potential for abuse of power which prevailed under the Wagner Act when a union could arbitrarily deprive a member of membership and under the union shop his/her employment as well.

V. Implementation: Scope and Machinery

The coverage of the proposed law would embrace all states, territories and possessions of the U.S. and any subdivision, including any town, city, county, borough, fire district and any person acting as an agent for these entities. Employees subject to the FNLMRA would include anyone engaged in the performance of work directly connected with the control and extinguishment of fires, the maintenance and use of fire-fighting equipment and apparatus, fire inspection services, the investigation of fires,, or communication operations, or rescue squad and paramedic personnel. It would exclude supervisors who are apparently limited to the fire department chief and assistants. Is interesting to note the Bill would turn over the jurisdiction of paramedical personnel to the fire fighters' unions, a group over whom there has been jurisdictional disputes between fire fighters, police and hospital unions. Once legislatively within the bailiwick of the fire fighters, the opportunity for self-determination by paramedical employees would be fully and completely terminated.

To administer its provisions, the Act would establish a Fire Fighters National Labor-Management Relations Commission of five members within the Department of Labor. Again, this marks a significant departure from the structure of the NLRA. Under the NLRA, the Board functions as an entity independent of any other Executive Department or Agency. By lodging the Commission within the Labor Department the Bill reinforces the Department's bias toward organized labor, an attitude independent of the political affiliation of the Secretary. Perhaps it will be remembered that the Labor Management Relations Act of 1947 removed the Conciliation Service from the Department of Labor, re-titled it as the Federal Mediation and Conciliation Service and established it as an independent agency in order to gain for it a more impartial perception in the field of labor management relations.

Members would be appointed by the President with the advice and consent of the Senate. Except for the initial appointments of four of the members, all five would be appointed to terms of 5 years. The Commission or its members may prosecute any inquiry necessary to its functions without disqualification as a participant in a subsequent decision of the Commission in the same case. This provision again departs from NLRB practice by permitting a Commissioner to be a prosecutor and judge on one and the same case.

The Commission is empowered to appoint an Executive Director and State or regional directors, attorneys and other individuals to implement the Act. Given the small scope of the Bill's application, it is easy to see where a new and large bureaucracy could be established with little to justify its creation.

The Bill calls for the appointment by the Secretary of Labor of a General Counsel, authorized to investigate alleged violations of the Act, to file and prosecute complaints and to exercise other powers delegated to the General Counsel by the Commission. No term of office is set for the General Counsel. Once more a departure from the structure of the NLRA where the General Counsel is appointed by the President with the advice and consent of the Senate for a period of four years. Once again, too, the Bill's leanings are quite evident and of course further undermine claims of impartiality by having the Secretary of Labor name the General Counsel.

VI. Implementation: Representation Procedures

To implement the rights of employees and employee organizations, the Bill authorizes the Commission to conduct representation elections. To that end, the Bill enumerates election procedures and duties of the Commission similar to those of the NLRB. However there are important differences.

Because of the extensive unionization of fire fighters which now exists, the Bill envisions public employer recognition of existing employee representatives of the Bill as the exclusive representative without an election or certification unless challenged under procedures under the Act. This was the practice adopted in Canada when the federal and provincial governments first adopted policies beginning in the 1960s to promote the New Unionism (Chapter II). If a contract exists, then the agreement is a bar to an election challenge until its expiration. A challenge to an existing unit can be raised by the employer, a member of the unit, or any employee organization. It is surprising to find that "a member of the unit," as the Bill unequivocally states, may challenge an existing bargaining relationship in legislation intended to strengthen unions. I would have expected a showing of interest of at least 30%.

In general, representation elections procedures may be invoked by a petition filed by an employer or an employee organization. A decertification election may be held if there is a claim by the employer or employees that the exclusive representative no longer represents the majority of the employees. While the Bill provides for decertification elections, it does not set forth what the necessary showing of interest would be. Would it be the single member of a unit, as the Bill specifies for challenges to units established prior to the legislation, or the 30 per cent required for a representation election? Decertification elections also can be invoked by an employer who has good faith doubts that the bargaining representative retains majority support.

A question of representation could arise on petition of the public employer, if the employer has good faith doubts as to the validity of the evidence demonstrating majority support for a bargaining representative. Another basis for an employer challenge is that the unit claimed by the bargaining representative is inappropriate. When an employer challenges the appropriateness of a unit, the Commission takes into account such criteria as the community of interest, the efficiency of operations and effective dealings, the rights of employees to effective representation and any other factors consistent with providing stable and continuing labor relations. Finally, public employers may also seek a representation election if there are competing claims by employee organizations for the right of representation.

An employee organization can petition for an election in an unorganized unit if it can demonstrate a showing of interest by at least 30 percent of the employees in the proposed bargaining unit.

When a question of representation does arise, the Commission will order an election using a secret ballot, or any other "suitable" method to determine the majority representative. By other "suitable" method, I presume the Bill refers to a check of membership cards signed by employees authorizing the employee organization to represent them, or perhaps secret ballots conducted by a State agency or other impartial third party. With regard to a card check, the NLRA and the Board limited this practice. Under the original Wagner Act, similar language enable the NLRB to use card checks as a means of determining the majority status of a petitioning labor organization, but the practice came to be suspect for many reasons, not the least of which that some cards were signed by employees under pressure, or may have been otherwise fraudulent. Despite this experience, the FNLMRA would give this authority to the Commission. It also parallels current practice in Canada in both the public and private sectors.

The Commission need not order a representation election if the parties consent to an election. This procedure follows the experience and practices of the NLRA.

After a representation election is held, the Commission is required to certify the results within 5 working days of the final vote count, barring any charge of an unfair labor practice. If a charge is filed, and the Commission has reason to believe the charge is valid, it would conduct a hearing within 2 weeks of the filing of the charge. If the Commission finds that the election was affected by the unfair labor practice charged, *or any other unfair labor practice it may deem existed*, it would require corrective action and order a new election. Thus, the Commission becomes a "policeman" and the responsibility for charging violations (unfair labor practices) would be transferred from those whose rights are the *raison d' etre* of the Bill to the Commission. If the Commission finds that the charged unfair labor practice did not exist, or that it did not affect the outcome of the election, it shall immediately certify the results of the election.

Once a bargaining representative has been chosen, the FNLMRA would prohibit a challenge to its bargaining rights for 12 months. In addition, if a contract is reached, the contract bars another election in the unit for a period of time determined by the Commission. As a rule, the maximum length of the contract bar rule is three years under procedures of the National Labor Relations Boar

VII. Implementation Procedures: Employer Unfair Labor Practices

Like the NLRA, the proposed FNLMRA identifies and separates the practices of employers from those of employee organizations which could interfere with the rights protected by the Bill. However, unlike the NLRA, the employer's unfair labor practices can be committed against an employee organization as well as an employee. Of course, this originates from the Bill's intention of establishing rights of employee organizations in addition to those of employees. Under the FNLMRA public employers could commit the following unfair labor practices. First, to impose or threaten reprisals on any employee, or to discriminate or threaten to discriminate against any employee, or otherwise interfere with or restrain, or coerce any employee because of the exercise of rights guaranteed by the proposed Act. This sweeping prohibition parallels that of the NLRA's first employer unfair labor practice. Likewise, the second which would make it unlawful for a public employer to dominate, interfere with, or assist in the formation or administration of any employee organization. Again, this follows the pattern set down by the NLRA.

When we come to the third unfair labor practice of a public employer, there is a significant departure from the comparable one in the NLRA and the experience of labor relations under the original Wagner Act. The proposed FNLMRA would make it unlawful for a public employer to encourage or discourage membership in any employee organization by discrimination in regard to hire, tenure of employment, or any term or condition of employment. The employer is not subject to an unlawful act if he dismisses an employee who fails to pay the agency shop fee, and dues payments required under a union shop.

Under the NLRA, the private employer is not required to discharge an employee subject to a union shop for the following two reasons: First, if the employer has reasonable grounds for believing that membership in the labor organization was not available to the employee on the same terms and conditions generally applicable to other members; second, if the private employer has reasonable grounds for believing that membership was denied or terminated to an employee for reasons other than the failure to pay the periodic dues and fees uniformly required as a condition of acquiring or retaining membership. Indeed, if the private employer were to discharge an employee at the demand of the labor organization with which it has a union shop agreement, he commits an unfair labor practice. The remedies include restoration of all wages lost (net of income earned elsewhere), with interest, and reinstatement of the employee with all rights restored. The union is subject to parallel remedies under the NLRA. As for the agency shop, the NLRA is silent on the matter, leaving it to collective bargaining and subject to state legislation under section 14 (b).

The distinctions made by the NLRA and absent in the proposed FNLMRA are significant and far reaching. Under the FNLMRA, as under the original Wagner Act, a union could deny or deprive membership to an employee for capricious or arbitrary reasons and then demand and lawfully force the employer to discharge the employee because he was no longer a member in good standing as required by the union shop. Thus, a member who asked too many questions, or the wrong ones at a union meeting could arbitrarily be deprived of membership and therefore his job. It is evident that these arrangements would vest enormous power over the economic life of workers in the leadership of a union. In amending the Wagner Act, the Taft-Hartley Act of 1947 severed the link between arbitrary denial or termination of union membership and employment. In contrast, the FNLMRA by permitting the union shop would give unions in fire fighting this power without any limitations.

The fourth unfair labor practice a public employer may commit it to deny any employee organization the rights guaranteed to it by the proposed legislation. Again, this departs from the NLRA because, as already pointed out, the FNLMRA grants rights to employee organizations, in contrast to the NLRA. Since employee organizations have a number of rights under the proposed legislation, the number of employer unfair labor practices is multiplied thereby. Of course, in going beyond the NLRA, the Bill would greatly enhance the strength of the fire fighters' unions.

The fifth public employer unfair labor practice would be to refuse to bargain collectively in good faith with the employee representative. The scope and significance of this provision would obliterate any differences between public and private sector bargaining with reference to the subjects of negotiation. It would bring about the full convergence in this particular area (matters subject to negotiation) between the public and private sector systems of industrial relations.

The most important consequence of the requirement to bargain in good faith with the union is the certain impact it would have on the fiscal integrity of local governments. If this becomes of the model for all of the New Unionism, insolvency will become far more widespread than it have ever been.

Another significant impact of the FNLMRA's would be on the separation of powers between the federal and state and local governments, and on representative government in this country. In defining the duty to bargain collectively, the FNLMRA states that the it shall extend to matters which are or may be the subject of a statute, ordinance, regulation or other enactment by a State, territory, or possession of the U.S., or subdivision thereof. Furthermore, if legislation is required to implement any agreement between the public employer and the union, it is the duty and obligation of the public employer to submit the agreement to the proper governmental body for action.

Thus, a federal law would compel state and local governments to negotiate over matters that are intimately tied to their budgets, over which they have historically had control and to a large extent substitute federal dicta for voters' decisions and priorities over a wide array of issues! But the matter does not end there. When there is an impasse, the FNLMRA would compel arbitration to resolve the differences, giving over to non-elected individuals influential if not decisive power over personnel costs. State sovereignty would be diminished to the point where states indeed would be mere provincial appendages of federal authority, and in particular of federal bureaucracy.

If the sweep of unfair labor practices chargeable to public employers was thought to be far reaching already, the Bill still has one more arrow in its quiver. The sixth unfair practice which public employers can commit it to otherwise fail to comply with any provision of the proposed Act. Thus, another large and relatively blank check is prescribed, one, I'm sure an activist Commission could stretch considerably.

VIII. Implementation: Employee Organization
    Unfair Labor Practices"

There are half as many unfair labor practices listed for employee organizations as for employers and all are routine if not innocuous. They are a gesture, not a serious consideration of employee rights which the union could violate.

The first is a general ban on union restraint or coercion of employees in exercising their rights under the proposed Act. At the same time, this prohibition is not intended to impair the right of an employee organization to prescribe its own rules with respect to the acquisition or retention of membership. Absent is any restraint on the union for denying membership for any reason other than the non-payment of dues. Under the NLRA, a labor organization may also prescribe its own rules for gaining and retaining membership, but it is an unfair labor practice for the union to deny membership for non-payment of dues or discriminate in the procedures and then demand and secure the discharge of a non-member. Thus, the NLRA makes it an unfair labor practice for both the employer to agree to such a dismissal and the labor organization to seek it. For example, a union and an employer have been found in violation of the NLRA in bringing about the discharge of an employee who offered to pay dues and fees, but refused to apply for union membership, attend a union meeting, or to take an oath of allegiance to the union. Likewise, discharge for failure to pay union fines, or assessments have been held unlawful (because they are not uniform dues or initiation fees).[4] Remedial action to "make the employee whole" apply to the union as well as the employer under the NLRA. All of this is totally absent from the FNLMRA.

The second employee organization unfair labor practice is to restrain or coerce an employer in the selection of its representative for purposes of collective bargaining. This is primarily directed to prevent a labor organization from interfering with management's choice in its representative (notably a supervisor) in adjusting grievances, or for that matter, in its selection of an arbitrator whether in reference to differences arising under an agreement or to the impasse procedures. This unfair labor practice would also apply, of course, to management selection of its representatives in bargaining over new terms and conditions of employment.

An employee organization may commit an unfair labor practice if it fails to bargain collectively in good faith with a public employer. This is the third unfair labor practice which an employee organization can commit. Again, this applies to both bargaining over new terms and conditions of employment and grievance negotiations. Under the NLRA unions can violate the parallel provision by not providing fair representation by maintaining or enforcing an agreement which discriminates against employees because of race. It should be noted that the fire fighters unions have been in the midst of numerous disputes dealing with affirmative action procedures arising out of alleged past discrimination and there appears to be no requirement of fair representation by an employee organization.

IX. Collective Bargaining and Impasses

Before dealing with bargaining over new terms and conditions of employment which lead to impasses, I will first note the FNLMRA's procedures for dealing with grievances. The certified bargaining representative alone is capable of negotiating over terms and conditions of employment for a new agreement. However, when it comes to grievances, any individual employee or group of employees have the right at any time to present grievances to employers and to have them adjusted without the intervention of the bargaining representative if the adjustment is not inconsistent with the collective bargaining agreement in effect. At the same time, the bargaining representative is entitled to be present at the grievance adjustment.

With respect to the new terms and conditions of employment, if an agreement cannot be reached the FNLMRA proposes compulsory arbitration. This is coupled with a ban on strikes, work stoppages and slowdowns. The procedure for invoking arbitration can be initiated by either the public employer or the exclusive bargaining representative. If an employer or exclusive bargaining representative declares that an impasse exists on any issue 60 days after the date on which collective bargaining for a new agreement begins, the Bill provides that the issues in dispute shall be brought before an arbitration panel for a final and binding resolution.

The arbitration panel would consist of 3 members, one chosen by each side and the impartial arbitrator, who becomes the chairman. If the management and union nominees cannot agree on the third member, they may select an individual from a panel provided by the Federal Mediation and Conciliation Services.

After the tri-partite panel is established it begins hearings within 14 days of the selection of the Chairman and he notifies the parties no less than 7 days prior to the commencement of the hearings of their date and location. The hearings must conclude within 30 days after the date they are started. Any person, organization, or governmental unit may permitted to intervene in the proceedings, for good cause. While the hearings are informal, a transcript is kept. The arbitrators may administer oaths and subpoena the attendance and testimony of witnesses, the production of records and other evidence. Anyone refusing to obey a subpoena will be subject to judicial proceedings for contempt.

Within 10 days of the conclusion of the hearings, the majority of the panel issues a statement of its findings and conclusions in writing. These are retroactive to the expiration date of the last contract. *The decision of the arbitration panel is final and binding upon the parties and upon the appropriate legislative body.* Awards are enforceable in the federal courts. Thus, the arbitration procedure culminates in a non-elective body having a decision making power superior to that of a duly elected legislative body and its award is enforceable upon that body by a federal court. In addition, the division of power between federal and state and local government is further eroded by the arbitration procedures envisioned by the FNLMRA. It will be recalled that the proposed Act also defined the scope of bargaining and thereby extended federal sway over what is negotiable. Furthermore, by prescribing an arbitration procedure, it does away with locally established procedures for resolving disputes which fall short of the federal mandate, taking away local determination of dispute resolution.

X. Commission Procedures

In general the procedures of the Commission set up to administer the FNLMRA appear to parallel those of the NLRB. Thus, it has the authority to prevent and remedy unfair labor practices enumerated in the Bill. On finding an unfair labor practice, the Commission is empowered to issue an order requiring the offending party to cease and desist from the unlawful act and to take whatever affirmative action deemed necessary to carry out the policies of the proposed Act. Commission orders may include the payment of income lost and the reinstatement of employees. Restoration of pay lost because of an unfair labor practice may be assessed against the employer or the employee organization. Orders of the Commission are enforceable by any federal court of appeals. Appeals of Commission decisions may be made to a court of appeals.

While the Commission, thus, has powers and would proceed generally like the National Labor Relations Board (NLRB), it has no power to seek injunctions to prevent certain types of unfair labor practices. The reason for this is the absence of unfair labor practices which employee organizations may commit under the FNLMRA, but which are found in the NLRA. The NLRA bans secondary boycotts, strikes with an element of violence (although these have occurred in fire fighting and would therefore justify an injunctive procedure), jurisdictional strikes, strikes defying NLRB certifications and featherbedding (also present in fire fighting, and therefore qualifying for injunctive relief).[5] Under the NLRA, the Board is required to give precedence to charges involving such unfair labor practices and if the evidence warrants, to seek an injunction from a federal district court to stop the unfair labor practice.

XI. Strikes

The Bill bans strikes and other methods of interrupting or slowing work, coupling this with the Bill's compulsory arbitration when there are impasses. Nevertheless, the ban on strikes and the like must be seen both in terms of the rights protected by the proposed legislation and the absence of any penalty either via an unfair labor practice or a specified punishment. Thus, in section 11, the Bill states: "No fire fighter or exclusive representative shall engage in a strike or induce, encourage, or condone any strike, work stoppage, slowdown, or withholding of services by fire fighters." At the same time, section 6, which lays out the rights of employees and employee organizations, states in subsection (a) (3), that employees have the right "to engage in other activities, individually or in concert, for the purpose of establishing, maintaining, or improving terms and conditions of employment and other matters of mutual concern relating thereto." Comparing these policies, it seems reasonable to conclude that "working to rule" and other methods of frustrating the ban on stoppages and slowdowns can succeed. Further, there is no penalty listed when an exclusive representative engages in strikes, stoppages and slowdowns. Nor are illegal strikes, stoppages, and slowdowns are listed by the FNLMRA as unfair labor practices. In other words, the ban on strikes and the like is toothless.

Experience in labor disputes involving fire fighters would seem to warrant that attention be paid to types of activity which would run afoul of a more balanced approach to a law governing labor relations in fire fighting. Indeed, as one study on union violence in labor disputes put it: " When strikes involve employees charged with protection of public safety they are inherently violent. It is not sophistry to suggest that denial of protection [to the public] is itself a form of violence".[6]

The evolution of the policy toward strikes by the International Association of Fire Fighters, the dominant union in fire protection, illustrates and underline how far public sector labor relations have moved toward convergence with private sector labor relations. Thus, if we go back some 40 years ago, to just after World War II, we find that an effort to weaken the historic no strike policy of the IAFF at its convention was defeated. According to the report on the convention at which a resolution to change the no-strike was presented, "it was asserted that the no-strike policy of the organization has been largely responsible for the prestige and tremendous strides which the International Association of Fire Fighters has made since it came into existence [the union was founded in 1918] and particularly during recent years".[7] (Incidentally, this is also evidence supporting my characterization of the IAFF and other public labor organizations of the time as "proto-unions" (Chapter II).

Of course, that is not the current policy of the IAFF. The change came largely as a result of the rapid rise of the New Unionism in the 1960's spurred by federal and state and local public policies encouraging unions and collective bargaining. As detailed in Chapter II, under the impetus of these changes public sector labor organizations underwent significant changes. Many transformed themselves from professional or quasi-professional associations to full blown unions. In the process, many, like the IAFF abandoned their no-strike policies as they transformed themselves from "proto-to full unionism. The IAFF removed the no-strike policy in 1968 when it was removed from the union's constitution.

When the IAFF abandoned its no-strike policy, many of its locals or members of locals turned to violence in the course of contract disputes. According to Thieblot and Haggard's study of union violence, 1975–1981, among ten large unions the IAFF ranked third in the number of violent incidents per 10,000 members, surpassed only by the United Mine Workers and Hospital and Health Care Employees.[8] Within the government sector over the same period, the IAFF and other fire fighters' organizations ranked third after the American Federation of State, County and Municipal Employees, AFL-CIO, and the two leading teachers' unions (the National Education Association and the American Federation of Teachers) in the total number of incidents of violence.[9]

Thieblot and Haggard expressed surprise at the presence of violence in the public sector for several reasons. They point to the strong bargaining position of many public sector unions, that their compensation generally exceed those of comparable workers in the private sector, enjoy job security greater than that found in the private sector, that the nature of their work, with some exceptions, is more characterized by tedium than hard physical labor and that this might be expected to inculcate habits and traits at odds with violence. Indeed, as trained professionals, in many instances, (the IAFF distinguishes itself as made up of **professional**, rather than amateur fire fighters) by training they should be expected to reject violence. Moreover, given the nature of their work, fighting fires, opposition and rejection of violence should be expected. But, as Thieblot and Haggard conclude, "...[such] is not the case".[10] In fact, they point out that over the period 1975–81, firemen and policemen "were involved in more incidents of violence than any other except the combination of the International Brotherhood of Teamsters (Teamsters) and the Independent Truckers Association".[11]

Not surprisingly, the chief weapon of violence used by fire fighters appears to be fire itself. In addition, vandalism, threats and harassment of supervisors trying to maintain fire protection, replacement fire fighters, and prevention of other fire fighting companies from dealing with fires are also used in disputes.[12]

The origin of fire fighters' use of strikes and at times violence has been attributed to their emulation of the tactics of other groups in the public sector, notably teachers. According to one analysis, "firemen ... and other public servants watched for years as teachers used the strike to raise their salaries above other public employee groups that abided by the old standards of achieving increases through more traditional, less disruptive methods".[13] It is ironic that teachers were so successful using "disruptive methods" set the example for others in unlawful activity. So well was the lesson learned that an editorial on a fire fighters' strike in Yonkers, New York commented: " The Yonkers firemen not only are refusing to carry out their essential duties. They also have persuaded paid and voluntary fire fighters from surrounding communities not to battle fires within their 'jurisdiction.' Let it burn, is their motto, and hang the consequences."[14]

There seems little doubt that unfair labor practices committed by a union could have been one way that the issue of violence could have been addressed in the FNLMRA, but as we have seen, there are none related to the issue in the Bill. Moreover, also absent is any penalty against a labor organization for engaging in a strike or any other form of related activity, even though the Bill does ban stoppages.

In the absence of any penalty, it hardly seems likely that the "ban" would have much impact on the strike propensity of fire fighters, as indicated by their record, 1974–1980, the only period available for detailed examination from data published by the Census. The amount of working time lost by fire fighters in that period exceeded its closest rival, the police, in five of the seven years available. Moreover, it exceeded time lost in education, all local government and the entire economy.

XII. Relationship to State and Local Laws

In a head-and-tails test of federal versus state and local labor law, the union wins either way. The proposed statute would preempt any Federal, State, or local law inconsistent with the Act. On the other hand, if any state or local government has a substantially equivalent law, then it would be exempt, if so attested by the Secretary of Labor. Where the state law goes meets or surpasses the provisions of the FNLMRA, it survives. It would hit hardest among southern and southwestern states, as I have already pointed out.

In the application of arbitration, the New Unionism argues for the broadest interpretation of scope. For example, unions would have it apply to matters historically subject to civil service regulations, such as promotion, demotion, job classification and manning levels. On the other hand, public employers would limit it to wages and other compensation, including fringes.

Although favored by many academics, the final offer method of arbitration is not viewed with the same benign attitude by municipal officials. Many mayors who have experienced it oppose it. Mayor Coleman Young of Detroit who voted for the Michigan statute when he was a member of the state legislature has a different view of it as chief executive officer of a major city. He complained that arbitrators "seem to believe that there is no limit to how much money they should spend" in reaching their decisions.[15] Mayor Young, together with other city and county officials in Michigan formed a Coalition to Improve Public Safety to repeal or reform the state law requiring binding final arbitration.

Opposed to the Coalition and its objectives are the Michigan State Fraternal Order of Police, the Michigan AFL-CIO, the Michigan Fire Fighters Association and the Detroit Fire Fighters Association.

Other members of the Coalition pointed out how the procedure erodes the sovereignty of local government and undermines representative government. One commented: "We feel it is imperative that contract decisions be made by local officials and an outside third party." Another said : "Public Act 312 destroys the traditional system for negotiating a contract and infringes on home rule rights by letting someone outside the city determine the city's ability to pay." Furthermore, he continued, "historically, the binding arbitrations have gone to the police or fire fighters [and] when the cities say they cannot pay the settlement, the arbitration panel says, 'That's your problem'."

Another criticism is that binding arbitration acts as a dis-incentive to bargaining in good faith. Knowing that public employers must come up with a proposal with any chance of winning the approval of many, if not most arbitrators, the downside risk of unions is limited and the incentive to go to arbitration is substantial. It is for this reason, most likely, that the difference between negotiated settlements and arbitrated awards do not differ all that much.

XIII. The Agency Shop, Fees and Their Expenditure

The landmark decision in the public sector was the *Abood* decision which came in 1977.[16] The key issues were the legality of the agency shop in public employment and the union's expenditure of funds collected under the agency shop on various political and ideological activities to which the non-member complainants objected.

In its decision, the Supreme Court found that public employees had no weightier rights under the First Amendment than private sector employees and therefore could be compelled to contribute to the costs of exclusive representation. The Court recognized that there are important differences in public and private sector collective bargaining, but that the "union security issue in the public sector is fundamentally the same issue ... as in the private sector" and that "no special dimension results from the fact that a union represents public rather than private employees."[17] As a result, the Court ruled that the agency shop was valid and that the union was entitled to a service fee for the purposes of collective bargaining, contract administration and grievance adjustment procedures.

However, the Court went on to say that the compelled payments could not be extended to political causes or ideological purposes not germane to the collective bargaining function of the exclusive bargaining representative. For that reason, the Court ruled that a dissenting non-member under an agency shop could not be required "to contribute to the support of an ideological cause he may oppose as a condition of holding a job as a public school teacher."[18] As to the dividing line between lawful and unlawful compelled payments, the Court acknowledged that "in the public sector the line may be somewhat hazier".

The Court did not decide on a specific remedy because, in the interim, the union had adopted an internal remedy to resolve the dissenters' claims for financial reimbursement. The Court made clear that a remedial procedure was required to "avoid the risk that non-members' funds will be used, even temporarily, to finance ideological activities unrelated to collective bargaining".

From my reading of the FNLMRA there is no hint that such a procedure is required. The proposed statute is silent on the matter; the closest it comes is the reference that agency shop "payments shall be made in accordance with rules and regulations prescribed for such purpose by the Commission." The intent is clear, however, and that intent is to strengthen the political might of the New Unionism and its support of political allies in government, federal, state and local.

XIV. Conclusions

The proposed legislation, although directed solely to labor relations in fire fighting, is actually a stalking horse, a model, for what might be expected from a future labor law governing all public sector employment. It will accelerate the diminution of sovereignty; the division of constitutional authority between the federal government on the one hand, and state and local governments on the other; and hasten convergence between the public and private systems of industrial relations. When accomplished, the comparative advantage of the New System of Industrial Relations (Chapter III) will approximate an absolute advantage.

It has been argued that the "sovereignty issue has, for the most part, been resolved by allowing public sector workers to organize, by forbidding most, particularly those in 'essential services' from striking".[19] As for the other, 'nonessential services,' it is argued that the sovereignty issue has been dealt with because strikes are short and the penalties moderate. The latter is akin to saying that a rape has left a virgin intact.

Completely bypassed by the foregoing characterization of the sovereignty issue is the budgetary process, not to mention policy matters no longer determined by officials elected by the community, but by collective bargaining and by arbitration.

Collective bargaining in the public sector does differ from private sector, but the changes which have taken place, the convergence between the two systems has shifted the balance of power between the public employer and public employees in favor of the employees. Professor Clyde Summers points to a number of reasons for the difference between the two sectors and why convergence has shifted the balance of power from the public employer to organized employees, the New Unionism at the local level.[20]

To begin with, public employment is unique because of the special character of the employer. Government is the employer, the agents of government are public officials, either directly elected or appointed by them, and that public officials are answerable to the citizenry and the voters. Public officials act according to constitutional and legislative principles; collective bargaining must accommodate, or should accommodate itself to those requirements. That, too, should make bargaining in the public sector different from the private sector, but it doesn't. To say that strikes may be moderate among 'nonessential' public employees, ignores strikes by 'essential' public employees, not to mention the violence that has often accompanied them, is hardly an accommodation to the unique nature of the public employer.

The difference, or what should be the difference between the two sectors, is seen from the differences in the decision making process within the two sectors. Public employers come to the bargaining table with governmental policies that are the product of constitutions and laws which circumscribe their authority and discretion. For example, wages and benefits are tied to taxes and those responsible for raising the funds are not those who face the unions across the negotiating table. Promotion and dismissal procedures may be subject to civil service regulations and/or legislative rules and cannot be (or should not be) altered by bargaining. Changes in pension programs are often subject to a state legislature, and are not within the discretion of the public official negotiating with a union. Thus, the bargaining over many issue is but an intermediate step to some legislative authority. The FNLMRA, it will be recalled, mandates a scope of bargaining which encompasses all such issues and also mandates that the public officials bring the bargaining agreement to the appropriate legislative authority. Under its arbitration procedures, the award is mandatory and imposed on the affected local governments. In addition, by bringing federal authority to bear it is further tearing away whatever is left of state authority under the Tenth Amendment of the Constitution.

Another characteristic setting apart public from private sector bargaining are the political aspects of the decision making process. First, in negotiating wages, hours, pensions and other terms and conditions of employment, their obvious impact on the taxes and budgets, leads to less obvious decisions on budget priorities. Such decisions are political in nature; the voters have chosen officials to carry out certain broadly understood goals. Collective bargaining will distort and re-allocate the budgetary resources to purposes which voters did not assent, but will have eventually to pay for. As for arbitration, "[t]he notion that we can or should insulate public employee bargaining from the political process either by arbitration or with some magic formula is a delusion of reality and a denigration of democratic government".[21]

Because of the political qualities of public sector negotiations, one must ask, what are some of the political consequences? Although outnumbered by voters, the political power of the New Unionism is dis-proportionately large. Exclusive representation focuses their power: the New Union can address the public employer with a single voice, provide a binding settlement, and give political weight to that economic voice. Next, the bargaining process highlights the authority and power of the union officials because they meet face to face with public officials and receive media attention in such sessions. Thus, the economic process of bargaining is translated into special political access. Negotiations over the organized employees' terms and conditions of employment generally gives them priority over other budgetary considerations, enhancing the public sector unions' access and influence on the political process. The same bargaining structure employed in economic negotiations becomes a formidable political structure which obviously has a decided impact on the politicians and public officials with whom the public sector union deals. As Victor Gotbaum, a former leader of the American Federation of State, County and Municipal Employees, AFL-CIO, once said in a moment of candor: "We have the ability ... to elect our own boss."[22]

Because bargaining in the public sector is so much a political process and the union a political body (Chapters II and III), the political power of unions, the nature of budget making and of budgetary priorities, of taxation, of governmental decision making will increasingly shift political power to one special interest group, the unions. With their political power so enhanced, public sector unions will be more capable of implementing their philosophy of more government intervention in the economy and political life of the nation. The philosophy of more government intervention in the economy is designed to re-allocate a larger share of the gross national product from the private to the public sectors in the form of more social services and transfer payments. This, of course, will stimulate the demand for public employment and with favorable legislation such as the proposed FNLMRA, increased growth of the New Unionism.

Another consequence of an enhanced power of the New Unionism which would be given by a federal law governing the entire public labor market will be an increasing demand for arbitration of disputes, such as proposed in the FNLMRA. The siren song sung by some academics on the virtues of arbitration has already won over many legislative bodies. Illustrative of this position is the following: "Arguments supporting interest arbitration are not wholly without merit. In certain situations arbitration may represent the only practical means of avoiding or terminating strikes that threaten vital public interests. ... In addition, experience indicates that some third party figures bring to negotiation disputes particular skill at resolving conflict ..."[23] The result of this will be to further shift public authority away from voters and taxpayers and lodge it with "experts." To that academic, the objections raised by sovereignty are "shopworn" and "fallacious." Moreover, the impact of collective bargaining is not viewed as a negation of public will and authority, but, as that writer observed, "it is precisely this opportunity to escape from responsibility that makes arbitration attractive to certain public officials".[24]

Looked at from an international perspective of what similar trends did in Britain, as one observer put it, "[t]he story of the growth of union power in the British public sector is not a happy one."[25] Why should it be different here?

End Notes

[1]See, for example, Arnold J. Thibault, Jr. and Thomas R. Haggard, *Union Violence: The Record and the Response, By Courts, Legislatures, And the NLRB*, (Philadelphia: Univ. of Penna., Wharton School, Industrial Relations Unit, 1983). Also, the Bureau of Census studies report strikes originating over recognition.

[2]Orley Ashenfelter, "The Effect of Unionization on Wages in the Public Sector: The Case of Fire Fighters", *Industrial and Labor Relations Review*, Vol. 24, No. 2, January 1971.

[3]Richard B. Freeman, "Unionism Comes to the Public Sector", *The Journal of Economic Literature*, Vol. XXIV, No. 1, March 1986.

[4]Commerce Clearing House. *Labor Law Course*, (CCH: Chicago, 1983) 25th Ed., p.1704.

[5]CCH, *Op. Cit.*, p. 5325.

[6]Armand J. Thieblot, Jr. and Thomas R. Haggard, *Union Violence: The Record and the Response By Courts, Legislatures, And the NLRB*, (Phila.: Univ. of Penna., Wharton School, Industrial Research Unit, Labor Relations and Public Policy Series, No. 25), p.120.

[7]American Federation of Labor, *American Federationist*, Nov. 1946.

[8]Armand Thieblot Jr. and Thomas R. Haggard, *Op. Cit.*, Table III-6 p. 59.

[9]*Ibid.*, Table III-7, p.62.

[10]*Ibid.*, p. 121.

[11]*Loc. Cit.*

[12]*Ibid.*, p. 136.

[13]John Herbers, "Public Safety In an Age of Self-Interest", *New York Times*, July 11, 1980.

[14]"Striking Against Public Safety", *New York Daily News*, April 17, 1981.

[15]John Herbers, *Op. Cit.*

[16]*Abood v. Detroit Board of Education*, 431 *U.S.* 209, 1977.

[17]431 *U.S.* 209, at 232.

[18]431 *U.S.* 209, at 235.

[19]Richard B. Freeman, *Op. Cit.*, pp.50–51.

[20]Clyde Summer, "Public Sector Bargaining: Problems of Governmental Decision-Making", 44 *Univ. of Cincinnati Law Review*, 660 (1976), quoted in Julius G. Getman, *Labor Relations: Law, Practice and Policy*, (Mineola: The Foundation Press, 1978).

[21]*Ibid.*, p. 445.

[22]Lloyd G. Reynolds, Stanley H. Masters, and Colletta H. Moser, *Labor Economics and Labor Relations*, (Englewood Cliffs: Prentice-Hall, 1986, 9th ed.), p.568.

[23]Raymond D. Horton, "Arbitration, Arbitrators, and the Public Interest", in David Lewin, Peter Feuille and Thomas Kochan, *Public Sector Labor Relations: Analysis and Readings*, (Thomas Horton & Daughters: 1977), pp. 305–306.

[24]*Ibid.*, p. 306.

[25]Arthur Shenfield, "Union Power in Government: The British Case", *Government Union Review*, Spring, 1980, p.19.

Appendix Table A-1
Density, the Old and the New Unionism, 1984 and 1988
By State

State	Old Unionism		New Unionism		Ratio of New to Old Unionism	
	1980	1988	1984	1988	1984	1988
Vermont	6.9%	5.2%	35.6%	40.5%	5.2	7.8
Florida	5.5%	4.4%	29.5%	26.6%	5.4	6.0
New Hampshire	6.2%	6.5%	31.8%	38.5%	5.1	5.9
Rhode Island	15.3%	11.9%	79.4%	66.9%	5.2	5.6
Maine	13.2%	9.8%	50.2%	53.4%	3.8	5.4
Utah	7.9%	5.9%	32.5%	31.4%	4.1	5.3
Massachusetts	17.5%	11.7%	52.1%	58.4%	3.0	5.0
South Dakota	6.6%	4.8%	14.9%	23.9%	2.3	5.0
Connecticut	12.8%	12.9%	69.2%	63.3%	5.4	4.9
North Carolina	4.6%	4.3%	23.7%	18.1%	5.2	4.2
Delaware	8.4%	10.8%	34.1%	43.0%	4.1	4.0
Nebraska	12.5%	7.5%	20.1%	29.6%	1.6	3.9
North Dakota	10.2%	6.7%	30.6%	25.6%	3.0	3.8
California	17.5%	12.8%	40.7%	47.6%	2.3	3.7
New York	23.0%	18.9%	66.3%	67.5%	2.9	3.6
Minnesota	18.3%	14.4%	44.6%	51.4%	2.4	3.6
Alaska	15.6%	13.2%	40.3%	46.3%	2.6	3.5
Arizona	5.2%	4.9%	22.7%	17.1%	4.4	3.5
Colorado	8.7%	7.1%	30.4%	24.2%	3.5	3.4
Texas	6.1%	4.9%	14.6%	16.2%	2.4	3.3
Oregon	18.1%	14.8%	42.6%	48.4%	2.4	3.3
New Jersey	17.2%	17.9%	53.2%	55.0%	3.1	3.1
Montana	8.0%	11.3%	33.0%	34.6%	4.1	3.1
Wisconsin	17.5%	16.3%	52.8%	48.8%	3.0	3.0
Maryland	15.0%	10.4%	28.5%	30.5%	1.9	2.9
Pennsylvania	20.2%	16.7%	45.8%	48.1%	2.3	2.9
Hawaii	19.3%	21.4%	50.7%	58.8%	2.6	2.7
Tennessee	12.3%	9.7%	19.9%	25.1%	1.6	2.6
Michigan	25.5%	21.3%	65.0%	54.8%	2.5	2.6
Oklahoma	10.3%	7.5%	23.8%	19.2%	2.3	2.6
Illinois	18.0%	17.4%	36.4%	43.2%	2.0	2.5
Washington	17.1%	18.7%	37.9%	44.5%	2.2	2.4
Ohio	21.5%	18.5%	39.0%	43.1%	1.8	2.3
Iowa	12.2%	11.6%	28.8%	26.7%	2.4	2.3
South Carolina	2.4%	4.2%	11.9%	9.6%	5.0	2.3
Louisiana	10.0%	7.7%	22.0%	17.4%	2.2	2.3
Nevada	16.6%	15.4%	41.0%	34.5%	2.5	2.2
Virginia	9.8%	7.4%	10.7%	15.8%	1.1	2.1
Arkansas	6.3%	8.0%	11.0%	16.6%	1.7	2.1
Dist of Col	10.3%	10.5%	23.1%	21.7%	2.2	2.1
Alabama	15.6%	11.7%	17.6%	23.8%	1.1	2.0
Georgia	10.0%	9.0%	7.5%	17.8%	0.8	2.0
Idaho	5.5%	9.4%	9.6%	18.1%	1.7	1.9
Wyoming	11.2%	10.4%	37.9%	20.0%	3.4	1.9
Kansas	11.1%	10.4%	24.3%	19.2%	2.2	1.8
Mississippi	6.8%	6.7%	20.1%	11.3%	3.0	1.7
Missouri	19.3%	15.1%	17.9%	24.7%	0.9	1.6
New Mexico	6.7%	7.2%	15.6%	11.3%	2.3	1.6
Kentucky	17.9%	15.8%	20.9%	19.9%	1.2	1.3
Indiana	25.1%	20.0%	40.0%	22.8%	1.6	1.1
West Virginia	25.6%	20.2%	23.6%	19.9%	0.9	1.0
U.S.	15.0%	12.6%	36.0%	36.5%	2.4	2.9

Chart 1
Share of Total Membership in the New Unionism 1960-91

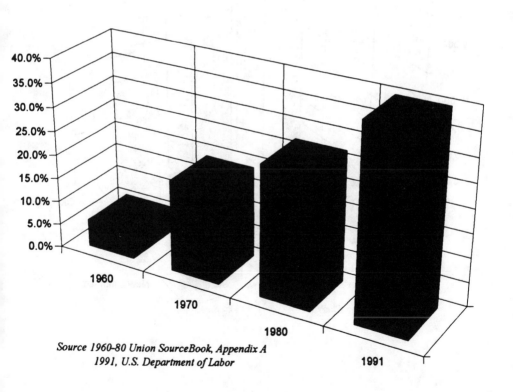

Source 1960–80 Union SourceBook, Appendix A
1991, U.S. Department of Labor

Chart 2
Membership, The New and Old Unionism, 1970-91

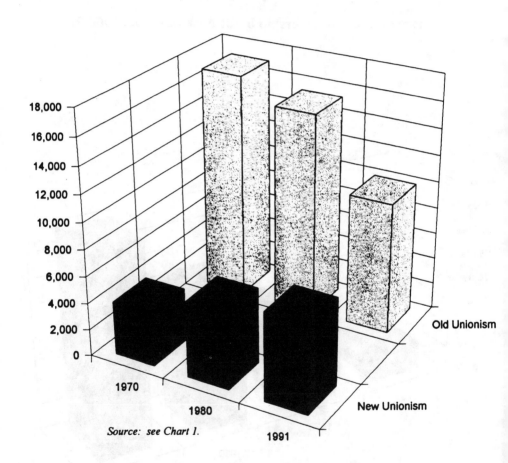

Source: see Chart 1.

Chart 3
Density, The New and Old Unionism, 1953-91

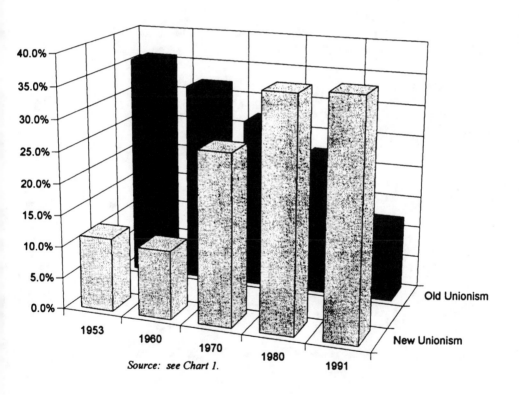

Source: see Chart 1.

Index